INFILTRATION

THE TRUE STORY OF THE MAN WHO CRACKED THE MAFIA

COLIN McLAREN

For two dolls … my treasured Ma and my gorgeous daughter, Chelsea

VICTORY BOOKS
An imprint of Melbourne University Publishing Limited
187 Grattan Street, Carlton, Victoria 3053, Australia
mup-info@unimelb.edu.au
www.mup.com.au

In association with x15 PTY LTD

First published 2009
Reprinted 2009 (twice)
This edition 2011
Reprinted 2011
Text © Scuttlebutt Media, 2009, 2011
Design and typography © Melbourne University Publishing Ltd, 2009, 2011

Text design by Phil Campbell
Cover design by Phil Campbell
Typeset by J&M Typesetting
Printed by Griffin Press, SA

National Library of Australia Cataloguing-in-Publication entry

McLaren, Colin.

9780522857467 (pbk)

McLaren, Colin.
Trimbole, Robert, 1931–1987
Police—Australia—Biography.
Undercover operations—Australia.
Organized crime—Australia.
Murder—Australia
Violent crimes—Australia
Criminal investigation—Australia.
Drug abuse and crime—Australia.
Mafia—Australia.

364.106092

PREFACE TO THIS EDITION

When I first embarked on writing *Infiltration* I had no idea how popular the book would be, or even dream of it becoming an *Underbelly* film production.

Many of my readers have told me the book appeals for a couple of reasons: not only because I share my story of what it's like growing up in Struggletown and joining the Police department at a young age but many readers were also fascinated by my infiltration of the Griffith mafia when the N'Drangheta was out of control during the 1990s.

This edition of *Infiltration* coincides with the telemovie release, which focuses on the mafia story: the dangerous journey of an undercover cop and his brave girlfriend who sting the mafia and close them down … for a time.

I hope you enjoy the ride.

Colin McLaren

CONTENTS

ACKNOWLEDGEMENTS

Thanks to … as is often the case in my life, the good guys are women. I thank the following for their help along my literary path: Philippa, A.B, Cathy, Foong Ling, Susan and, most of all, Alison, who often quipped: 'You can do better than that!'

Alterations … for reasons to do with covert identities and old-fashioned privacy, a couple of names in the book have been altered.

The sum total of two decades.

It's a naive individual who believes that, just because a cop carries a badge, he has a flawless character. Many are heroes, some fall well short. It's just as gullible to think that every crook is necessarily rotten. Cops and crooks are, after all, merely representative of our society. There is good, bad and mediocre in both professions. I have worked with (and against), delighted in and been frustrated by many magnificent examples of each. Throughout this book, I recall many of them, and thank them all. It was a fair ride!

Colin McLaren
aka
Cole Goodwin
Tommy Paul
cm@scuttlebuttmedia.net

PROLOGUE

Antonio invited me for a stroll, through the orange groves. The sun warmed our backs and I allowed Antonio to play host. My tape was on.

He walked with confidence, taking the occasional glance at his fruit trees. He was wearing a pair of Italian jeans, soft calf-leather shoes and a brilliant white Versace shirt, pressed to impress. He had the classic look of Italian style, as well as charm. We were the same age, nudging forty.

'You like our ways, Cole,' he said, handing me an orange as he peeled his own.

'Always have, since I was a boy,' I explained.

'You know the Italian life well.'

'It's the family ways that work for me,' I replied, enjoying my fruit.

'Why do you feel for family so much?'

Antonio stopped walking, throwing his peel onto the ground, and, taking a bite of his juicy orange, waited for my answer. He looked neither at me nor his fruit as the sun hit his face and he squinted.

'My road's been different from yours, Antonio. I have always wanted this.'

'Your road has been hard?' he asked.

'You could say that.'

'Don't ever make our road hard, Cole ... ever,' Antonio said, as he shifted his piercing gaze to me. He finished his orange before wiping his hands on a perfectly clean white handkerchief. As we strolled back to the crowd, he placed his hand on my shoulder and spoke his final word on the subject. '*Ever.*'

I accepted his words as we wandered back, smiling, to the rich collection of men, women and children mingling in an atmosphere akin to what I had experienced twenty-five years earlier with my best friend Vinnie and his Sicilian family.

Antonio moved between the other guests, all Italians, all family except for myself. The Calabrian dialect was spoken often that afternoon, the perfect way for the Italians to converse without me understanding. I sensed the occasional sideways glance from the bewhiskered men; Antonio, obviously, was seeking comment from his clan. In a way, I felt like I was back in school, being assessed for an exam. I had studied my subject well and wanted desperately to pass. As I too mingled, I came to realise that each glance I caught was accompanied by the faintest smile. I liked that, and realised as I filled the wine glasses of many out-reached hands that my invitation to a sausage-making day was merely a ruse. What was really in play was my membership to the N'Drangheta, the Calabrian Mafia.

At the end of our day Antonio made sure that I left the farm laden with wine, trays of sausages, and boxes of oranges. As I walked to my car, fresh-faced kids with peppermint smiles held my hand and Antonio opened the car door for me, whispering, 'Welcome to our family.'

I
A HARD ROAD

1

'IF YOU'RE GOOD'

I think it's fair to say that I have danced on the edge of crazy throughout most of my life. My earliest memory itself was filled with that sense of folly. It was 1960 and summer, the relentless February sun made sure of that. I gazed out across the top of the high, thin grass in the paddock over the back fence. Grass that cut like paper, was as tall as the sheep, the colour of their fleece and the colour of my hair, and was interspersed with golden tussocks. It seemed to go on forever, standing sentry, breaking the boredom of the rolling fawn hills.

As sunset fell over my paddock, a regiment of shadows formed, the silhouettes of dead gum trees on the landscape. I had a name for each tree as well as for the few head of cattle who ambled on, heads down, looking for green, but grudgingly accepting less. I stared wide-eyed into this paddock each day at dusk, watching the rabbits come to life and seeing the eagle take its dinner. As little as I was, at times I felt like a giant target, as scores of grasshoppers took aim and hurled themselves incessantly at my head. The paddock was always silent, as I took stock of it and all that was within it.

My paddock was in Clarkefield, just an hour's drive away from Melbourne. Clarkefield itself was, and is, a tiny town, nestled, almost as if it were asleep, on the other side of an airport freeway. It looks as if it crawled to its location and plopped there, having decided it had no more strength to continue. In the days when I explored my paddock, there was no airport, nor was there any freeway. Clarkefield was nowhere in particular, and no-one passed by.

Suburbia never did extend Clarkefield's way, didn't even tickle a kiss on the dull face of our town. Ma once said, 'You don't live in Clarkefield, you exist.' And existing consisted of drinking beer and telling tall stories in the big bluestone pub, or flirting with the neighbours in the main street. But I was a kid then, and kids are happy anywhere, at least they were in my day.

'I'll catch dinner', I thought, as I sat alongside a rabbit burrow. The sun was settling in a lazy buttery haze across my paddock and my cheeks were flushed scarlet and warm. My four-and-a-half-year-old arm stretched deep inside the burrow, scouring the dark hole.

Anyone who has lived on a farm knows that this is reckless. Rabbit burrows were often taken over by goannas, which fed on the young bunnies and slept it off in their warrens, out of the blazing heat. More common, and even worse, were the deadly tiger snakes that evicted the rabbits and took up residence themselves. Ma was a matter-of-fact woman; her advice was short, strong and spot-on: 'There's only one good snake Colin—a dead 'un.'

Oblivious to the danger, arm still reaching into the burrow, I touched something. It wriggled and disappeared from my fingertips, making me even more determined to seek it out. My arm plunged deeper, until there was no more arm. With a child's enthusiasm, my fingers twinkled, desperate to reconnect with whatever was in the hole. I was born with an abundance of enthusiasm and determination, and I exercised both on that balmy, late afternoon as I lay belly down on top of fresh dirt and fresher rabbit droppings.

Bingo, I was onto it! I grabbed and held on tight, my legs working my body away from the hole, like I was pedalling a bike. I pulled out my arm, as my prey fought hard, furiously, like a fully grown giant lion. I turned red dirt into red dust, and sucked in the excitement.

The thrill of my first catch! Maybe my father, Dougal, would be proud of me, maybe not. I will never forget his advice from an earlier outing: 'If you grab hold of it … then bloody well hold onto it tight,' he bellowed as he ground his teeth and riveted his bulging, watery eyes on me. In the years we spent together, he only ever told me two or three things of any consequence, and that was possibly his most profound advice. My arm came out and my prize was raised in the air. Just a kitten, as they are called, perhaps only days old. It wriggled madly in my grip, kicking its rear legs, as rabbits instinctively do. It was mine, my first ever toy, my first ever pet.

I clambered to my feet, covered in soil, and raced off with my catch pressed firmly to my chest, wriggling and weeing everywhere. I ran through the tall grass, hurdling tussocks, and dived under the barbed-wire fence into our backyard. Ma was at the clothes-line. She knew I was headed her way and finished off a sheet. I bounced into her arms with my trophy and she looked delighted, careful not to hurt the prize, and making sure she rewarded me with what all little boys want to be rewarded with, a hug and comments of being 'brave' and 'strong'. She'd often say, 'You big strong cowboy', which had me running about madly, chest out and feeling on top of my world.

She dropped her big wooden pegs and we walked together, just her, me and bunny. She found a box and called it a 'bunny house'. I dug up clumps of clover for feed and spent the next few hours telling my entire life story and family history to the rabbit, who offered nothing about himself. Then darkness fell.

As morning finally nudged its way through our heavy drapes, I scrambled out of bed, kicking off my bedclothes faster than usual. I raced from the bedroom, into the kitchen, dodging the table, hitting the flywire door and onto the back porch to greet my pet, asleep in the laundry overnight. It was time for my new toy, and I had a whole day planned, but my excitement was short lived. Bunny lay motionless. I was too young to understand just what a bunny needed as a safe place to sleep for a night; to my mind, a large empty preserving jar was the ideal resting place. The bunny seemed to fit snugly inside and the lid went on easy enough. Perfect, I had thought. Unscrewing the lid of the jar, my world caved in. I was stunned to find my new pet lifeless.

I dropped the lid onto the bare dirt and cried, loud and hard. I pulled the bunny out and held my dead, stiff pet in one hand and the empty jar in the other. There were running steps in the background and the wire door pinged as it was hit again. Ma had come to the rescue, wiping her hands on her apron as she towered over me. She too looked shocked, and a little pale, but she gave me a faint smile, as she gently reached for the corpse, explaining, 'Rabbits need air holes to breathe, and room to move. Any wonder the poor bunny died. Colin, give it to me.' She kissed my forehead and glided away to sort out her morning chores. I was left on the back porch, shattered, holding onto an empty jar and the offending lid. Dougal soon appeared on the scene, having been told of the morning's disaster. The flywire door banged more heavily as he walked past, carrying an armful of empty beer bottles. He pulled up, turned and glared at me with his watery eyes, offering his only words on the subject: 'Stupid bastard.'

That's my earliest memory. It's a memory I cherish. Ma is the chocolate among the liquorice allsorts. I often fall back on that memory and enjoy its mood. I replay it in my mind's eye, reliving the nose-tickling odour of fur, the stench of rabbit droppings, the aromas of red earth and clover. And the comforting fragrance of my mother, a pot-pourri of cheap scent, kitchen soap and perhaps cinnamon, or nutmeg, or whatever else might have found its way into her oven that day. There's another indelible smell too, that of the rancid stench given off from empty beer bottles and Dougal's breath: that instantly recognisable smell of stale hops and day-old beer.

For me it's almost impossible to recall early memories based on addresses. By the time I had left home, on my sixteenth birthday, I had lived at fifty-four addresses, and attended thirteen different schools. That was life for my family. The early years were more stable: we lived in and around Clarkefield at a few different places, different farmhouses, for a number of years and also managed a respectable stint in Coburg, but later there were times when we only stayed somewhere for a few weeks. We travelled back and forth, wearing out the pages of the street directory, trying to find somewhere to live.

The reason for our house moving was simple: we came from struggle town, a knockabout Aussie family, the stuff of sad lyrics in a Slim Dusty song. A classic postwar family who amounted to nothing much, led by a father who may have been the original dole bludger, as well as a drunk and a womaniser. Being evicted was par for the course. It was a while before I was old enough to work out the pattern to our moving but we always moved far enough away from the old address to avoid the debt collectors and revenge-seeking husbands.

Suitcases and packing boxes were never discarded; they formed an important part of our furnishings. They were carefully stored away, as we knew they'd be needed again. We had a system in place with our treasured cardboard packing boxes. Ma wrote 'Kitchen' or 'Lounge room' or other destinations on the box flaps, depending on what was being packed. When we needed to hit the road, it certainly streamlined the packing process. We repacked the boxes according to the appropriate room markings, and off we'd go, again. I thought it was all very exciting, each time we were on the move. I knew how to pack, what to pack, in what order, and the best way to arrange precious possessions so that they'd be well preserved. I'd close the flaps, tape them in place, and deliver a box of my worldly possessions into the trailer, all in no time at all.

When I caught the bunny, we were living on a beat-up little dirt block, a five-minute walk from Dougal's family farm. Our house was just down from the railway station and Clarkefield pub. Apart from those two colonial structures there was not much else, except for an asphalt tennis court and the general store that was as big as a country barn, with 'Bushell's tea' signs plastered across the huge glazed windows.

I visited the store every day. It was no more than two hundred dusty steps from our house. The bell above the rickety door tinkled as I charged inside with coins in hand and a note from Ma. Often our purchases were on the tick, carefully recorded in a book until the end of the month when all accounts were to be paid. Usually we paid late and it was me who copped the sour looks from the shopkeeper, as if I had anything to do with the current account deficits of our clan. The store owners, Mrs Farley and her husband, seemed ancient to me. They looked like general store owners too: well fed and always wearing cardigans under their aprons, even in summer.

My Ma had this wonderful saying when I was little, which carried until I left home at sixteen. 'If you're good,' she'd say. This was her constant pre-emptive comment to us kids, no matter what we were doing. When we asked for homemade cakes or a treat, she would reply, 'If you're good,' thereby ensuring her four children behaved like perfect angels for the time it took to secure our much-desired reward. Generally, though, we always were well behaved; sure, we acted up at times and as we grew into teenagers, there must have been occasions when we were a handful. But, on the whole, the inner discipline we had still amazes me. My siblings and I had great respect for our Ma, and conscious concern for all the hard roads she travelled. So, when my mother requested discipline by saying, 'If you're good,' we were, invariably, very good. I love those three words; they'll stay with me forever.

The weatherboards of our two-bedroom timber house in Clarkefield were a deep charcoal in colour, had never seen a paintbrush, and were as dry as the Simpson Desert. There was one room to the left and one room to the right, with a door in the middle and a tin roof, verandahs at the front and rear. We didn't have hot water, unless we chopped kindling for the wood heater; lighting was a handful of bare bulbs dangling from twisted black flex. Each wall inside the old cottage was covered with unpainted tongue-and-groove lining boards with dog-eared calendars nailed to them; some of the floorboards were broken. It was only worth being bulldozed, or used as firewood.

All four of us kids slept in one bedroom. My little brother, Titch, was coming out of nappies and my kid sister, Bubby, was walking everywhere flat-out. Our bedroom never had the problem of being cluttered with toys—we didn't have any. Toys cost money and we had very little of that; besides, there were more important, far better uses for money when it did come our way.

Apart from the ruckus of the bedroom there was also a 'family' room, although we were more a group of people flung together and living in the same place than a family. This was the room where we all ate, Ma cooked and sewed, Dougal drank and the resident black snake made its occasional unwelcome appearance to scare the bejesus out of us all. My older sister, Sandra, who we called Sambo, stuck to my mother's side learning it all; I guess she was being groomed, though I can't imagine what for. 'The perfect family, just like in the *Women's Weekly*, girl, boy, girl, boy,' said Dougal proudly to guests over the years. I was boy number one, the second eldest; we were all one year apart in age.

I was a sweet-looking kid, I know, as I have the only two photographs of myself as a child. We didn't ever own a camera. Ma sometimes souvenired the neighbours' photographs, and put them in a blue cake-tin, which she kept in a drawer of an old battered dresser. The tin had a picture of a pretty Islander girl on the lid; I can still see the cleavage on the girl as she leaned forward. My Ma treasured that tin of memories. I treasured the lid. As a youngster, I opened the tin many times: the only official record of my family. There was one photograph of my parents on their wedding day. I looked at that photograph a thousand times over the years. I used to think, 'This is proof that she did really and truly and absolutely marry him!'

I know as the years moved on and I went about my life, Ma was always pleased with the way I turned out. She was happy with the sum total of what I had done and become, always interested in what I was doing, exploring, thinking. She liked following my zigzag progress and delighted in my stories, saying they were her adventures too. Despite our obvious closeness, she never once told me she loved me.

My father was a man trapped in an era of compliance and conformity. He escaped only through the beer bottle and his mates. His world offered little, expecting each man to be a cardboard cut-out of each other, with a family, house, one motor car and regular employment. Dougal was incapable of sustaining any of those key ingredients, falling back to mateship and the safe haven offered by like-minded souls in the public bar. He had no respect for anyone or anything, or himself. Sadly, alcoholism grabbed hold of him at far too early an age, ensuring that those trapped within his world were also victims themselves. I hated my father deeply as a growing boy. While I felt saddened at his miserable existence, I was never able to forgive him.

We stayed in Clarkefield just long enough for me to start at the little school, with its single classroom. My parents, by then, were arguing on a far too regular basis. At least, it was Dougal doing most of the yelling, and occasionally throwing punches, as Ma suffered. One afternoon after school I walked home to find the local police sergeant pounding on our front door and hollering at Dougal, wanting his attention. Dougal was on notice: 'Pull up or move on' was the warning. The boxes came out and we started packing.

2

CHIP ON MY SHOULDER

could see the heat haze rising from the concrete footpath, so hot the
thin soles of my plastic sandals would have stuck to it. The footpath
ran conspiratorially along beside the neatly trimmed nature strips, one
after the other, after another, after another. Sunset fell over the car park
of Dougal's beloved watering hole, creating one massive shadow, blan-
keting the blistering hot cars. At the age of eleven, I already could tell
the make and model of each car. I stared at that familiar hotel, with
tired eyes, watching the drunks come to life as they entered the public
bar. As young as I was, I knew well what lay ahead as I sat in Dougal's
car with the constant heat beating at my head.

Our house was a few blocks away in suburban Coburg, a war-
service suburb with nowhere to run, hide or play except the cemetery.
Like Clarkefield, Coburg was nowhere in particular and no-one
passed by.

I should have been in Year Seven at my local school but on this hot
summer day I was at a different school—Dougal's drinking school—
along with my two sisters and Titch. We were sitting inside our ivory-
coloured Vauxhall sedan, waiting. We were in the car park of the First
and Last Hotel in Sydney Road. It was an unforgiving 110 degrees

Fahrenheit outside, and there hadn't been a cloud in the sky for weeks: 1966 was a record year for Beatles hits and extreme heat.

I was alone in the front seat of Dougal's car. I had pulled rank and thrown my kid brother into the back, alongside our two sisters. No-one dared sit in the driver's seat. My siblings were purple faced, wet haired and bothered, as was I. We were desperately in need of water, fluid of any kind. We had stopped acting like kids long ago: no more wisecracks, wriggling or changing of seating positions. There hadn't been an argument for at least an hour, just a heat-induced, breathless silence, rapidly turning into a dangerous stupor. We'd been in this car park many times before.

The windows were wound down, to no effect; flies meticulously patrolled every inch of the inside of the windscreen. The remnants of our lunch lay on the floor of the car: four empty potato crisp wrappers, passed to us by our father hours earlier, after he came storming out to the car.

'Why can't you bloody kids just sit there and be quiet, for Chrissake, is that too much to bloody well ask?' He had forced his face into my open window.

He had ground his teeth harder and longer than normal and, with two of his freckled, ginger-haired fingers, he had grabbed hold of my nose and squeezed hard, as if he was attempting to prise it from my flushed face. I'd closed my eyes, tight as possible, taking one massive deep breath.

I hadn't been scared. I had lost most of my fear a long time before, along with respect and admiration. All I had was an overwhelming desire to see him gone—gone from our lives and gone from my world. He had thrown the bags of crisps onto my lap, as if he'd predetermined we'd be ungrateful for his gift of sustenance, and vanished into his sanctuary.

Stupidly, we kids ate the crisps in double-quick time. We were too hungry to even notice what flavour they were. I then felt sicker than a last-born pup; my lips became crinkled and cracked from the salt and heat. The worry of being punished for being away from the car was being overridden by the need to consume water. We looked at each other, without talking, knowing that something had to be done: I had to walk into the bar and face the music. Full of trepidation and dread, I legged it across the hot gravel. The stones of purgatory burned the soles of my bare feet. I had recklessly bee-lined barefoot, my sandals long since abandoned in an attempt to cool down.

As it was a rough-house pub, the patrons were mostly interstate truckies, hard-nosed drinkers and thieves. Sitting in the car park over the years I had seen scores of no-hopers empty car-loads of brand-new kitchen appliances or electrical goods into the back door of the public bar. I got the drift of what was really going on inside the bar. Occasionally Dougal would arrive home carrying a new toaster or set of knives, naively believing all would be forgiven.

The hotel door was covered with a sheet of metal. I knocked hard; the waiting went on for a while, then the door burst open to the sound of beer swilling, laughter and a racecaller's voice, before a huge frame of a man walked out. 'Wez me dad?' I asked the giant, a mono-lith in a navy blue singlet, his arms covered in homemade tattoos. His extraordinary-sized beer belly hung low over his jeans.

'Fuck off you little prick before I kick your arse.'

I backed away from the door; my left leg trembled. I was too scrawny for this caper.

'Jesus, young fella, you're hot—are ya all right?' came from behind me, from a man not much taller than I was. He too had a beer belly but much smaller; he was pleasant, clean-shaven and carried an armful of transistor radios, all new and in boxes. He sized me up. 'Err … is your dad inside, young fella, is that the worry?' I wobbled a nod to him. He shook his head, in a mix of disgust and concern, shifted his grip on his load and placed a reassuring hand on my shoulder.

'Poor bastard. What's your dad's name, young fella?'

'Dougal, sir,' I replied, as if answering a schoolteacher.

'My God, you're Dougal's boy, wait there, young fella, and I'll hunt him home.' The kindly man made me stand up straight.

'Now, young fella, open the door for me. I'll unload this lot, and sort out your Dad.'

He was gone for just a few minutes before returning, carrying a large freezing-cold pot of ambrosial lemon squash, with icy drops of condensation running down the side. He handed me the glass and I drank, as fast as I could, slurping the freezing, sweet drink. It sent instant pain to my head and ran over my chin. Seconds later I was staring at the crushed ice at the bottom. 'Didn't touch the sides, hey, I'll get one for your sisters,' he said.

Just then, Dougal barged his way through the door, his arm raised to deal with the flash of sun after the cool darkness. He stumbled and almost knocked the empty glass from the kindly man's grip. 'He's in a bad way, Dougal, it's not good, get 'em home.'

Dougal didn't respond. He searched his bib pocket for the car keys and guided me firmly towards the car, hand behind my head. He was fuming. My good samaritan slipped inside the public bar, never to be seen again.

'I've told you fifty bloody times, you bastard, not to come into the pub. What do you think you are playing at?' he slurred. 'I had important things to discuss, without you kids muckin' it up!'

My little brother and sister started sobbing as the car sped along at breakneck speed. Everything was screaming: the engine, Dougal, the flies and my siblings. Intersection after intersection flew past.

The Vauxhall bounced up the driveway of our slime-green house, coming to an abrupt stop; we all tumbled out and headed straight for the rear garden tap, where we jostled for positions to drink the hot water from a hose that had lain in the sun all day. Dougal slammed the car door with as much might as he could muster, and stormed past us into the house.

From the front yard of our Newlands Road home, we were offered a view of Australia's most notorious prison—HMS Pentridge— the exercise yards as well as the cells caging murderers and armed robbers as well as lesser villains. I saw it as an exciting bonus to be so close to the worst kind in society. I'd often stand on tiptoes, and imagine the goings on in the prison, trying to see any murderers skulking in the grounds.

Sambo and I walked down the road each morning to the prison wall and awaited the passing school bus. After school we made the return journey, hiking up the hill to our home. Each day I had my eyes peeled, watching the prison guard in his sentry box, rifle slung over his shoulder. I used to walk home backwards, aching for a prisoner to hoist his rope over the prison wall and jump to his freedom, right in front of me, wearing black-and-white stripes and a big number on his back. My imagination had him landing safely on his feet and running to a waiting car, desperate. Looking left, looking right. Then, as the escapee tries to get into the getaway car, the prison guard springs into action and trains his Winchester 'Marksman' series 11 rifle onto the fleeing felon. A number of shots ring out and the escapee is cut down, dead. The car speeds off, fishtailing along the street with more shots at its rear, as the prisoner lies like a maggot on my nature strip. My daydreams ended with the guard smiling victoriously and sirens blaring in the background.

Our family life was sliding down a similarly tragic slippery slope, largely due to Dougal's inevitable decline. He wasn't a very tall man and his body weight had started to shift after years of drinking and very little physical work. His bullish profile, jowled and bellied, was in line with his street-thug manner. We were all at home one afternoon. It was a warmish day and we had been whingeing how we never had a swimming pool, like the lucky kids in the neighbourhood.

Dougal stormed out of the house to the front yard and grabbed the garden hose. He turned the tap on hard and marched back inside with water spurting at full bore, proceeding to spray water in every room of the house. We ran in all directions, bumping into each other in the hallway, getting doused with water. Initially I thought it was a joke and smiled, only to receive a faceful of water and realise that Dougal was blind with rage. I ran and hid under the kitchen table. Ma stood there soaking wet, as did my sisters and brother, trying to understand his madness. So much water had been set free that most of our clothes and carpets were awash; the lounge suite was ruined. He stood in the hallway like a fireman, holding his thin green garden hose and yelling at the top of his voice.

'There you are … is that better now? … Have you all cooled off yet, you bastards? … There's your fuckin' swimming pool.'

A couple of weeks later, I went for a walk with my Ma. She often took an evening stroll, once the dinner was over and the house was quiet. It was on this night that I had my first grown-up chat with my mother. Life was becoming drastic. I looked at Ma, thin, yet remarkably stylish, especially considering the life she was forced to lead. She was wearing a fashionable pink-coloured twinset and a skirt. She looked a bit like a movie star with her scarf around her neck and her sunglasses over her eyes; important accessories to hide the black eye and marks on her neck.

'We've got to get away from him.'

'I know,' Ma replied.

'I can't stand him. We have to get away, now. I hate him.'

'I don't know where we'd go or how we'd cope.'

'We'd cope, you do the work, not him, he's never here.'

'Let me think about it. I can't lose you kids. I can't have you in a social welfare home,' she said.

'Let's just run, I hate him,' I pleaded.

'Soon, I need to think it over. Soon, I need to think.'

The next day was like any other. I was to meet Ma at the local shops on the way home from school to help carry some shopping. We turned the corner of our street and were headed down the last stretch when a catastrophic image hit us both in the face. We stopped, in tearful disbelief.

All our possessions were strewn outside our home—stacked haphazardly, one piece on top of another, from driveway to driveway, covering the entire nature strip. Most visible were the beds, which were piled on cupboards, a tower of tired furnishings. The collection included our clothing and personal items; our toothbrushes lay in the open air on top of a mattress, along with a half-used cake of soap and a few half-full bottles of cheap shampoo. We had been evicted, again. The locks to the doors had been changed, making it impossible to get back into what had been our home. My sisters and brother appeared from the neighbour's house, glum and silent.

Some neighbours chose just that time to water their gardens, while others peeped through their drapes. Venetian blinds were rea-ligning their slats. No-one offered a wave or greeting. In silence, the neighbourhood watched our downfall, as we failed the quintessential family test of achieving the great Australian dream.

My mother dropped her shopping where she stood and collapsed onto a chair. She surveyed the poorly packed stack that was once her furniture and then the mess of weatherboards that was once, until moments ago, her own home; her only chance at suburbia, taken, in one swift movement, by an anonymous group of men who came and went, leaving behind a slip of paper.

The official-looking page explained a history of default payments on the mortgage—her mortgage. She had worked five days a week for two long hard years to pay that mortgage, toiling in the heat at a local factory on a huge industrial sewing machine, leaving lifelong scars on her skinny, skilled fingers. She had worked overtime some Saturdays and still made time for her family. She knew all along there was a greater picture at stake. Wiping a face full of tears with one hand and with an eviction notice in the other, my mother came to the realisa-tion that her husband had not directed her hard-earned salary to the mortgage; it was the local publican he had given it to, month after month. She sat and nodded quietly to herself.

We spent the next three years running, from house to house, bed-sitter to flat, in a desperate bid to shake off Dougal. It was a hard three years, sometimes winning and other times losing the race. It was like being on a merry-go-round, each of us clutching onto a pretty col-oured pony as the ride was cranked up. Our problem was the man controlling our merry-go-round: Dougal. Often he set the speed on full throttle as we tried to evade his advances. There were moments when we spun so fast that any one of us could have fallen off, and crashed firmly into a miserable mess. But for three years we hung on, tight, as Ma guided us along.

During our ride of madness we stayed for a stretch of time in the Housing Commission flats in North Melbourne with our kindly Auntie Gwen and tough guy Uncle Bill, and their four daughters. I could feel my mother's shame, having to sleep on the floor of a commission flat in a rough-house suburb.

Gwen worked in a local cigarette factory; she always had a biscuit tin full of loose cigarettes on the kitchen table and a pot of tea on the go. She easily smoked sixty a day and drank ten cups of tea. Ridiculously skinny, she had the look of an anxious pigeon, so sprung was her system with nicotine and caffeine. I adored Auntie Gwen for many reasons, but most of all for the way in which she never passed judgement. Bill was a wharfie and a hardened drinker. For all his drinking he never missed an hour of work. Work was fun to Bill. It allowed him to indulge his pastime: stealing from shipping containers. Before we got too cosy, Bill sent us packing. Thinking back, it was the right thing to do, to move on, before Gwen's biscuit tin of cigarettes had us all smoking.

We found accommodation just up the road at a mostly ramshackle house, behind an equally dilapidated dry-cleaning store. The owner allowed us the dive rent-free, as long as Ma ran the dry-cleaning shop. This seemed like a perfect solution. Ma's independence flourished as we began to see less of our father, and there was no doubt that running the little business provided her with a new outlook on life.

That was until one night, when Dougal turned up in a blusterous rage. He had been drinking for days and his entire body reeked of booze. He was stony broke and went through the house like a hurricane, abusing us all.

By the time the police finally arrived, Ma had discovered that the dry-cleaning float money was gone. After trying in vain to come up with a solution, she had no other choice than to talk with the shop owners. They saw my mother's swollen face, savaged her over the stolen money, and told us to move on. The packing boxes came out again. Within the hour, the smallest and worst car in the suburb shuddered to a halt at the front of the shop. It was a car I knew well, a two-tone brown-and-cream Morris Minor, driven by the crazy Gwen. It was parked with doors open and the engine revving.

How do you get two adult women, four children, a houseful of clothing, a bathroom full of toiletries and a kitchen of utensils into a Morris Minor? Answer—quickly.

Once we crammed ourselves in, we fled. Keen to put distance between us and North Melbourne, Ma turned to Gwen and yelled stirringly: 'Come on, Gwen! Give 'er the herbs, give 'er the herbs!' The Morris Minor raced forward, picking up speed and charging towards the city, away from Dougal, wherever he was. We laughed and laughed, and my mother cried a great laugh herself. She was free, again!

Despite our many moves Dougal always seemed to find us. He'd be able to play on my mother's emotions, promising better times ahead. One time he teamed up with a local thug and paid us a visit for dinner. They'd been hours at a city pub, and were both already stupefied. After dinner we kids were sent to bed but we lay awake, listening to the slurred nonsense in the lounge room.

Dougal fronted Ma in her bedroom, cornering her and calling out aggressively, demanding sex; the atmosphere was terrifying. Then his mate padded across our bedroom floor. He was completely naked and with an erection. I watched and counted his every step as he got closer to his prey. Ten paces later he was standing at Sambo's bed. Her head was covered with the bedclothes. As his hand reached towards her face, I sat bolt upright and glared in his direction, shivering madly, and saying as loudly as I could, 'Sambo, Sambo, what are you doing?' They were the only words that came out. I was so scared that the volume of my voice was less then it should have been. Thankfully,

Sambo stirred and three other voices joined in, enough to spur the naked lowlife aggressor to sprint for the kitchen and to run from our home, grabbing his strides and shirt on the way out.

After a few stop-starts, we settled at a bedsitter in Elfin Grove, Hawthorn. It was a divine little place: one lounge room with a tiny kitchenette in the corner and a separate bedroom that slept the five of us, virtually on top of each other.

Living at Elfin Grove was possibly the most influential time of my childhood. Most of the confusion with growing up seemed to get sorted there, or at least began to start making sense. It was where I first became interested in girls. I also got to know about Italians, their home-ly culture and ways of dealing with their own. Living next door to us was another single mother, with six kids of her own, Mrs Bongiorno; we called her Kath. An Italian immigrant, she came to Australia to marry her Australian beau and build her family. After the birth of their sixth child, her husband died, but she carried on in good Italian fashion, raising the children on her own. She was utterly Italian, it was as if she had never left Sicily, still speaking with a strong accent and looking the quintessential Italian mother. Her children were of similar ages to our clan and there were four girls and two boys. I envied them all.

Good things never lasted for us. An ever-vigilant Department of Social Welfare decided that our family unit needed to be split into two. Titch and I were to live with Dougal, and the two girls were to stay with Ma. No amount of protest could muster change in the marsh-mallow brains of the case officers assigned to our file. The department allowed Dougal to find whatever accommodation he felt was adequate. I can still see Ma politely, patiently working with these people, only to be met with prejudice. It was the way of the times: women had to justify themselves and men could do whatever they pleased.

So Titch and I started sharing my father's single man's room in a run-down boarding house full of drunks; a mice-infested, weathered dump. Every night down-and-out boozers visited our room, chasing grog. Titch and I headed off to school each morning hungry.

Our lunch was usually pie and sauce in the student canteen; dinner—snags with tinned peas—was eaten among aged alcoholics, shifties and no-hopers.

Our clothes were never washed and our general appearance was that of street kids. Dougal was rarely home, so mostly Titch and I put ourselves to bed. We came under the eye of at least one old paedophile, who took any opportunity he could to visit our room with his slimy befriending ideas. Titch and I spent all of our time watching each other's backs. It wasn't long before we started avoiding our 'home' and disappeared onto the streets, and into the laneways. Inevitably, thieving found its way into our modus operandi and we began stealing anything that wasn't tied down.

Never staying long in one place, Dougal soon moved us into the 'blood-house', the Vine Hotel in Richmond. Titch and I shared a room upstairs and Dougal had his own room. Like a pair of artful dodgers we were into everything. Down the road from the pub was Leo Berry's boxing gym, a mecca for con men. We started hanging out there after school. When I wasn't punching the bag, I'd hit the broom and help clean the gym. I looked forward to smelling the ripe stench of sweat and lanolin, and I loved the sound of the speed ball being thrashed or the rhythmic noise of a skipping rope hitting the timbers.

But we couldn't continue existing among beaten drunks, avoiding the reek of vomit in the hallways, watching 'hot' goods coming in the back door, or listening to the long-winded bullshit stories of amount-to-nothing wannabes. Nor should we have been glaring at the fat-titted hookers with their faces full of bad make-up, working the pay cheques on Friday nights. Dougal disappeared for a while and Titch and I were reunited with our sisters and Ma.

Our return to Ma's little pad also meant a reunion with the Bongiorno family. Both mothers fostered a closeness that would last through the rest of their years. For the first time in my life I had come to truly appreciate my own siblings, seeing them as individuals, not as opponents jostling for the same small slice of our tiny pie.

As I approached fourteen years of age I became totally besotted with each of the Bongiorno girls, with their stunning dark Italian features and masses of long dark hair. My pubescent male hormones were racing out of control and there seemed to be only one track in my mind, leading straight to the bosom of my next-door neighbours. Foolishly, I had come to believe that the elder two, Elizabeth and Mary, both in their late teens, were flirting with me, and I would sneak a splash of the landlord's Old Spice aftershave lotion and practice suave lines just before 'bumping' into them. Both girls eventually did break my heart when they took up with seriously older men. Devastated, I sought solace in the company of my kid sister Bubby, desperately hoping that she might introduce me to some equally busty girlfriends.

But our family mantra should have been 'nothing good lasts forever'. One quiet night, as we were all snuggled up in bed, Dougal came calling. He'd brought his best temper with him, pounding clenched fists angrily on the walls. Ma hushed my sisters to a petrified silence. Dougal's language became viler as he hurled his obese body against the door to our sanctuary.

I ran into the garden and took cover under a Norfolk pine, watching the anger ooze from his face, both hands clenched firmly around the door lock. Filth sprayed from his mouth as he pulled and pushed on the handle. I wanted to kill him. Police sirens wailed as they approached. My heart dropped from my chest as I watched him break the lock away from its housing, snapping the metal spindle. Finding the entire locking mechanism in his hand, he tossed it aside, and charged forward into the dark. Ma fell to the floor as I, cowardly, cried under my tree, hearing the sirens get louder.

A team of cops handcuffed Dougal after his violence moved into the front yard, in full view of the petrified landlord and midnight neighbours. As he was led away by six uniforms, one of them winked at me and smiled as he jerked the handcuffs hard up Dougal's back, causing him to yelp and jump a foot in the air. I knew absolutely that Dougal would receive a well-deserved flogging that night at the hands of those chesty men, and I sensed they'd enjoy dishing out their summary justice to a wife beater. He yelled his usual parting abuse, 'Fuckin' cop callers', as they forced him into the rear of the divvy van.

In that moment, as the divvy van cruised away, I dreamed of being a policeman one day. I saw the immediate effect a uniform could have and that effect proved intoxicating; for years we had suffered the abuse of this man, never able to cut ourselves free from his aggressive and selfish ways. Yet, in the space of a few minutes, a blue uniform had made the wolf disappear from our door, just like that.

Dougal was taken to a mental health institution for violent alcoholics where he was locked up for a time. All we found out was that he was induced into a four-day sleep before receiving shock treatment, a supposed remedy prevalent in the late 1960s.

Despite the help offered by the police that night, the boffins at Social Welfare chose to lock Titch and me up as well. The Box Hill Boys Home was a cruel place for two growing boys, housing, as it did, some of the state's worst young offenders. I'd never understand what 'care and protection' could come from living amongst teenage thugs and thieves. We had escaped our mad father for a gang of a hundred violent young desperadoes.

Institutional life for Titch and me was made somewhat easier because of our upbringing, which gave us credibility. I offered up wild stories about my Uncle Bill and his wharfie activities that were listened to with genuine zeal. It's the way of the world on the wrong side of the street, a way that we both worked hard at delivering during our time in the Home. Each day we kept one step ahead of a beating and two steps ahead of the influences that could turn us rotten. We had to survive, and we survived with dignity, rarely letting anyone get the better of us. Titch toughed it out like a much bigger kid and no-one got any free punches on him.

After much frustration Ma convinced the boffins that we should be freed from the institution and we were sent home. If we had stayed just a few weeks more, there's little doubt Titch and I would have been on a one-way ride to criminality. Sadly, Dougal was hovering again.

It was my turn to mop up the dishes but I was madly studying for my exams and we had a house deal that we could be excused from chores—especially Sambo and I, as we were in higher grades—under these circumstances. Ma asked Titch to dry the dishes. Our father was loafing on the sofa, itching for a blue. He and I hadn't communicated in any real sense since being evicted from our slime-green house more than three years earlier.

'Colin can dry the dishes Clare,' he yelled from the sofa.

'No he can't, he's got exams tomorrow,' returned Ma.

'I said Colin can do the fuckin' dishes, Clare, and that's it.'

I dropped my pen onto the table.

He swaggered into the kitchen, grabbing a tea towel from the nail on the wall where Ma hung them to dry. He walked over to the table where I was studying and threw it provocatively at me, showing his yellow teeth. 'You're drying mate!' My 14-year-old chest expanded to its maximum, as I took hold of my allotted tea towel. He poked his face close to mine. I saw hatred, and just then, my own eyes went blurry. That was the exact moment when rationality went out the window and rage took over. I threw the tea towel to the floor, yelling, 'Get fucked!'

There was no turning back. I charged him.

Our bodies bashed against the wall. Our joined mass caused the walls to shake and my sister to start crying. I held on as tight as my might could muster, believing he would surely get the advantage of me, but he was shocked by my aggression. I pounded his body against the wall again. The toaster fell, then the salt and pepper canisters. Ma was yelling, pleading, in a vain attempt to pull us free: 'Let go of him, he has to study.'

I stood back and faced the man I had hated all these years. Then I lurched forward with my right fist and clipped the side of his face, landing a poor punch. He looked rattled, being struck by his own son or more likely because he was involved in an actual fight with a male, as opposed to a woman. I swung again, with a better result. He charged me, hoping to end it with his bulk; in return, he received the hate and frustration of his entire family as my brother and sisters came to my aid and grabbed hold of him, pushing him away. Ma too joined in and the odds looked beautifully in favour of good instead of evil.

We five teamed well as we pulled, scratched and punched our way at him. Hitting him at times and hitting each other by mistake. His arms were raised to fend the blows as we mustered strength from years of forced submission, hatred and humiliation.

The old boy was weakening, succumbing to our superior combined strength. His body rocked towards me and I felt his flagging bulk. I needed to get that weight away from me and took in as much oxygen as my burning lungs could inhale. I looked over his shoulder and saw that the tea towels had fallen from the nail on the wall. I lined the nail up in my sight and, with as much force as my skinny body could summon, I pushed. He gathered momentum, moving back towards the wall, as my siblings joined the push and Ma stood aside exhausted. Dougal landed firmly on the nail. It pierced into his back and he looked up at the ceiling; his fight had ended.

Somehow Ma opened the back door to our forty-fifth house in fourteen years, and we all pushed our injured, but very alive, father out into the backyard, into his own darkness. The door shuddered close and I never saw him again.

3

CROSSROADS

My love for Italians began while living next door to the Bongiorno family, a priceless addition to my upbringing. The deal was sealed by another Italian: Vinnie, my best mate. We met as fifteen year olds and formed a gang: John, Joey, Bobby, Vinnie and I. Not a gang for violence or anything like that; a gang of wannabes, looking for action in the form of girls and parties. We became inseparable—did it all together: drinking, shooting pool, chasing girls, sharing girls, getting into fights, driving cars, fixing cars, chasing more girls, sharing more girls. On Saturday nights most of the gang would get inebriated at the local pub or band room, but—because of my father's influence, I think—I didn't drink as much as the others. I was also less likely to get into a fight, because by this age I had seen more than a lifetime's worth of violence.

I couldn't imagine a better bunch of guys to grow up with. We felt closer than brothers, and watched out for each other on a daily basis. A code of sorts held between us, making it mandatory to do whatever we could for each other. Vinnie moved out of home for a while after an argument with his father and took a flat across the road from where I lived. Naturally, he didn't have any furniture or any food, so we 'borrowed' whatever we could, including the bread and milk deliveries from the front yards of our neighbours. We convinced ourselves that the neighbours wouldn't have minded had they known the plight of our Vinnie.

Vinnie was the glue for our little group. The son of an immigrant, he came from a strict Italian upbringing. His parents were orthodox Catholic Italians. There is something about an Italian family that attracted me then, as now. Their 'old country' stories were filled with tales of poverty, yet also a unique family closeness and a determined desire to improve their lot.

I had seen these traits in Mrs Bongiorno, as she strived alone to provide, and saw them again in Vinnie's mother, Mrs Messina, who held together her perfect family with her very own apron strings. I would take my place most days at Vinnie's dinner table with Vinnie, his two younger brothers and both parents. All held faithful to the traditional ritual of dining together, sharing a wine and discussing the day. Mrs Messina was the world's second-best cook and Mr Messina pottered in the back garden, where he planted the mandatory tomatoes, zucchinis, grapes, olives, peppers, onions and everything else a good Italian father should grow. He also made his own wine. It was horrible but we drank it in copious amounts anyway and praised him profusely for it, ensuring a return pour came our way.

Music filled their welcoming home. There might be Mrs Messina's Italian classics wafting through the outdoor speakers, competing vigorously with Vinnie's Led Zeppelin or Black Sabbath. His younger brothers fought a miserable battle to have their Beatles albums played, only to be howled down by Vinnie's oh-so-mature cries of 'You're not playing that crap on my stereo!' The brothers drove Vinnie nuts with their incessant poking about in his motorcycle workshop and snooping through his precious record collection.

To sit in their backyard was a cultural bonanza: laughter, aromas, food and arguments. Mr Messina had great difficulty with Vinnie's shoulder-length ringlets and not a day passed without him reminding Vinnie of his embarrassment. Mrs Messina wove her way quietly between the two, with offerings of stuffed zucchini flowers or roasted peppers. I watched father and son struggling to reach a unanimous position on hair length or where motorcycles should be parked. Such theatre, and all this with soothing glances from the elegant and amused mother, serving antipasto; of course, there was always the occasional jibing from the two brothers, Joe and Mario, just to stir the pot.

On Sundays half the former population of Sicily descended on the small backyard. Car-loads of aunties appeared, laden with recently prepared delicacies, accompanying uncles with offerings of their own brews of house wine. Invariably, the afternoon would progress to Italian food, music and dancing. Most of the festivities took place under the lush wisteria-covered arbour, Mr Messina's proudly discussed handiwork. As he held court boasting of his timber craftsmanship, Vinnie would stand behind him with eyebrows raised to the heavens. The crowd always laughed loudly.

I was the token skippy. There was always a birthday being celebrated, or an engagement or a christening—never a divorce. The group was the same each Sunday, and every person present was dressed to the nines. The older folk had the sun-sheltered seats on the sidelines, allowing them to watch the dancing in comfort. From here these patriarchs sat back, looking slow and considered, observing, like sheepdogs watching their flock. Vinnie said they were the ones you never fucked with, the respected ones. Their craggy faces housed a few broken teeth, and they were rarely clean-shaven, looking just the type who might have dodged the law in the old country. Everyone acknowledged them on arrival, shook their withered hands and tended to their food and wine needs. The old boys intrigued me. Vinnie called them his godfathers, well before Hollywood dramatised the word.

Occasionally, as I meandered through the crowd, I suffered a cheek pinching or smooch from the sharper of the aunties. After a king's helping of Sicilian food and too much bad red wine, Vinnie usually made a declaration of utter disappointment. 'Enough of this wog stuff!' He argued with his parents for the right to leave the party and usually won, whereupon he gathered me up and charged into the night, leaving behind an adoring crowd.

Strangely, Vinnie might tell you he had a dysfunctional upbringing. Apart from the occasional generally good-humoured squabble, his upbringing always looked perfect to me. I guess another man's grass is always greener. When I, years later, returned home to Australia to await the birth of my child, it was Vinnie and the boys who made life bearable, with their regular madness and great calamity, and my frequent visits to the Messina household to indulge in Mrs Messina's antipasto. It was my daily exposure to my Italian friends that allowed me to appreciate their community and envy their ways. I still do.

It was not just Italian culture that seized my imagination in my late teenage years. The first of many journeys to Europe began with a trip to Amsterdam as a nineteen year old. It was a time of awakening for me, a boy from struggle town with a longing for more. Like most adolescent Australians I had it in my head that my time was getting away and I craved to see north of the equator. The action always seemed to be 'over there' and being stuck 'down under' was driving me crazy. I had a thirst that could never be quenched in my native environment.

The 1970s proved to be a fabulous time to be nineteen. The era of young people being able to afford to travel was just getting underway; the term 'backpacker' hadn't even been thought of. Travel luggage was generally a sturdy leather suitcase and a tiny carry-on bag, given to passengers by the airline when they purchased a ticket. I had arrived with mine in London in the northern autumn and took a variety of odd jobs. I shared a house with a dozen other travellers, one of whom, Norman, was heading over to continental Europe. He suggested we team up. We did.

I arrived in Amsterdam in the middle of winter. My body ached from the sheer cold but my mind was alive in a visual feast, absorbing the daily treats, tastes and adventures available on every street. My morning crawl from the hull of a houseboat began with an ice-cold wash from a basin of water fetched from a canal. Then, once I was dressed in as many layers of clothes as I could comfortably walk in, I hit the streets. During the day I teamed up with Norman, my strapping white South African friend, who I thought possessed great maturity. I was fascinated by his intriguing accent, one that I had never heard previously, and hung on his every word—he was so un-Australian. Norman was a quiet twenty-one year old, with matted blond hair that reached to the middle of his back, and a long wispy beard. The more I travelled with him, the more I started to look like him.

On fair-weather days I'd disappear into the narrow streets alone to explore the dozens of small art galleries, or stop and chat to the artists, absorbing the winter sun from the fronts of their bohemian studios. It was the beginning of my love affair with the world of art. Often I lost hours in the newly renovated Rembrandt House Museum, ogling art until the security staff booted me out so they could lock up. I was captivated by the avant-garde architecture of the suburbs running off the Spuistraat Canal; there was an interesting design at every turn, and shapes and materials I'd never seen before. I meandered blissfully, studying the mixed construction methods and unique facades.

It was a time when popular culture ruled, and there was plenty of it. I felt a growing sense of impatience, wanting to see what was next while desperately hoping not to miss anything along the way. Bands played all over town and the world's youth seemed to all be in the same place at the same time. The world had only just come out of the 'make love, not war' era. In Amsterdam, ideas were discussed openly and without caution, in stark contrast to other parts of Europe, firmly in the grip of the Cold War.

Most 'free speech' was voiced in the student cafes and bars in the centre of town. I headed that way at least once a day, just to be a part of it all. Then there was Dam Square, the thirteenth-century centre littered with young people, hippies, pigeons, music and the smell of dope. Drugs weren't illegal: in fact, an abundance of cafes specialised in selling a comprehensive range of choof, Afghani black hash, Moroccan heads and Spanish green, Lebanese gold and locally grown varieties. It was as easy as sitting and choosing your potion from a menu. I wasn't a junkie or even a heavy user of any 'recreational' drug but, like many going through the teenage years, I sampled a slice of this and that, including a smoke of choof every now and again. Norman and I looked dishevelled, which meant we were usually offered a pre-rolled joint of locally grown product or a tiny piece of hash, and off we went, choofing away, like two New World lords, sucking in not only the smoke but everything else that this Old World town could offer. Our walks were alive with long-winded, esoteric chats about life, history, art, music, lyrics and the words that filled our lives. It was the way of our times and they were, as we were reminded by the lyrics relayed by the outdoor speakers over Dam Square, a-changing.

Amsterdam exposed me to Vincent Van Gogh for the first time. There was a wing of the Rijksmuseum dedicated to his works. It was during one of those periods when European art was not in vogue and sometimes the gallery would be empty, except for me. I would stand alone for ages, staring at the collected works of this extraordinary artist. His images left me thinking, dwelling and a little melancholy. I think it was the rawness of humanity juxtaposed with the brightness in colour of his childlike painterly strokes that first drew me to his pictures. The understanding of desperation evident in his many self-portraits moved me; I'd seen a similar harrowing look on my Ma's face in younger years. His series of 'chair' paintings turned a pathetic old chair into an object of simple beauty. I *saw* the rattly old house in Clarkefield in Van Gogh's works. And the honesty and struggle that surfaced in his depiction of the Arles farm-workers was breathtaking. I was developing a deep appreciation of art, an appreciation that would carry on throughout my lifetime.

Norman and I had been shuffling the streets for months and had probably seen most of what there was of this wonderful town; we were due to talk of where to head next. Having spent a night at a YMCA near the Stormsteeg Bridge, we had risen and ventured out into the crisp daylight. We had gotten halfway across the Stormsteeg Bridge and the centre of Amsterdam was in front of us. The station was to our right. Norman looked in both directions.

'I think I'm going home mon,' he said with a hint of conviction.

'Back to London?' I asked, curious and surprised.

'No mon, I'm going all the way home,' he offered.

'South Africa, home?' I asked, with a sense of loss.

'It's time, I'm finished with travel mon, back to school in two weeks,' he said, working it out as he spoke. He wasn't one to waste words.

'How will you get there?' I asked, knowing that Norman had worked it all out in the previous thirty seconds.

'There's a bus from Dam Square through to Paris, then I'll fly.'

'When will you go?' I asked, knowing the answer by the look on his face.

'Now—it's time Colin, mon,' he said, as he turned to me and shook my hand.

'Why don't you come along mon … come to South Africa, you're a traveller.'

I knew in my heart I had no desire for South Africa. Apart from maybe ten more words, Norman and I parted company, never to see each other again. I stood alone on Stormsteeg Bridge, watching him head towards the centre of town, and taking his beautiful accent with him. Fading into the traffic, he was, plain and simple, a traveller going home.

This seemingly insignificant moment was more than just the parting of two friends. I had arrived at my crossroads, beginning a chain of events that forever altered the course of my life. At the time, all I saw in front of me was the need to make a decision on where I'd travel, now that I was alone. I turned towards the railway station and booked my passage to London.

When I was living in London, I briefly dated an Australian girl who was working as a nurse in a hospital on the outskirts of the city. She was a couple of years older than I was and was travelling and working with another nurse friend of hers. They had taken a bedsitter in Earls Court, and for reasons that were both convenient and cosy, I took up her invitation to stay with them and headed off on the ferry to London, to share her bed.

By week's end, my Aussie girl and I had fallen into a rut. Inclement weather does that to people; it reduces activity to the most basic. It was all to do with conserving energy and keeping warm, I guess. Each morning the three of us went off to our daily jobs—I had picked up a job in a butcher's shop and spent my days making sausages. We'd return home in the darkness of late afternoon, rug up for the evening and prepare a meal. The rest of the time would be spent huddled in bed or watching television. By March there was still no sign of winter letting go. Nights were cold, and the only heating we had was a small heater, worked by a coin-operated gas meter.

Nightly, we slapped together starch-driven meals of pasta or rice. The overall cost of living in London was horrendous compared to the meagre salaries offered. I remembered Ma's description of Clarkefield: 'merely existing'. It wasn't long before boredom had seeped into me. I missed the buzz that comes from travelling, and so I conjured up a plan to leave, within days, to take up Norman's offer and travel to South Africa. I went home to the bedsitter, to tell of my plans. I remember thinking how nervous I was, pacing the tiny bedsitter and fidgeting. At precisely the moment I had summoned the courage to break my news, she turned to me from the tiny kitchenette and said, 'I'm pregnant Colin'.

I stood dumbfounded.

The rest of the night was an awkward blend of forced discussion and tortured query. We resolved nothing. As tiredness overcame us and I lay in the bed—a mattress on the floor—I thought back to the Stormsteeg Bridge. I wondered, and I always would, about the decision I had made on that bridge; 'what ifs' ran through my mind as often as the image of the pregnancy.

The London weather started to improve, but the pregnancy didn't. Soon we were on a plane home. I was numb as the Qantas jet lifted off from Heathrow airport and I wondered if I'd ever return. I didn't sleep.

After landing in Melbourne, my girlfriend went to stay with her mother and deal with the run of questions and lack of answers. I stayed with Ma and ate very well again. I slept for sixteen hours that first night in the spare bed; my siblings waiting eagerly outside the bedroom door, to see me and to hear the stories of my adventures. The first story I told cast all my others deep to the outfield: 'A girl you have never met is pregnant.'

We didn't get off to a great start as a happy couple. Within a short time, we had nosedived; neither of us seemed to have any real feelings for the other and we had left our sex life, such as it was, back in London. We simply waited for the clock to tick around to October, when the baby was due: tick, tick, tick.

Tick, tick, tick … and so came 13 October, and the birth of Chelsea-Leigh. Literally, emotionally and individually, it was a great day. Like most fathers, I felt overawed by the sheer complexity, grit, pain and achievement of childbirth. 'The birth went without incident and mother and daughter are doing well'—I think that was what the doctor said. I know I felt half a metre taller, yet, at the same time, very insignificant. I smoked a big cigar.

With a new baby came a new job offer. On my return from London, I had gone back to my old job as a logistics manager; now, out of nowhere, I was asked to manage a new builders' hardware company that had opened in the outer eastern suburbs. Although the offer meant moving to a small house, the living conditions were better and the salary was higher.

Sadly, life in our new home was no better. It was a tough period and there were few luxuries in our life. Most of our furnishings were ones either that I had made, using offcuts of timber from work, or that we had purchased at trash-and-treasure markets. We were a long way from enjoying the lifestyle that our mortgage-belt neighbours had. Chelsea's mother was from a well-to-do family and I sensed she felt lower than the bottom rung on her ladder of life. Our baby daughter was still in nappies. She was growing fast, and each day there were moments of real pleasure as her personality started to show through. I relished my time at home after work and felt a close tie to her. She had become the cutest bundle of cheekiness, yet she and her mother couldn't seem to bond.

One weekend I was at home making a pine sideboard in the backyard. I stepped inside for a drink to be confronted by a sad and sorry sight of mother and child, a sight that flashed me back to my own childhood. Chelsea was lying helpless on the floor, crying hard. She wasn't seriously hurt but she was very distressed. While I appreciated that many new mothers are under great physical and emotional strain and are, at times, exhausted, it was worrying how Chelsea's mother stood over her, full of frustration, and clearly startled by my entry. Thankfully, only part of her initial angst had been delivered to Chelsea, but I feared for the future. My own history could not allow me to accept the incident, under any circumstances. We sat down and tried to talk about what had just happened, and about the hopeless situation we had found ourselves in, raising a child together. We were only kids ourselves and neither of us was ready for such a task.

As we talked, a great weight fell from her shoulders. We spoke honestly for perhaps the first time in our union, both agreeing that there was no future for us as a couple: we were too different to ever make a go of it. We found a furnished apartment block near her mother and close to town; there was a vacancy. It was decided I would move to another smaller house and take care of the baby. In a few hours, I was driving the mother of my child and some possessions to her new apartment. The only vehicle I had was a truck I had borrowed from work to remove rubbish from home, so we three bounced along in the front cabin together in stony silence.

My journey back home was surreal, with my bunny-rugged daughter sitting alongside me, her dirty-nappy smell wafting through the cabin: I was a single parent. As I drove through the night I thought back yet again to Amsterdam and my crossroads decision to head to London. I stopped myself from losing my head to memory by realising that London would be forever represented by the beautiful baby girl who slept beside me. Everything started to drop into place that night; it was a drive that I'll never forget. Chelsea was what it was all about.

I approached the task of caring for a baby like any other production or despatch issue. Chelsea needed three key things to work properly and efficiently. Firstly, she needed a vast supply of nappies. I introduced myself to the old washing machine and quickly learned how to use it. I rolled it as close to the back door as possible, allowing valuable time to be saved when taking the washed nappies to the clothes-line (disposable nappies were not yet common). Next, I set up a table in the kitchen, close to the washing machine. I kept all the nappy needs on the table, out and ready to go. No wasting time with ironing, folding or stacking clean nappies in cupboards, only to devote more time to hauling them out again. No walking from one room to another in search of the accessories associated with a clean baby. It was more efficient to gather everything at one central point. Formal dining got the shove for a year.

Chelsea was changed on the table and a new nappy selected from the large stack waiting nearby. The dirty nappy was tossed into a waiting bucket of water next to the washing machine, soaking before being put through the wash. Every peg I could muster was placed at an equal distance—the exact width of a nappy—from the next on the clothes-line, thereby shortening the time it took to hang out washed nappies. Chelsea and I had developed a sound and economical nappy replacement system that could be worked in parallel with feeding.

Feeding was the next problem; I saw it as the start of the nappy process. Chelsea had been on a formula since birth, which made life simple; she was now playing happily with some solids. I purchased baby food from the local wholesaler in bulk each fortnight, varying the recipe each time. To streamline matters we kept a large boiler on the cook-top laden with water, bottles and baby food, ready to be warmed.

The final task to be sorted was getting Chelsea to and from her crèche, and me to work. I had to be at work each day at seven o'clock. The upside was that I could easily be away from work by four o'clock.

My first trick was to convince the crèche to accept Chelsea at such a young age. Their policy had never allowed for a baby still in nappies, so I had to present myself to the owners and explain myself. I worded up the cute one and took her along as well. She performed beautifully, smiling and gurgling continuously. The position of a single parent was nothing new to the owners but the single parent being the father was a complete novelty. Not only were they amazed that I was undertaking the role but they were fabulously supportive. It helped that most of the child-care staff were girls of my age and they took an immediate liking to me—I guess because of the novelty factor. By the end of our first week, Chelsea and I had sorted the ideal working relationship between us. And so it went.

My God, it's hard bringing up a child alone! Maddeningly, crazily and stupidly hard! After two months I was as thin as a rake. By four months I was almost dead. When will these bloody nappies cease? When will this baby stand up, put on a dress and walk to school? When will she start dating and get married and leave my house?

Anyone visiting our little house may have noticed a few faded brown streaks running down one of the internal walls, near the nappy factory. There were times when frustrations took over in the parenting department. Sometimes life just gets the better of you, and sometimes a loaded nappy might be flung at the wall. Not a pretty sight, seeing a nappy projectile fly across the room, hit the wall at about head height, stop momentarily, and then slide ever so slowly downwards. But I could never, ever take my frustrations out on my cute little bundle of joy.

For all the ups and downs, I liked my life as it was, then. And I loved my little blonde-haired girl. She was doing as much for me as I did for her.

4

THE CUBICLE GIRL

'**A**tten-*tion*!' came the loud holler of the sergeant, almost bursting the veins in his bull neck as he fully extended his chest.

'Forwarrrrd … march!' Off we went, like tin soldiers: *left, right, left, right, left, right*, arms outstretched, thumbs pressed down onto clenched fists, eyes straight ahead, *left, right, left, right*.

'Squaaad … right wheel!' and turn right we did, just as we should, just as we had to, in perfect timing. My God, we're getting good at this. I can't wait till I march out of this godforsaken joint.

'Annnnd … squaaad … halt!' Twenty-eight dutiful police recruits did just that, stopping dead. 'Squaaaad! … At ease … stand easy.' By now the sergeant was clean out of steam.

'Listen up! Your graduation parade is in two hours. Don't forget squad 10/80, the chief and the media will be watching. Get it right. Get it absolllluttttely … right! Squaaad … dismissed!'

'Shut the fuck up, you'll give yourself a heart attack,' I whispered, riling against the strong discipline.

What had I been thinking five months earlier when I had sheepishly strolled in the front gates with a head of hair and an attitude? During the ensuing twenty weeks of classes and this nauseating drill sergeant, I had questioned everything, especially this stupid marching.

I hadn't minded the English classes, despite the way the gay teacher had gone all gooey and faint over the twenty-eight uniforms. I had been okay with the report writing sessions, but nosedived when it came to typing, remaining an aficionado of the two-finger work-out. I had loved the law classes, taking to them like a duck to water, though I don't know why. It was law that had got me through.

As I dawdled off the parade ground with my squad mates, heading for the dorm, there was an undeniable sense of relief. Now, at last, it was over, just as we were getting sick of each other. I was twenty-four years old.

Two hours later and we were all spit-polished in full dress uni-form. A bit more *left, right, left, right*, and then *halt*! For the last time. We stood in formation and listened to a longwinded speech by the police minister about increased budgets and police numbers.

I glanced across at my Ma, standing with her new husband Ray and fidgeting with the cuffs of her pale blue cardigan. She saw the parade as one of her proudest days. Finally, our names were called, in slow, alphabetical order. I waited patiently, 'A, B, C ...', the 'Macks' are always in the middle of a roll call. Dead centre, middle of the road, average—I liked that: it allowed room to move up, or crash down. My thoughts were drifting off again, to car chases, murderers, cops and robbers. I looked at the few squad mates I could see without turning my head, and wondered how many villains they had just arrested in their daydreams.

As recruit Lockwood was getting his handshake from the chief, I noticed Dee, looking sensational in her white fur wrap-around; a deli-cious mix of Dutch and Sri Lankan ancestry. 'Is this the one?' I asked myself as I stared at her. I hoped so, seeing I had had an earlier girl-friend's name crossed out from my tattoo and replaced with 'Dee'. Before I could come to an answer—*left, right, left, right*.

I saluted and took my diploma. I didn't hear a word the chief said, although I knew everyone respected Mick Miller. His mouth just seemed to open and close a few times, as if in slow motion, and I nod-ded. His collar looked way too tight and he had tiny beads of sweat on his brow. I must have been asked something, as he waited for a reply that never came; he frowned as I marched away. Waiting for the end, I drifted off again, back to my entrance interview, to a panel of three old-time coppers firing questions. They had worked halfway through their list and stopped, dropped their pens and sat back in their hard chairs. Luckily, they had seen stuff that I couldn't place on my paperwork.

They had chatted away then, recalling the past, and making scathing comments about the new breed of criminal, junkies. One of them had eventually looked down at his paperwork, then up again. He had asked about my Uncle Bill, who had a history with police. I offered up my past freely, believing they would have had it on file anyway. They did, and my honesty was what they had sought. One of them had met Uncle Bill and liked his character, just didn't agree with his hobbies. Then they had focused on my travels to Amsterdam and London, believing it a fine way for a young person to grow up. I had nodded. None of them had worried about me having been a disc jockey in a dozen different nightclubs. They had seemed to notice my wry smile at this point and dropped their eyes back to their reports. I had noticed two similar smiles on the panel.

The other panel member had a teenage daughter about to head overseas. He had asked a host of questions about where his angel should visit, and what to watch out for. I'm sure it was those travel escapades that got me recruited, not the mere 70 per cent I received in the exams, or any grandiose statement I might have made about good versus evil.

A whining feedback squeal rang through the Chief's microphone. He tapped madly at the offending mouthpiece, deafening everyone. The commotion snapped me back to the present. I grabbed my cap and threw it into the air, along with twenty-seven others. My guests enjoyed a round of applause and far too much gossip about life as a recruit. Lecturers slipped in between the gossip to tell them what a bright recruit I was and then mingled with the others, telling them the exact same thing. Two cups of tea, a few handshakes, and off we went, out the same academy gate through which I had entered, this time with a royal-blue uniform and loads of trepidation.

Walking to the car, I spared a thought for my younger days, the life I shared with Titch and the stupid things we had done, and shivered for a moment. Too many home addresses flashed through my mind: some that I had forgotten, others that hurt. I saw Dougal sitting, romancing a bottle of beer, at our kitchen table. I turned away, chest out, enjoying the fresh air and a strange sensation, one that I experienced for the first and only time in my police career, one that embraced me, held me close. I felt like a new centurion. I let my breath out, slowly, sensing many different battles ahead, and forever dropped that line of thought.

My post-graduation weekend was spent at home. Dee and I did a lot of catching up and the rest of the weekend was spent worrying about Monday and my rookie period at Oakleigh, a tough station about 15 kilometres from the centre of town. From the beginning I harboured a constant longing, one that only got stronger. I wanted to be a detective. I wouldn't settle for anything less. I knew that uniform work was just a stepping stone, and the way ahead was to be an outstanding uniform cop.

I tried on my uniform countless times, getting the feel of it, hoping to relax the stiff woollen fabric, the thick cotton shirts and heavy black leather boots. Dee caught me a dozen times, standing in front of the mirror, talking to invisible crooks, reaching quickly for my handcuffs, spouting, 'You're under arrest!' Of course, it was a bit of a buzz wearing the belt, handcuffs and baton, and I stuck a police issue notebook in the top pocket with a pen and strutted about the house booking Dee for being too gorgeous and Manny the dog for gulping his food. But in the end I surrendered to the simple truth: I hated the uniform. Never had I felt so restricted, so formal, so copperish. I was so down on the whole uniform caper that at no time did I ever allow my neighbours, best friends or old workmates to see me dressed in it. I realised I wasn't a loyalist, or a purist, and probably not a true centurion. I just wanted to be a detective and wear a suit.

The first thing I learned was that being a street copper was no breeze; that, in fact, at times it was as hard as hell and almost as dangerous. Rookie life at Oakleigh was full of Greeks, old-time knockabout Aussies, and a swelling population of Asians.

On my first day in uniform, I arrived sharp at the appointed time of seven, driving my beat-up Volkswagen Beetle, which was spewing black smoke. I had bought it for only 500 bucks six months earlier from a stoned surfie on the beach. The motor was buggered and it coughed, spluttered and pigrooted its way forward, trying to get there. I hadn't paid the rego, although I had meant to—I had just always been busy. The tyres were bald to the wire. As I rolled into the rear car park, the old bomb just died. I got out, facing a stiff sergeant who stood looking at me, guts hanging over his belt.

'Did you seize that shitheap?'

'What?'

'Did you just fuckin' seize that?' The sergeant tried a little harder.

'Oh … well … yes.'

'Are you the new connie?'

'Connie … yes.'

'Well done son, a pinch on your first day.' He glared at the car.

'Thanks.'

'Call the towies to get rid of the shitheap.'

It felt odd, walking into that police station, like being in a 1950s time warp. I wandered through the chemical smell of high-gloss paint on the walls and over the fresh beige linoleum on the floors, looking, I'm sure, like a startled rabbit, still pulling on my collar.

What I quickly learned was that cops cost governments money. There's no dough in locking up crooks or in prosecuting baddies. From a government's perspective, the best way to deal with cops in need of new office equipment is to throw the old junk at them. Everything was second-hand: the clapped-out typewriters, rejected by the Ministry of Justice; the redundant office desks, dumped by the Department of Public Prosecutions; and the swivel chairs that had lost their swivel. My allocated locker was one of those tiny vented steel jobs given to schoolkids, about the size of a bread box. I was told to hang my uniform on a hook on the verandah. There were never any pens. I was constantly knocking them off or buying my own—there was always someone with their eyes fixed on your pen.

Every station had a 'watch-house' counter, a reception, where the public came to whinge, or where the crooks were checked in and issued a room and discussed their frequent flyer points. I was sure the watch-house was really just a museum of ancient office equipment. The oldest desk was lined with ink pads: red, blue, black, and about twenty different stamps, one for every occasion. The watch-house keeper was normally a young rookie, riddled with nerves and pimples. Rarely were they given any instructions on how to handle complaints, write reports or help the public. Most of them were so new to The Job they just stood there, nodding, listening to the grievance, unable to offer anything.

The reception door was fitted with a buzzer. When it sounded, the more senior cops scampered to the back of the station to avoid dealing with complaints. Sometimes they got jammed together in the hallway as they fled, leaving the naive rookie to stare blankly at his customer. The senior cops were consumed with driving around the back streets in the police cars hunting the 'Top Ten' most wanted crooks and local riff-raff. It wasn't long before I understood where the 'us against them' mentality came from. It thrived in the cops.

Every minute there was something happening. It all started the second the rookie clocked on for duty and didn't end until he was well into unpaid overtime. One minute a stabbing, the next a domestic argument, then a report of a beat-up letterbox, then a car accident, then a drug overdose and on it went. It was as though all the car accidents, fights, injuries, thefts and arguments lined themselves up waiting for the rookie to punch his clock card, and then—*bang*! It all started.

I was a rookie for four months, the usual period. There was no guidance, no post-graduate instruction. I had to pick it up as I went, learn as I worked, run as fast as the next guy. There were many shifts, particularly at night, when I was alone at the station, juggling job after job. After a while I was begging for a day at the office to finish some of the zillion forms that had to be completed for each incident.

I reckoned my upbringing helped me, as I knew (mostly) how riff-raff thought and the ways to deal with them. Sometimes talking was cool, sometimes talking was a sheer waste of time. It depended on an endless list of variables. What I knew absolutely was that there were no rules for trying to fathom human behaviour. The answers weren't in any textbook, nor were they posted on the noticeboard of any police patrol room. You had to work them out as you went along, based on the person in front of you; based on whether you were dealing with the world's worst individual or whether you were simply faced with a drunk who only wanted someone to take notice and tell him things were okay.

I soon realised that some of the locals on my beat treated cops with disdain, refusing to have anything to do with us. To many we were lepers, to be studiously avoided. The exceptions were the elderly, who often called on us for reassurance and support. I watched them become more vulnerable, calling us off the street, often just for a cup of tea and a chat. What they were really doing was asking, 'Is everything all right?' Their neighbourhood was changing so fast and they could only sit by looking, bewildered, at it all.

On the whole most people just kept to themselves. They didn't want to know—about crime, their neighbour's break-in, the whereabouts of so-and-so, or any other matter. No-one leaned over the back fence anymore or got to know the people next door; the sense of community was fading.

The biggest surprise was the number of drug users on the streets. I don't mean teenagers who snuck an occasional choof but desperate heroin addicts. I hadn't really taken much notice of them before, yet, here they were in the shopping centres, squatting in derelict houses and hanging out in many of the pubs. Those early days were a rude awakening.

The number of household burglaries was at an all-time high, as were office break-ins and car thefts. Street violence was at such a level that concerned parents simply refused to let their kids visit some areas. There were stories of junkies brutally bashing elderly people while they made off with their housekeeping money. Addicts would ransack a back shed for a set of golf clubs or an electric drill set; they were stealing anything they could get their hands on, to momentarily assuage their insatiable habits. The newspapers were full of headlines and addicts were full of junk, mostly speed or heroin. The real calamity was that it was the white powder doing the burglary, not the 18-year-old syringe cushion waving the knife. It was also the white powder that woke the junkie in the morning with aches and shivers and sent him over your back fence, again.

When I was a boy, a crook was someone you might hear about on the grapevine—a hard-nose who lived in the next-door bungalow, only venturing out at night with his kit bag, in the days when tattoos were reserved for crooks and sailors. Most people never saw an old-style crook. Why would they? It was the banks, payroll vans and container ships that they preyed on, not your television set. The closest Mr and Mrs Jones got to a crook was reading the weekend news round-up, which was mostly blunt tabloid journalism, accompanied by black-and-white photos of a blown safe or a robbed paymaster.

Old-world crooks were tough guys, blooded by a tough father or uncle, rising through the ranks, not dissimilar to apprentices really, until one day they were jumping bank counters themselves. In those days there was honour among thieves, at least until the shit hit the fan and the detectives started warming up with telephone books. A bit like my Uncle Bill, crooks had their own codes of conduct, as did the detectives. Wives, kids and the elderly were never interfered with. The family was sacred, as was the family home, to both sides of the fence. But times had changed.

After Oakleigh I was shipped off to 'the Castle', the police head-quarters at the northern end of Russell Street, opposite the old court building and jail that had been around since Ned Kelly's day. The start of the 1980s was a time of street protests and rallies. It wasn't uncommon for a crowd of a thousand or more left-wing socialists to take over the central business district and cause havoc, all under the guise of an official street march. Every uniform was called upon to do their bit.

Often I found myself standing at the front of a police line, placidly taking the abuse and insults hurled vehemently at us. Our instructions were always, 'allow them to let off some steam, don't make any arrests'. Of course, the leadership of the leftist groups took full advantage. We were spat on and had marbles thrown under our feet. Big, butch, hairy students would spew bad breath vitriol, centimetres away from our faces, then let fly with sharp kicks to the shins and knees to our groins. I lost count of the number of times I took my uniform coat to the dry-cleaners to have the spit cleaned out.

At least when the builders' labourers marched, they didn't resort to spitting. There were a few times they'd cut up rough and everyone had a free for all, with haymakers and punches going in all directions. The union boss, Norm Gallagher, was going through grief with the courts, so in his defence and as a show of strength, his membership took to the streets, and old Norm would waddle out every now and again to stir them up. Most were just looking to score a few hours off work and take in a few laughs; many of them got to know us and we'd say 'hello' before the noise started up and 'goodbye' at the end. It was a bit like a Monty Python skit.

Russell Street offered more of the same that I had experienced in Oakleigh; more walking the beat, more car accidents, more drug overdoses, more fights, more pub brawls and more of wearing that silly uniform. The bonus for working at the Castle was the intensity of jobs. Like a magnet, the city drew in crazies and all the bent and damaged individuals seeking extreme experiences. One of those misfits could explode any night of the week and all hell would break loose for an hour or two. It was these experiences that made my job a sliver or two more exciting than being stuck in the suburbs.

I never avoided assignments and always put my hand up for an extra shift or overtime. It is a peculiar job; this sort of work becomes addictive. You can find yourself lost to the adrenalin that the beat delivers, always wanting more, often seeking a greater level of intensity. I had a friend at that time, Jenny, a nurse who was employed in the casualty section of a large hospital. She had the same addiction to her workplace, thriving on the challenges that sprang up. We sat around for hours swapping stories.

Jenny felt that she was achieving a great deal, being a charge nurse in one of the busiest casualty rooms in Australia. She dealt with the weekend rush of ailments and misery, desperate people all wanting her to 'help', to react and to save them. Her 8-hour shift was often twice that, most of it unpaid overtime. She hung around for the buzz, for the rush—for selfish reasons, yet reasons that were ultimately unselfish. I could identify with every word Jenny said. It is the 'what next' buzz that holds you to The Job, stops you from going home. It's indescribable, the thrill of not knowing what's about to walk in the door.

In amongst the euphoria, there were occasions when I felt I was going a little stir crazy with my constant search and need for intensity. This is the dangerous period, the period when all the lines become fuzzy and reality starts to fade. It is the time when cops can either start to actually believe they are new centurions, consumed in their own self-importance and their delusion, or they lose themselves to alcohol, and crash, falling onto the growing scrap heap of burnt-out police. I was beginning my own journey along that first track.

The months rolled by, as did the heartache I saw and the violence I witnessed, until, one night, it reached a peak.

It could have been any other rookie on patrol that night. There was a call about a young girl in distress at the McDonald's on Swanston Street in the city centre. I was the first to arrive. The female toilets were the focus of a dozen blank stares from customers, frozen to their seats. An obscenely youthful counter kid ushered me forward. There was a sort of post-traumatic numbness at McDonald's that night, a numbness that is often present at the very worst crime scenes once the initial horror passes. I was walked down some stairs, past a sea of faces, into the unventilated rest rooms to the rancid smell of trapped urine.

Cautiously I opened the toilet cubicle doors, one by one. At the third door I was faced with a young girl, sitting on the pan. Her face was beautiful. Her fragile shoulder was resting against the side wall, legs sprawled, and her head drooped. Saliva dribbled to the floor from her loosely gaping mouth, and her eyes stared at me. A hostile syringe was embedded deep in her arm, the needle bent, probably from a shoddy attempt to remove it. Her left wrist was crudely lacerated and congealed blood dampened her jeans, covering the floor, all the way to the vanity basin. A razor blade lay at the bottom of the toilet water. She had injected a monstrous load of heroin into herself and then slashed her wrists. The heroin had sent her to noddy-land and the blood had drained from her body. She was dead.

I don't know what affected me more: the sight of the congealed blood, the syringe, or the undeniable beauty of the sixteen year old. A street gang, the Lebanese Tigers, had sold her the heroin. Although I was expected to spring into action, I couldn't; I just stood frozen, feeling a deep sadness for what could have been. A girl, on the edge of womanhood, her innocence stolen and yet, as I bent down to check for her pulse, I still saw it in her dead eyes.

The raw stench of her blood crawled into my nostrils. My boots were slippery underneath. I wanted to run, to get out, to breathe again. As I stepped away from the toilet to radio for an ambulance, I left sticky red footprints.

Once the paramedics had dealt with her body and she was taken to the morgue, I walked off on my own. Initially I headed to the busiest intersection in the city and stood, watching the hustle and bustle, quietly scraping the remaining blood from my boots onto the gutter's edge. I listened to the sounds of night: car engines, passing trams and giggling revellers. I drifted along the busy streets, wondering what sort of career I had entered, and why such obscene, cheap thrills plagued my work. I needed to escape and go travelling again, to disappear to some place nice and safe—but I was stuck with the knowledge that the dead girl was going nowhere, at least nowhere on this planet.

The street noises irritated me to a point where I ached for silence, so I headed into a park and found a quiet bench. I thought about what I was doing for a career and how it was changing me. I wondered what the dead girl's parents would be feeling at that moment, as I sat with drunken teenagers staggering past. I was absent without leave from my beat, but I needed to question my world. My thoughts took me back to my own home, back to the little house I was renovating by the beach, and to who was sound asleep in the second bedroom.

Perhaps it was the memory of Chelsea that jolted me back to reality, or maybe the growing noise of the late-night stragglers who were still roaming through the park. I had lost myself to an hour of deep thought. The image of the cubicle girl would prove impossible to remove for a long, long time. I openly feared what sort of world Chelsea might walk in when she was sixteen. I wanted to be put in a position where I could make a difference, any difference, to this madness. After twelve months on the beat I came to realise the brave coalface work of uniform cops had no real impact on the agonies generated by heroin abuse. I sat, confused about life, until it was time to knock off, and then I ventured home and sat some more, at the foot of Chelsea's bed as she slept.

Chance or fate, or whatever you want to call it, stepped in, and out of the blue came an offer to work in plain clothes, to escape the uniform, pull out my old jeans and maybe grow a beard. It was an opportunity to focus on street crime and, I hoped, make a contribution to stemming the rising tide of gangs and drugs in the city. It was as if some high-ranking officer in the Castle had heard my silent pleas as I stood at that McDonald's toilet cubicle, praying for the chance to make a difference.

In 1980, Melbourne had as bad a gang problem as at any period in its urban history. Gangs with tags like the Lebanese Tigers or Thomastown Tuffs or the Sydenham Boys descended on the Botanical

Gardens each weekend for a little warfare, mostly bashing themselves from head to toe. Most of the time speed or amphetamines promoted the action. Once they were bored with that intoxicating elixir of drugs, alcohol and violence, the gangs would splinter off into the streets of the central city, in search of the flashing lights of the pinball parlours.

The reality about gangs of young toughs is that, once they take hold, they are difficult to move on. That toxic mix of bravado and testosterone—hero stuff when you're in a gang of ten angry hoons with nothing but spit and time on your hands—is hard to eradicate. Each night they moved onto Russell Street, a few blocks away from police headquarters, where they preyed on kids far too young to fight, schoolkids in town for a movie or to spend their pocket money.

My plain-clothes partner, Wayne, and I were stepping in and out of vacant doorways one night, dressed in jeans and T-shirts. The trick was to blend in. It was easy to spot a plain-clothes cop, with a short-back-and-sides haircut and regulation-size moustaches: creativity was the key. There were times when we went all out and dressed like bums, in the worst clothes we could find. Wayne's nickname was the 'Master Blaster', because of his cool attitude under pressure. Like me, he had joined the force after working here and there; he had travelled the world for a few years and had joined the cops to make his mark. We were mates. He was not only street cunning, he was solid to work with. He got the job done. And, like me, Wayne was grooming himself for something better.

This night, my denim jeans were sticking to me like a leotard. The sweltering sun had been boring down all day, leaving a claustrophobic closeness in the evening air. Then I saw three ominous shadows walking up my dark laneway. Some Lebanese Tigers were on the loose; their timing was perfect. I nudged Wayne.

It was well after midnight. We had heard the last of the roar from the crowd at an open-air rock concert, who were now heading into the city. A wave of Saturday night trouble was on its way. The Lebanese Tigers were looking to dole out a flogging to an old vagrant, or perhaps break into a building to lighten the owner of some of his possessions. We waited for the shadows.

'Shhh,' Wayne said, abruptly pulling me into our dark niche. I held my breath. They moved clumsily from one door alcove to the next, trying out their jemmy. We sensed a potentially dangerous situation; our response had to be quick and firm. Wayne eased out his firearm, stowing it behind his back, and we sank deeper into the piss-stinking alcove.

'Two doors away, they'll step in,' he said.

'Guess who?'

'Snake.'

'Good one,' I whispered, reaching nervously for my firearm.

Snake was in his mid-twenties and thought to be the leader of the Tigers. He had a nose the size of an axe head and was one of the city's worst thugs. It was rumoured that he had given the cubicle girl, and many others, their heroin. There were two low-level thugs with him, probably full of poison, but both were far bigger than we might have hoped for. Their shadows loomed as the laneway light guided them to us. Snake's foul mouth was bossing his boys: 'Try this, quick, quick, fuckin' try this fuckin' door, quick.' He was talking fast, the common side effect of too much speed. We could hear the jemmy working; no luck at that door—they moved closer. One metre away, then they stepped into our square; three to two in a doorway face to face, not a good ratio.

'Freeze … Police,' we yelled in tandem, our firearms drawn. It is strange how unmistakably authoritarian those two words can sound. The jemmy hit the asphalt. *Clanggg!* Wayne and I both felt the initial blows to our heads as fists flew. Our three bad boys jumped high, turned in mid-air and attempted to flee. Comically, they only bumped into each other. More fists, more chaos.

In a situation like this you have less than a split second to grab the first body that presents itself. Wayne jumped on his closest body and I jumped on mine. Another bout of 'Freeze…' as well as the hard touch of a cold steel barrel under the chin. They dropped to the putrid asphalt, breathing in vagrant piss and pigeon shit. The third one was gone quicker than a hot pie at half-time at the football. Snake was good at avoiding arrest.

'Who was your mate?' we hollered. 'Who?'

'What mate?'

'Who was your mate?' Wayne barked, forcing his Tiger's head into the asphalt.

'Don't know nothing, cunt.'

Wayne's strong suit was not infinite patience, nor was he fond of gratuitous insults. There are a lot of tricks you learn to encourage street punks to talk. Some work, some don't; depends on the resolve of the one who might be enjoying it, so to speak. Wayne deployed his favourite stategy and the response was immediate. The former tough now looked nothing like a fearful modern-day crook; all the tough had run out of him. He now belonged to the Master Blaster.

'Who was the prick who ran away?' Wayne asked, with quiet confidence this time.

'Sorry sir, I'll tell you, I'll tell you,' came the well-mannered reply.

And so he did, tell us everything, and more. Both toughs then went gingerly into the Castle to be charged; we picked up Snake later for half-a-dozen break-ins and for drug dealing, and then back on the prowl we went, wandering the streets all night looking like a couple of desperadoes as we looked for real desperadoes.

At the end of our shift Wayne and I usually sat around and drank enough coffee to keep us awake for a month. Often the coffee was replaced by a few boutique beers at a favourite 'shit-head-free' bar. We cop-talked for hours, about our work lives, our careers; we talked about our problems. Once you were a cop, you found a few thousand mates to talk to and that's how it was. There was often strife to discuss, whether it was a marriage that went sour or an internal police investigation that was worrying someone. But this morning I was heading home, and strife was the last thing on my mind.

I was about to get married. Dee was sublime, far too heavenly to let go; marriage seemed my only solution. I wondered why women wanted so desperately to be married and why men so openly obliged. I also wondered whether I was making a mistake. I loved her, sure, but 'for ever and ever'? That concept confused me. Certainly my own parents weren't too good at holding that one down. I imagined my life without her and saw a lonely man living in a city apartment with time on his hands. I shook my head and saw a nicer image, that of a cosy wedding at the police chapel and some fine food and wine. I saw two happy people.

We had been weaving a fine tapestry together. I only hoped Dee, at twenty-four years of age, would allow us to grow together, and leave the having children part for a few years. There were good times to be had, and a career to explore first. The last thing I wanted was for cracks to appear in our otherwise rich relationship. I brushed it off as I drove home to catch a few winks.

It was a big day; a great day. Titch was my best man and most of the friends I had gathered in life were there: Vinnie, Thomas and the beautiful Sally, Rico and his gorgeous wife Gina, and right up the front was my darling mother, looking a treat, standing proudly alongside her husband Ray. Chelsea was the flower girl, naturally, and did all her little jobs to perfection. Then down the aisle came Dee, looking better than any girl had the right to look. As she walked towards me, with her wondrous father guiding her, I felt lucky.

The months on my calendar just seemed to peel away. Wayne and I were soon looked upon as two of the 'old boys' at Russell Street, though I wasn't yet twenty-seven years old. I was still enjoying plain-clothes work. 'Our time will come', we thought.

5

SECRET SQUIRRELS

I got the word. A vacancy in the drug squad surveillance unit was to be advertised and I should put in for it. The 'dogs', or 'secret squirrels', were an elite four-man team working exclusively on drug traffickers. They were the cops who followed the big crooks at a time when stamping out drug dealing was top priority. This was the break I had been waiting for since I stood staring at the cubicle girl more than two years earlier.

The secret squirrels were considered a privileged team, hidden in a secret cell inside the drug squad. Working covertly, with an arsenal of vehicles and photographic and video equipment, they could go anywhere, any time, enjoying full anonymity. To enable them to do so, their whole existence was falsified. I wanted the job badly, so I studied my arse off, digging out drug legislation, notes and case histories.

They put me through the wringer, poring over my background, firing question after question, to the point where even I started to wonder who I was. The field of thirty-seven was narrowed to a handful, and I was one of them; another round of interviews, and then, finally, I received an internal letter, instructing me to 'come Monday, and leave your police uniform behind'. I went home to celebrate.

The drive home that night was not as exhilarating as it could have been. Instead of feeling elated, I found my mind turning to the many problems that were developing in my marriage. Cracks that I had hoped might heal kept getting deeper, wider. Dee had become envious of my closeness to Chelsea. I was torn, struggling to comfort and reassure her, but frustrated that any affection I showed to Chelsea, if witnessed by Dee, was taken as a slight against her. She didn't seem to understand the bond that there often is between single parents and their kids; she had no need to be jealous, I cared deeply for her. Most of the time I let it slide, other times I'd get annoyed and voice my disappointment. I think we both realised how different we really were, and both feared that our time together might be running out. I started juggling—home versus work—as many other cops did.

The secret squirrels' office was part of the drug squad's muster room. We had to park our cars in an underground car park across the road, then, covering our faces with a magazine or newspaper, we sprinted across the street. Once in through the back gate, we wove our way through the uniform section, past the CIB block, up a few flights of stairs and into our office. There we walked past Jan, the receptionist, who had spent twenty-five years sneaking people in and out, and then into the muster room, past the narcotic detectives: Murph, Parsons, Blob, Bingo, Steel, Furzo, Two Dicks, Belly—no-one was ever called by his real name. Each of the detectives kept a cheap bottle of aftershave in his top drawer, just for Friday night, play night.

The drug squad office was a haze of cigarette smoke and a maze of posters, drug paraphernalia and junk, confiscated from drug dealers. Bongs were used as ashtrays; Bob Marley was on every wall. Minute weighing scales sat on top of desks, glass syringe kits lay idle, mug shots were pinned here and there, some with a dart in the forehead, or 'caught' written in texta. Sledgehammers and jemmy bars, maps of state forests, images of marijuana leaves and opium poppies and clutter was the design. The professional buzz within this group was addictive, just like the drugs.

At the very back was the squirrels' office, full of toys. Spy toys—cameras, binoculars, monoculars, tripods, video equipment, listening devices, trackers, battery packs, aerials, tinting sheets, rolls of film, cartridges and anything else that could fit—filled the lockable cabinets that lined the walls. I moved in.

The part of the office that attracted the most attention was the photo wall or pinboard where photos, either confiscated or stolen on raids, were on display. Every squad had one. The photos, of some of the country's toughest crims, were invaluable, ideal for detectives trying to identify a suspect. They were mostly happy snaps and solved countless crimes. Often a few juicy photos of crooks' molls were placed on the wall; these girls were certainly not camera shy. Explicit snaps of lovelies flashing their tits and more; shots of a girl and a few guys, all sharing a bit of lovin'—just your typical bad-guy family-album stuff. There would be at least one detective gazing at that wall most times during the day.

It was there that I spent my first months understanding the life of a secret squirrel. We had six vehicles in our fleet, a car for every occasion, including a utility, a panel van and a coupé. They were cars that blended in with the traffic, making it possible for surveillance; we had one that could look like a plumber's van one day, a food-delivery truck the next or a hippie love machine on yet another. They were full of gadgets: recording devices, cameras, tinted windows—even a swivel chair that worked.

Our targets were the upper echelon of the criminal world. We were after the kingpins, the guys who either made the junk or imported it from places like China, Burma, Colombia, Lebanon, Afghanistan, Thailand … so many locations, so many different types of poison. The top-end drug traffickers could expect to triple or quadruple their initial outlay with each importation. Sometimes the rewards were even greater. It wasn't a bad earner, if you could stomach the risk. A mere million-dollar funding of a successful load could return a larger fortune. The guys who chose to manufacture speed were achieving even bigger profits. No wonder they drove around in flash imported cars.

Many were living in penthouses on the edge of the water, overlooking the city they controlled. Most had lawyers on retainers, private eyes on the end of their phones and goons taking care of business.

Some of the smarter crooks were well versed in surveillance. They had to be; it was just risk management for them. They were so clever, often adopting anti-surveillance moves to shake off the squirrels, especially as we got close to their homes or, more importantly, close to their place of drug dealing. It's something else to see a criminal's paranoia, especially if he had been tipped off that the squirrels might be working on him. A good crook would just presume he was being worked on. We knew that and were happy to outsmart them, most of the time. I learnt quickly that drug dealers weren't anything like the dumb-arse nongs usually portrayed on television shows.

Whenever we got a new car, it went through the garage to be fitted with gadgets, switches and buttons. Each car had highfalutin radio frequencies to talk car-to-car, to the office, to other detectives' cars or to common police radio operators, depending on the need-to-know basis. Radio devices were secreted under the seats and dashboard so sticky-noses wouldn't be able to see. Our car-to-car radio was tucked away in the roof lining and operated with foot buttons near the accelerator. Nothing was visible, even to a junkie, should he smash a side window looking to lift a quick purse or wallet.

Also hidden were a heap of switches to alter the many lights of the car. We avoided detection by flicking switches to dim the headlights, or turn them off, or kill the reverse lights or indicators and many other combinations. A surveillance-savvy crim will check his rear-view mirror, watching for the same headlights. (Each model of car gives off a different pattern in the headlight glow.) We could change the character of our headlights, bluffing the target into believing the car behind him was not the one he had spied earlier, all in a switch. The brake light kill-switch was effective when 'following' someone from the front, again during the night. Once you got a reasonable distance on the crook and were temporarily out of sight (around a corner or curve in the road) the idea was to kill the tail lights, do a quick U-turn and come back on the target, without him seeing the glow of the tail lights. The tricks were endless and great fun.

Some of our cars were fitted with high-powered engines, well over the manufacturer's specifications, allowing us to drag down fleeing criminals. We also had state-of-the-art trackers to hide on a target car, which was really useful if the driver was holding large amounts of drugs or cash. A tracker meant you didn't have to be all over him at a time when he was hot, allowing him to do what he did best: deal drugs. Then, when he was done, we could get up close and bust him.

It was the bust that was the real fun, often at the end of many weeks of dogging: weeks of gathering evidence meant swapping cars many times, following the crooks on foot, through airports, on planes, through shopping centres, even in and out of banks and chemical supply companies. Foot surveillance needed a separate range of equipment, from covert radio kits with microphones sewn into jackets or shirt collars to carry bags fitted with micro video cameras, to tape crucial evidence. We even had jackets and belts fitted with hidden camera kits, and a baseball cap with a camera the size of a lolly hidden inside. The list of gadgets was endless; as soon as one was invented, the technicians were hard at it creating another, often smaller device. It was a lot like playing between the pages of an Ian Fleming novel.

The cameras we used were many and varied, from the most capable 35 mm SLR cameras and long-distance lens and myriad smaller lenses to tiny hand-held cameras designed to catch one photo at an exact moment. I tended to hog the cameras a lot of the time, trying to get that one magic photo.

The worth of photographic evidence was proved the time we dogged an amphetamines cook to Ballarat. Oclat was one of the biggest manufacturers of speed in the country; he had been making vast amounts for years and was closely involved with the Hell's Angels, supplying them with kilos at a time. We dogged him around chemical supply companies for weeks, watching him buy the chemicals needed to create his potion. We had him cold, buying precursors and the intricate glassware used in the long process of making speed. Much of the evidence was on secret film and videotape. The only thing missing was his laboratory.

Then one Sunday Oclat took a country drive in his fully laden four-wheel drive, leaving his wife and kids behind—that's always a good sign that someone's up to no good, especially when the forecast is for wet weather. It was raining cats and dogs, and the squirrels were failing to keep up with him on the slippery highway. Blinding sheets of water made it almost impossible to follow. Luck came our way a few minutes before Ballarat, when he turned onto a network of lane-ways alongside the state forest. The tracking device did the rest, putting him to bed on a small farm in the middle of nowhere. We knew we had him this time.

During the night, as he slept, Vag and I did some serious snooping on the property. Vag was nicknamed Vagrant because of the extreme lengths he went to in dressing down to blend in on the street. He was an extraordinary operative. No-one was better with a camera. We snuck around in the dead of night wearing thick hiking socks, perfect for spying. Boots and shoes make telltale marks in the mud; socks just make soft blobs that fade away by morning.

A few hours later we had what we needed. Oclat had set up a laboratory inside a glasshouse on the property. We crept with a timorous forensic chemist into the laboratory and he nervously confirmed it was a speed lab and then bolted back to his hotel room. Meanwhile, Vag and I went to work setting up an observation post, so that we could watch the cook at work until it was time to bust him with his finished product. This is the exact time in any investigation when everyone starts to get toey, excited. There was a sniff in the air, and each of us worked a fraction harder and faster than normal.

Oclat's property backed onto a state forest with a border of shady gum trees. Overnight, we fashioned the best little hidey-hole, gathering branches from nearby trees to create a lair that would have done a family of wombats proud. It was big enough to hide two squirrels for the five days we sat and photographed our man busy in his lab, coming and going to and from his farmhouse carrying glassware, tubes, beakers and chemicals. A sense of danger returns to The Job as you sit in stony silence throughout the night, waiting, watching and hoping like hell the crook doesn't sneak up behind you with a double-barrelled shotgun.

On the fifth day, while Oclat slept, we snuck back into the laboratory with our still nervous forensic chemist. He told us the good news: the cooking process would be complete the following day. We escorted the poor chemist back to his warm hotel room and we in turn went back to our breezy apartment, knowing our target's life was about to change forever. We waited in the rain.

It was about an hour before the scheduled bust and the detectives and Special Operations Group (SOG) raid team were ready. The state forest was crawling with cops. We expected to seize about 20 kilograms of speed, worth millions of dollars on the street. Vag and I sat behind the camera tripod with itchy fingers. Our target had only just walked back into his lab from his house. He looked as if he was counting his money as he walked. He was inside for no more than minutes when, without warning—*boom*! An enormous accidental explosion ripped through the night and the entire laboratory exploded before our eyes. Poor ventilation had caused flammable gases to collect, then they ignited. A massive bubble of flames plumed into the sky. The noise was deafening as we clicked off the motor drives on our cameras: tishink … tishink … tishink.

Frame after frame captured the catastrophe, and Oclat running from deep inside the explosion, across the paddock, covered in flames. The big man fled desperately towards his house in a maddening attempt to get to water, stumbling as he went, rubbing his wretched burning face. Our photographs showed the flames coming off his entire body. The faster he ran, the more the fresh air whipped up the flames. By the time his contorted body got to his front door he was almost done for. But he made it inside and to water. He still suffered burns to most of his body. The following hours delivered chaos to the unsuspecting countryside, with MICA ambulance units and fire brigades descending from all directions.

Eventually Oclat was taken off to intensive care. He was under police guard for months, and ultimately needed to wear a body stocking for the rest of his life. The trial was shorter than we'd normally expect because of the fantastic photos. The Supreme Court judge, in his final summing up, commented as he passed sentence, 'Mr Oclat, a picture is worth a thousand words.'

Not all the crooks we worked on had connections to the Hell's Angels. Some were merely desperate drug addicts who, due to dire circumstances, found themselves dealing poison. Every now and again one would come up with a real smart scam, an innovative way of dealing. We liked the smart ones! We received reports on a junkie who was making his own heroin and on-selling it. Manufacturing heroin is rare and always attracts an immediate investigation, as heroin is one of the most destructive drugs in the community.

Within a few days we were onto him. He got the thumbs up from most of us at the office for his entrepreneurial ways. Our cook was a third-year university student, studying chemistry. With a little extra-curricular research he had found out that heroin is made from opium, grown mostly in the 'golden triangle' where Thailand, Laos and Burma border one another. A little more homework told our student that heroin is refined to produce morphine. If the morphine is then refined, codeine is produced—the simple active ingredient in pharmaceutical headache pills. Cookie worked out that if he was able to gather enough codeine together and reverse the chemical process, he would eventually come up with heroin. He was right.

The university student became a university-trained drug dealer. He gathered some basic pharmaceutical glassware, set up a makeshift laboratory and produced enough heroin for his own habit and that of a list of clients. Business and pleasure mixed together in one profitable operation.

The trouble was that cookie needed a continual supply of codeine tablets. A heroin addict can be a very determined creature; we followed him. He visited dozens of chemist shops a week, around and around Melbourne. After he parked out the front of the chemist shops, his junked-out girlfriend raced into the store and bought packs of codeine tablets. Back into the car and off they went again, and again. By week's end they had gathered a car-load of tablets, enough to crank up the laboratory and turn headaches into heartache.

Our task was made more arduous by his extraordinary level of paranoia. He was a compulsive rubberneck, looking at every car that came near him. At times we were certain he suspected surveillance but each day we got away with it, gathering the evidence, photos, video-tapes, even the address of his clandestine lab in St Kilda. The reason for his paranoia became obvious, in time. Our target was the son of one of the country's most prominent persons. Daddy was a royal commissioner, listening to evidence on organised crime, and a man highly respected by police and the legal profession.

The squad was at a loss with this news: what was the correct thing to do? Should we abandon the investigation, approach his father and allow the family to deal with it? It seemed like a possible solution but it would have been hugely improper. We decided to treat our suspect like anyone else. The son of the royal commissioner was eventually busted, without fear or favour; more importantly, his clever clandestine laboratory was closed down and his midnight oil recipe destroyed.

This was about the time I welcomed two new boys, Mick and Charles, to our team. They were great characters, both of them mad as hatters. Mick came from a worldly background in policing and went on to become a master at covert work and a great friend. Charles was different. He came from a similar background to mine, with a dysfunctional family life in the western suburb of Braybrook, slumsville in those days, followed by numerous inconsequential jobs and overseas jaunts until he joined the cops. He was an ex-champion boxer and loose cannon. I called him 'the last of the knucklemen'. He was extremely capable with his fists, preferring a fight to a feed. Why he was selected for the squirrels was anyone's guess, but I was glad he was; he brought light to my cloudy days.

We welcomed the boys with one of the saddest investigations we undertook. There was a gang of bad-arse Turks living in the Richmond Housing Commission flats. They were prone to serious violence and had gradually taken over a major heroin dealing network. Their centre of operations was a Turkish cafe in Church Street, just down the road from one of my old schools, Richmond Tech. We set up an observation post across the road from the cafe in an office building whose occupants were only too pleased to help eradicate the scourge of heroin dealers.

As we watched the front door of the cafe, we filmed the sophisticated distribution business. About a dozen people were involved. Many were also suspects for stabbings, as well as causing fatal overdoses from heroin that was too high grade. It was fascinating to study these criminals in action, with 'nit-keepers' watching the street, keeping a lookout for the filth, and the runners whose primary role was to stash the heroin in secret hidey-holes in the cafe, retrieving small amounts each time they closed a sale with a junkie. There were even a few fake card players, trying to make the place look busy. Then there was the boss, grossly overweight, unshaven, probably sixty years old. He sat at the back of the cafe, waving instructions and smoking his pungent Turkish cigarettes.

Our vantage point allowed a full view of all the players and the cafe. We filmed blissfully away, filling folder after folder with surveillance sheets. A hundred junkies visited the cafe each day; taxis arrived from all over Melbourne.

One sunny afternoon a taxi arrived with a tall thin woman. She didn't look like the usual junkie; she was well presented, nicely dressed. She certainly got the attention of four dulled squirrels; we needed a bit of livening up as it had become a textbook job. She was in and out of the cafe, scoring her poison in only moments and slipping back into her waiting taxi. A closer examination of her facial features on the film yielded two curious results. Firstly, she was struggling in the pretty department: her face was that of a junkie in real trouble; the poison had a hard grip on her. Secondly, she was once a well-known pop singer.

There are times when you see something that you just don't want to know about. Something that cuts deep causes you to put down your camera. This was one of those times. It is fair to say that each of us would rather that she hadn't gotten out of that taxi that day. Our popstar obviously had a habit that hurt, one that controlled her. On about her fifth visit she staggered noticeably as she stepped out of the taxi; her whole being was in disarray as she scrambled into the cafe. Equally clear was the fact that she had no money. An argument ensued as she hassled, begging for her poison. Then, our camera lens witnessed the ultimate self-demeaning act. Our celebrity unzipped the trousers of the fat Turkish boss and, dropping to her knees, the popstar popped the old Turk, in exchange for her heroin. Then, as fast as lightning, she returned to her waiting taxi to go back to her miserable life. Everything on the Turkish job seemed boring after that day. We were glad when the job ended a couple weeks later.

It seemed that the more success we had in the squirrels, the more we worked. Investigation after investigation, target after target. Like the Italian importer who was bringing kilo lots of cocaine from Sydney every six weeks. He lived in a swish beachside suburb and we found a little cottage across the road occupied by an elderly lady. She took great comfort in letting the squirrels sit in her front room for weeks, believing we were trying to catch a rapist.

Every six weeks we trained the camera on his front door and his glossy red Alfa Romeo. We heard him on our listening devices, counting his big bag of money; our cameras snapped him walking to the car, putting the bag in boot, looking up and down the street to assuage his paranoia. Then off he would drive to the airport. One of us jumped the flight as the rest of us snuck into the luggage handling area behind the carousel where, thanks to the federal police at the airport, his bag was sneakily searched. We pulled it apart, photographed the money, marked some notes for later identification and replaced the bag so that it could join the unsuspecting target in Sydney. Our northern brothers then took over and covertly snapped the pick-up. Then more of the same as he returned home with the cocaine.

We did the run with him a few times to prove his enterprise, and then he was busted driving back from the airport with a million dollars worth of junk. He lied all night to the detectives, until the photographic and video evidence was dropped on him. Then he begged for help, offering hopeless promises, before being locked away for half a lifetime.

This was the job that almost got us into a lot of strife. The Italian was meeting his suppliers in a park near his house, for talks. We had bugged the park bench but also needed to get photos of the meetings. We found a little apartment, which was owned by a Qantas hostess, that overlooked the park. She allowed us to use her flat, as she was away working for three days. We had been sitting in the apartment for a couple of days, getting bored. Charles was usually the first to find boredom. The next thing we knew, he was ratting through the girl's bedroom, snooping. He walked into the lounge room wearing a pair of her knickers on his head, waving his arms. Things got a bit carried away, and all of a sudden we were all running up and down the hallway with knickers on our heads, in fits of laughter. Then the front door opened; she had arrived home a day early! God, Charles was bad—but great fun.

By this time, home for me had become very unfunny. Dee and I were really struggling after two years of marriage. I felt trapped; I was suffocating. Any good times were few and far between. We had started to drift apart and, strangely, there had developed a real pressure for us to have children. I weighed up my heavy lot, day by day. There was Chelsea, who was now nine years old, to consider. And there lay the worry. Dee's jealousy was getting worse; I was tiring of being close to Chelsea and then observing the sad looks from Dee. I also knew I would never have another child until I was completely ready.

I battled my failing marriage at a time when I was trying to move closer to my personal dream: to become a detective. In hindsight, I know how selfish I was at that time, yet I realised our marriage was not meant to be. I adored Dee, yet we would admit being too different. While we remained friends, I was deeply saddened by our end.

Professionally, I was looking for my next challenge in my life as a squirrel.

It presented itself when Cody, a detective who went on to become Australia's expert on undercover work, joined our squad. Cody was a great strategist and became a dear friend. A tall and strapping man, he looked remarkably like Clint Eastwood in *Dirty Harry*. The drug squad had a policy allowing select cops to work undercover, buying drugs and climbing up the ladder to the level of the main dealers. Cody thought I might be okay at it, so I became an undercover operative, using the name Tommy Paul. I saw it as a great opportunity to infiltrate some of the worst criminal groups in the country. I also welcomed it as a distraction from the sorrow I was feeling with the end of my marriage.

This would be the start of many years of working with Cody on drug dealers throughout Australia, with the extraordinary help of an informer we shared, codenamed Bunsen. Good old Bunsen was probably responsible for seeing a hundred drug dealers jailed; he was a man who should have been given a medal for his contribution to the police department, which not once said 'thanks'. He deserved better.

One of my most challenging covert jobs involved an outlaw motorcycle gang. Their main man was becoming too successful, selling high-grade heroin in large quantities. Bunsen wangled an introduction to the leader, a thug who never drank alcohol, took drugs or socialised, and only dealt in pure rock heroin. He was as hard a target as I ever worked on. It didn't matter if I wanted half a kilo of the stuff; he dealt only in ounce (30 gram) lots, believing undercover cops wouldn't play with him for ounce deals. A good theory, but this time around we didn't care, knowing that each ounce would put him away for five years.

Our biggest concern was getting him to shake off his paranoia. He told Bunsen he only dealt with crooks from interstate. We got onto a friendly detective from Sydney. That in itself was difficult, finding a 'friendly' anything in Sydney in the 1980s. Most Sydney squads at that time were on the nose, stinking of corruption. Luckily Cody had a safe contact; even luckier, the contact had a cousin who owned a vacant house near Balmain. The cousin was overseas for an extended period, so we had the use of the house. Wayne, whose career had paralleled mine, and I went to live in Sydney for a while, he acting as my body guard, social secretary and issuer of suntan oil, enabling me to make contact with our heroin-dealing warlock.

While I was in Sydney, Chelsea was well cared for by her Nana. They shared an ever-growing bond. My Ma had always been my greatest supporter and the help she gave me with her granddaughter was invaluable. I have never taken her love for Chelsea and me for granted. Chelsea often spent time with her Nana.

I had done about six or seven undercover jobs up till then, all in Melbourne. This was my first time interstate. Once we had the phone hooked up in my covert name, I sent down a message for the bikie to call and the waiting game started. We knew the bikie would tap into his contacts and work out our address, so we transferred the electricity bills to my name and had a mess of mail sent to me and left it sitting in the letterbox.

Our home away from home was in need of serious renovation. Wayne and I put a few ladders out front to make it look as if I was playing handyman. In truth, we often had nothing more to do than lie in the backyard and catch the sun, day after day. One afternoon I strolled to the letterbox, just to stick my head out, in case anyone was watching, and *bingo*—we had hit pay dirt. All the letters were missing from the letterbox.

I was being scrutinised; someone was interested enough to spirit away my mail, nibbling the bait. When the phone rang the next day, we almost jumped out of our skins.

'How's the renovations?' a sober voice asked.

'Fine, I could do with a hand.'

'Next week for you,' the sober one said.

'One or two?' I asked, hoping it was two.

'One now … we'll see about more later.'

The phone went dead. Wayne and I nearly went through the roof; we had snared our target. We simply had to wait a week in Sydney and suffer more scrutiny. We just hung around. It occurred to us that we didn't need to stay in the house during the night. Our target believed my cover story: that I ran a couple of seedy nightclubs. So, off we went into the Sydney night, checking on my supposed nightclubs. It was important for us to visit as many seedy nightclubs as we could, for covert reasons of course. We played from one Kings Cross bar to another.

By midnight we found ourselves in the Texas Tavern and Bourbon & Beef Steakhouse, both known for serving bad women, toughs and shonky cops. These were dens of iniquity in those days; it was a hoot mixing it with the trash of Sydney. Somehow, at the end of our night, we had crawled our way into a bar on George Street. Wayne was still up for as much drinking and dancing as he could muster. I stood aside and stared at a stunning blonde with a deep tan, wearing a tiny white dress. Cindy was celebrating her twenty-sixth birthday; I was thirty.

For the next fortnight I spent every available night in Cindy's little attic, perched high above an old mansion by the harbour in Drummoyne. We had fallen hopelessly in lust. She was a psychiatric nurse and had a skill for delving into people. She asked the curliest of questions, trying to work out what I really did for a living. She too had come from a broken family, leaving home at sixteen to walk her own road in life. She tried unravelling me many times, but was continually frustrated.

Up and down to Sydney I travelled. I flew to Melbourne for meetings with my bikie, to discuss and buy drugs, then back up to Sydney, as if I was returning home to run my nightclubs. But it was really back to Cindy and long nights of drinking Heathcote shiraz and making love, overlooking the sensual soft lights of Sydney Harbour. Before long, 'Cindy' was tattooed on my arm. Wayne lucked in meeting an airline hostess, ensuring we were both blissfully occupied of an evening. The hardest trick in this balancing act was to keep the management of the drug squad from knowing about our social lives. Occasionally a detective rang our house at night and then followed up with a pager call, wondering where we were. Wayne and I juggled our stories, telling lies so we could see our new-found loves.

My infiltration of the bikie boss' operation had gone better than planned, with him dealing freely. He was a hard-arse who trusted no-one, not even his own group of greased thugs. In the end we got the better of him for reasons of pure greed. Like most drug dealers, the bigger the amount of cash involved, the bigger the temptation. Even the smartest are bothered by temptation. Money does that.

Cindy and I lasted for more than a year, even though I had told her untruths in the beginning. I had to. I was never going to compromise the investigation or Wayne's and my safety. Initially, I swung my cover story into Melbourne, not Sydney, telling her I owned a couple of nightclubs and was often travelling around the country on business. She kept frowning but went with it for a while. She found it weird that I wouldn't give out my private telephone number. I ended up supplying her with the number of the 'yellow' phone, a handset we had in our office that any detective passing by answered with merely a 'hello', then allowed the caller to do all the talking. This way we were able to offer targets an untraceable phone number. It worked most of the time.

Cindy was more suspicious than most drug dealers, maybe because her judgement wasn't fuzzy with greed. One day she went straight at me.

'What do you really do, Colin?'

'Run my nightclubs,' I said, lying through my teeth.

'Bullshit … you're a drug dealer!' she said with a firmness in her voice.

'What? No way.'

'You have to be, you're never anywhere and no-one can live like that.'

'No way, I run a couple of nightclubs, I'm just busy.'

'You're a drug dealer and unless you tell me, we're finished.'

I told her everything. Well, most things. I blurted it all out, as her strong personality wouldn't let up. She knew something was odd. I also felt she had a right to know.

She sat there numb and silent, biting her nails down, as she often did; she was a little annoyed that she had gotten in so deep with a 'narc'. She took a few minutes to mull it over, offering a faint smile and a shake of her head. Her biggest fear was eating away at her: was she going to be busted for smoking dope? Cindy enjoyed smoking choof occasionally. After a few giggles and reflecting on all the times we had spent together, she relaxed and accepted the revelation. For the next year she genuinely struggled with my lifestyle. Always full of uncertainty, often worried for where I might be and what I might be working on.

During this period, Chelsea and I were living in a glorious two-storey house in St Kilda with another detective, Dick, and his girl-friend, Pam. Both were wonderfully decent people who were there for me time and time again, making sure Chelsea was fine, making sure I was just as fine. My home life was running on perfect, as was Chelsea, at ten. I knew then, as I had known a hundred times before, that I was blessed with this kid, truly and divinely blessed. Other kids might have reacted badly to the unorthodox life I was leading but my girl just rolled with the punches.

But at work, pressure was building. I felt that I was ready to implode. I was chewing through the undercover jobs like I was eating lollies, one job after another. Once our targets were locked away, I lined up for another job, another hit of adrenalin. A quick change of appearance and identity and back on the merry-go-round I spun. The masking-tape glue had hardly been washed away from my stom-ach when it was time to tape another recording device to my body. I had even befriended a tailor who made me a leather coat to hide a tape recorder in the lining of the waistband; I was totally geared to working undercover.

Naively, I believed I was making a difference. My obsession for work was starting to take me over. My judgement was both obsessive and clouded. I had become driven by an insatiable need to prove myself, to do bigger, better, best, to stand out above all others. Thankfully, I wasn't altogether blind in my professional pursuits. I had come to understand the root of my trouble: Dougal. I had created a career and had worked as hard and as constantly as I could, all to show my world that I was a better person than Dougal. In doing so, Dougal had become the chip on my shoulder, and I didn't know how to shake him off.

6

LOSING THE PLOT

My career was developing at a fast pace. There's no denying under-cover work is dangerous. Most of the time the operative lives in a world of second-guessing, trying desperately to understand what the target's next move will be. There lies the problem. The operative must constantly rely on his own judgement. Yet, by now, mine was becoming clouded. My personal standards were bumping into the chip I carried on my shoulder.

This was at a time when I was introduced to some lowlifes in an outlaw motorcycle gang. They were moving loads of speed and our objective was simple: to take a few of them out and destabilise their group. The detectives had bowled over a bikie underling for dealing and turned him into an informer. Next, I was in a house full of rubbish, all tough guys, spitting and snarling. None of them had any handkerchiefs. I had been reluctant to do this job because the pressure I was feeling was heightening. I was forgetting things, making poor decisions.

After a few weeks we had our two main targets on toast: video evidence of drug buys, tape recordings, photos, the lot. Vag, Mick and Charles were having a field day taking care of business. Well, Vag and Mick were. Charles was often asleep in a car tucked away in a back street somewhere; that was his way. The guy was always taking naps. One day we caught him, sound asleep, with the car seat down flat and using a newspaper as a blanket. He was snoring his head off—until Vag dropped a couple of firecrackers into the car. The last of the knuckle-men sprang to his feet, sparring the air, ready for a fight.

On the final day of the bikie job I put in an order for a kilo of powder, which the bikies cheerfully agreed to supply. They also offered as much hashish as I wanted, explaining that they had a container full, fresh from Afghanistan. The drug squad had a tip-off that a full container of hashish had just arrived in the country; the shipment was worth many millions of dollars but, typically, the feds had no idea where it was.

Naturally, I asked to see a sample, which proved pure. Each slab weighed a kilo. As a result of the hashish buy, I met four more players. They were serious heavyweights from a group that had been on the books at the drug squad for years. One was so violent that he did time for murder years later, after beating some poor guy to death. Our only trouble was that I couldn't get enough show money to buy the whole container at such short notice. We ordered twenty-one slabs, figuring the squirrels would find the container when the crooks went to collect the drugs.

We settled on a time and location to do the exchange. The only concession I could gain was that my mate would carry my money, a couple of hundred thousand dollars, wholesale price of course. My mate was a slimy Turk, Joe, who happened to be a very talented under-cover operative who looked as if he would cut anyone's throat. Joe and I worked a fair bit together and knew each other's thoughts, which was handy in covert work.

The gig was that I would go to their house in the suburbs and inspect the hashish and speed. Then I would page Joe, who'd carry the money into the address in a Foster's lager box. We would do a quick exchange and be out of there. In reality, detectives would come burst-ing through the front door with shotguns and it would all be over.

Easy, I thought. Our signal to bust was Joe and the Foster's box disappearing into the house.

'Eighteen, nineteen, twenty': I counted the slabs of hashish, dropping each kilo onto the billiard table in the upstairs room of the two-storey home, owned by one of the bikies. As I counted I gawked at the faces before me; everyone in the house was too quiet. My sixth sense was telling me something was definitely on the nose.

'Twenty-one.' All the hashish was there, along with the big bag of speed. But then the room swelled with bodies; there were now seven crooks around the billiard table instead of two. 'What is happening here?' I thought. Why, all of a sudden, do seven guys want to be part of a drug deal? Didn't they have anything else to do? I wasn't thinking straight.

I signalled Joe by pager for the money. And all I could do was stand there and wait, with the drugs strewn over the billiard table. The crooks began to get toey, pacing the room like television wrestlers. The biggest and toughest was getting hot for the cash, yelling, 'Where's the money?' Another walked over to a cupboard, opened it to reveal a hidden safe and ferreted around inside. Another two walked behind me in stony silence. I was fuzzy; I had lost my sharpness and was unable to keep up with everyone's movements.

'Joe, where the fuck are you?' I thought desperately. Should I bolt downstairs and out of there, or stay and let my covert recorder tape the transaction? Judgement was failing me and my armpits were warming up. I tried to find things to talk about, knowing that it was either a rip-off or I was about to be searched. One of the heavyweights smiled at me, asked where I got my leather jacket, and if he could try it on. If the jacket came off, my tape would be seen as well as my gun.

Just then, Joe turned up, carrying the Foster's box. 'At fuckin' last,' I thought. 'The posse will be here soon.'

'Forget trying on my jacket, here comes the loot,' I muttered to the heavyweight.

Joe got to the top of the stairs, took one look at me and knew something was rotten. I flicked my head to the billiard table and he tipped the cash out. The dude at the safe reached inside and pulled out a handgun, keeping it at his side. My heart almost dropped through to my shoes. It was a rip-off.

I should have seen it coming. Seven crooks never turn up for a drug buy. I tried desperately to make eye contact with Joe, who was busy playing out his role of a smelly bad Turk with money. The two dudes behind me signalled to their mate at the safe. It was about to be on, big time. Joe caught on to the vibe and locked his eyes on me. I reached behind to the small of my back for my hidden .32 pistol, placed my shaking hand on the grip and flicked off the safety catch.

'Police … Freeze!'

The yells echoed from downstairs, as twelve detectives crashed through the hallway. Our dirty seven dropped the loot, the handgun was thrown back into the safe and the door slammed shut. They looked frantically at each other and then at the doorway, minds ticking. Whatever ill intent they had considered, they had certainly had a change of plans, and began sprinting for the staircase, only to be met by shotguns coming the other way.

As the detectives thundered up the stairs I dropped to the floor and listened. 'Freeze! Police … Freeze!' There's nothing quite like it!

Thank God for the detectives. I hate to think what could have happened to Joe, or me. I was blind to the warning signs, too wound up in my own ego. And thank God for Joe's cool head; mine had become fuzzy to the dangers of our world.

My biggest single worry was that there had been three firearms found in the billiard room; two handguns in the safe and a rifle against a wall. The bikies were up to no good that day, and I had failed badly. I walked away knowing I had fucked up, despite catching a bag of crooks. I should have called the job off as soon as I walked into the billiard room and saw far too many crooks for one drug deal. The warning signs were all over their desperate, greedy faces—warning signs that I had failed to see.

After hours, when Charles, Mick and I went painting the town red, we were getting more out of control. None of us seemed to have any sense of danger, nor did we question the madness in our lives. Everything had become a sea of work, crooks, undercover, secret squirrels, guns, infiltrations, stings, cunning, drugs, drinking, show-money, big talk, women and nightlife. I'm sure the latter two were merely there to help digest the rest. The three of us celebrated sting after sting, laughing all the way to the following morning. Responsibility was second to good times. As we ran amok, we told some absurd lies. We were potato farmers, or airline pilots, television scriptwriters, film directors, and gangsters, world-champion marksmen, undertakers and on the rubbish went. Our stories changed as often as the girls. After a few years, reality went missing. We had gotten away with it for too long. Yet the bosses all laughed along with us, relishing the tales of our escapades every Monday morning. Charles was in the middle of it all, director of lunacy.

The 1980s were a time of great excess; it was as if the whole world was going a little mad. Life was too many big-haired girls and loud clothes. Hollywood churned out movies that stylised drugs and gangsters, and the public took to the clubs and discos and mimicked the cinema.

Royal commissions were following one another, exposing bent politicians and even more bent cops. Mafia stories were serialised in the Sunday papers and a few brave journalists were doing more to fight organised crime than the collective efforts of the police departments of this country. One brave politician who did confront crime in his community finished up living with the fishes. It was getting out of hand. In Victoria, cops were starting to fall into a pattern of shooting first and asking questions later; luckily, dead crooks can't talk.

Interest rates were at an all-time high and people were stretching themselves like never before. 'Greed is good' became the mantra and talk was cheap. In the middle of all this nonsense, I was playing a big-shot drug dealer, with carte blanche to catch as many crooks as I could. My life had become a mess of false identities, bullshit cover stories, changing looks and lies.

It was time to slow down, to go back to being normal again. It had been a long time since I had thought of anything other than my career. A long time since I'd been to the cinema, sat in a great restaurant and studied the menu, stared at a beautiful painting, read a good book. The most reading I had done over the past few years was the label on the back of a shiraz bottle. Others in my squad had noticed my downward spiral. The head man, Belly, was a kindly old detective, revered by his men; when he told me to take a couple of months leave and stop thinking about crooks, I did. I also forgot about the girl in the cubicle. The next week I booked a flight to the States and took an overdue holiday with my lifelong mate, Jenny, the nurse.

Chelsea, too, was in need of a better slice of life and went happily to stay with her Nana and Ray for a while. They were now living on the coast at Port Macquarie, in a little house 50 metres from the ocean. The break did Chelsea the world of good. So, too, it was for Jenny and I; we went from state to state eating hot dogs, driving T-Birds and being normal.

Belly had been good enough to write me a letter of introduction to the three premier undercover teams in America: Miami Vice (Metro Dade), New York Police and the LAPD. All I had to do was knock on their doors and say hello. It took a month of hotdogs and Rolling Rock beers before I broke away on some useful work experience with these guys. I spent a few days with each team playing shadow on infiltration operations, watching the action from a distance, either from a covert observation post or from within a static truck, their version of a van filled with spy gear. At Metro Dade undercover unit I was attached to the team that inspired the *Miami Vice* television series, working alongside Mike and Raul, the alter egos of the two main characters from the show. They were buying machine guns from a gang of nasty Cubans and took me along for the ride.

They were light years ahead of Australian law enforcement as far as covert equipment and gadgetry was concerned, but the stories we swapped over a couple of late-night drinking sessions were similar, as were the many issues the operatives had with higher-ranking police officers. I gave a briefing to the unit on the efforts of my squad and they were complimentary about our work.

I was further impressed at the long-term infiltration work undertaken by the New York Police Department undercover unit. Their operatives could go deep undercover for up to a year, infiltrating the Mafia. I was given two days access to the Mafiosi cell and delighted in reading folders of information reports on suspects who would make headlines around the world, names like Giotto and Gambino that would splash across the pages of newspapers for years to come.

I finally returned to Australia, both rested and ready for change. I relaxed into the habit of staying home, watching television and hanging out with Chelsea. I was fully at peace and knew it was time for this hamster to jump off his wheel. So I left the drug squad after three long years and went to become a real detective. I also flicked away that rotten chip on my shoulder.

II
RUNNING WITH EXECUTIONERS

7

DENNIS-VILLE

'Come on, Anzac,' I yelled, running the red light.

Anzac was tiring. He had started off full of beans, salivating, ball in mouth and aching for the front door to open. Once it did, he was off; it was me who had to push the barriers to keep up with him. He had an extraordinary memory for streets, intersections and traffic lights. A smart blue heeler, at the edge of leafy Studley Park he knew we'd do away with the rules and off he'd be able to go, romping through the grass, itching for the ball.

My life was more settled. Chelsea and I were living in a terrace house in Abbotsford and I was living more like a normal person. I could even find time for a dog. Chelsea had become a junior gourmand at the age of thirteen, and at least once a week we found ourselves at one of the many eateries in spitting distance of home. Our weekly dining sojourns were completed with wine tasting and armchair critiques of the food put in front of us. We scored each restaurant on our own system of merit: 'bad', 'good' or 'fabulous'. Each week we came up with a new and sometimes crazy idea about what we would do, should we ever own a restaurant. All questions were covered on the night: what style of food we'd serve, what the decor would be like, how many entrées on the menu compared to main courses, the type of produce served, and so on. Most weeks we settled our ambitions on an Italian trattoria; an idyllic, country-style eatery serving simple peasant food and authentic Italian wines. We worked on that idea time and time again, relishing the day it might happen. In the meantime, I paid attention to my waistline as well as my tastebuds and made sure I worked off my excesses in line with my healthier lifestyle.

Anzac and I ran most days, at least 5 kilometres, often ten. It was my only sport; I was useless at anything else. I thrived on running; it's the loner's sport. Somehow, running allowed me to find the seemingly infinite time and inner peace to do my thinking, unravel my issues. Anzac was the ideal running partner; he kept his conversation to himself and was always up for a trot at any hour.

And there was certainly plenty to occupy a cop's mind. Police murders are rare in our community. We're fortunate not to suffer such crimes too often, as police killings tear at the very fabric of law enforcement, striking at the heart of our community. In a modern society, the police and the judiciary must be protected at all costs, must be exempt from the madness that society musters at times. To abandon this principal is to invite chaos. Yet this had now occurred in Melbourne. A bunch of lowlifes who had decided that they didn't like being locked up had bombed the Castle. A young policewoman, Angela Taylor, died in the explosion. Although I had no ongoing involvement with the investigation—the homicide squad had taken instant control, although I had done some basic crime scene stuff—the callous murder also had implications for me. The Russell Street bombing marked a turning point in the relationship between criminals and police: thugs were now prepared to set cold-blooded ambushes against police, not personally, but as a symbol. Melbourne had lost its innocence.

Anzac picked up the pace as he recognised the row of terraces alongside ours in the soon-to-be-trendy working-class suburb. As always, we sprinted for home. I came in in a respectable third place, as I usually did, behind the dog and the ball.

Within the hour I was dressed in the worst rags I could find and heading for work. I had promised Errol I'd help him out on a jailhouse sting. He had a burglar in the cells and no loot. He had locked up a 'docket-head', a local crook with a page or more of prior convictions (the page being the 'docket'). Richmond detectives were always locking up docket-heads; the area was crawling with young toughs who roamed the streets doing burglaries. Errol's docket-head was from another area, a bloke who happened into Richmond to try his luck. He had 'fessed up to a few burgs, but Errol couldn't locate the stolen goods and the crook wasn't giving any hints.

The gig was that—since the crook had never met me—I would turn up at the watch-house looking like rubbish, dressed in scruffy clothes and pretending to be a local docket-head. Errol would stick me in the same cell as the crook, making sure I had my charge sheets with me. The idea was to get talking to the crook, hoping he would believe I had also been locked up for burglaries, and try to get him to tell me where his loot was.

This day was like most stings we did. As the cell door opened, I was shoved in, swearing and snarling. Once the handcuffs came off, Errol swung a couple of punches to my guts and I fell in a heap alongside the burglar. One of the 'show' punches had landed the wrong way and winded me. After a few well-delivered words from Errol, I sat in the company of a bad-arse burglar, who came to my aid as soon as the cell door was locked. The docket-head helped me sit up, straightened my clothes and handed me my charge sheets, which had fallen on the floor—but not before he had glanced at my four charges of burglary. I ran this one like any other, staying on small talk for half an hour, swearing, bad-mouthing the 'fuckin' filth' and ingratiating myself with my new buddy, who appeared happy for the company. Then, when the time was right, I went for the jugular.

'You came into my town to kick some doors in, hey?'

'Yeah mate … I'm from Flemington, cool with you?' said my buddy.

'Cool … anyone watching your back?'

'Nope, alone.'

'Yeah, me neither … did the jacks get your gear?' I eased on him.

'Silly fucks, no way,' he bragged, but I needed more.

'Hah, same here, I hid some stuff near the flat I broke into and they never found it. I'll go back and get it when I get bail, dumb fucks,' I teased.

'My shit's in my car, hidden a street away, in my girlfriend's name,' he offered, whispering as he leaned into me, 'Got a shit-load of jewellery'.

'Cool one, hope the car's locked.'

'Not a problem, the keys are on top of the wheel.'

We both settled back and told exaggerated yarns about how bad we were and asked each other do-you-know-so-and-so questions for a while. Then, lucky me, out of the blue, the watch-house keeper called my false name.

'Time for bail, you. Get your shit together, you're being released.'

The big key opened the big door and I was away. As I left the cell I high-fived my new pal and we promised to 'stay cool'. The whole sting took merely one hour and I got to lie about and snarl as much as I liked, bad-mouthing my workmates. I debriefed Errol and off he went. In thirty minutes he had the car, two television sets, two video players and a bag of jewellery.

We did lots of cell stings at Richmond detectives. While stings were good fun, what I really thrived on was being a suit-and-tie detective. I especially enjoyed working in the suburb where I had spent much of my youth. It was a bit odd at times, working a beat I had walked as a kid, seeing blighters who had shared the same back lane-ways with me and Titch and been over the same hurdles, the only difference being they'd chosen to keep going, taking the road to serious crime. Occasionally it was sad, especially the ones who were true battlers, trying to free themselves from the back-street poverty. When an old schoolmate was brought in for questioning I often excused myself from the interview, although once or twice I stepped forward and tried to make their path a little easier.

Our success at Richmond was due largely to the close relationship we actively fostered with our community. It was still very much
struggle town, made up largely of low-income earners, immigrants,
battlers, crooks and a few smart homeowners who jumped in early at
the start of the gentrification. Other important players in this socio-
economic equation were the shopkeepers and publicans: there were
thirty-six pubs in our 'village', so they were a voice to be heard. The
odd ones out in this eclectic mix were the crooks. They preyed on the
locals with burglaries, thefts and violence.

We gained the confidence of these different and important sub-
groups and together we became a team. The role of the shopkeepers,
publicans and residents was to keep us supplied with a constant flow
of information. We needed to know what the thieves were up to, who
was breaking into the houses, shops and factories, who ran the gangs,
and where the villains could be found. The system worked well. One
of its great features was the Christmas party thrown by the Richmond
police. The Town Hall donated the building for this extravaganza and
the entire community looked forward to it for months. Up to a thousand people attended an event that offered music, dancing, a barbecue,
pig-on-the-spit, free alcohol, speeches and a million handshakes. It was
an old-fashioned Policemen's Ball, without the suits and gowns.

Each cop invited up to ten guests who helped to fight the good
fight. People like the butcher, the baker and the candlestick-maker,
literally. Local resident Molly Meldrum and some of his protégés made
sure they were there, as did other celebrities. Channel Nine's Melbourne
studios were down the road and they turned off their cameras for the
night and got a bit sozzled. The only class of people excluded were the
crooks, although each year, out of sheer stupidity, a few did gatecrash—
and what fun they presented. This yearly event galvanised strong community links with the police, links that got results. For weeks after the
party the station was abuzz with fresh information.

During almost every shift at Richmond, I found time to cruise the
area, often with Errol, killing time, taking in the back streets. Inevitably

we'd happen into 'Dennis-ville', in the back blocks, near the Yarra. 'Dennis-ville' won't be found in any street directory, yet everyone knows how to get there, or get out, in a hurry. There's a list of things guaranteed to happen in places like Dennis-ville, like the sound of gun-shots peppering the night. Equally there's a list of things that never hap-pen, like seeing a private-school uniform hanging on a clothes-line. It's a maze of a dozen one-way streets, bordered by noisy, late- night cargo trains, a relentless freeway and a shopping strip peddling to the riff-raff, with TABs, two-dollar stores and too many Chinese takeaways.

'Dennis-ville' was named after its most entrepreneurial citizen, Dennis Bruce Allen.

As Errol and I drove around, we talked most often about the Pettingill clan, our infamous family of gangsters who lived among the industry, near the old Rosella tomato sauce factory, in Dennis-ville. The clan consisted of the matriarch, Kath, and her daughter and six sons, most of them in their thirties. All the boys were docket-heads, with priors that went back years: drug dealing, shootings, stand-overs, the lot. Dennis was the eldest and by far the smartest and most ruthless of his half-brothers. He didn't have any full brothers—Kath had a busy life mothering children to different men, many of them just passing through. Dennis was often written up as the 'worst criminal in Australia', a level of notoriety he relished. He was reputed to have committed at least ten murders, depending on what newspaper you read or which bar-room story you tuned into. Dennis was certainly evil, one criminal who truly deserved his reputation. His crimes were the stuff of a B-grade Hollywood movie: he had chainsawed a Hell's Angel's body into roast-size pieces, drowned a prostitute junkie, emptied a pistol of bullets into one nit-keeper (lookout) and cut the throat of another.

Not a big man, possibly 175 centimetres tall, he was wiry and had a voice that sounded like a broken-down tractor. At least half his body was covered in tattoos, many drawn inside prison. If he was known for one thing, it was his propensity, like a Russian pimp, to wear extraor-dinary amounts of bling, mostly necklaces: big, brassy looking and riddled with diamonds. In reality, each piece was 18 carat solid gold and all the diamonds were real, many the size of rice grains; at any given time he might have $250 000 around his neck.

Dennis made his money dealing vast amounts of heroin and speed. Over the years he and Kath had amassed ten houses that I knew of, all within a couple of streets of each other, some side by side like Monopoly assets. They were all Victorian terraces and on his tax return Dennis listed himself as a 'renovator'. A strange renovator, as he had neither tools nor blackened fingernails to show but he had the wealth to pay for the upgrades, and the goons to do them. He and Kath moved around, living in a different house every few months. It was their way of keeping the cops on their toes.

Driving down the narrow streets of Dennis-ville, you could smell the odour of criminality in the air. Two of Dennis's houses had been renovated to become the area's brothels, employing a string of pathetic female junkies who doled out unprotected sex for a few dollars. Unlike many other crooks, Dennis had a commercial brain. He realised the benefit of employing drug-addicted hookers for a triple win. He made his initial 50 per cent on every trick, and then won the other 50 per cent as the sole supplier of junk to the girls' raging habits. For a bonus, he took his daily sexual fringe benefit.

Kath was nicknamed 'Cyclops': she had had one eye shot out during a fight inside one of the brothels. She had a hide of galvanised iron; no tougher woman existed in Australia, yet she wasn't much over 150 centimetres tall. Once she locked her single eye onto you, it was time to put your smarts into drive. I always seemed to get on well with old Kath; I often deliberately found ten minutes of my day to listen to her complain about a court case, or too severe a jail sentence for one of her boys. Eventually, as age took over, she became a caricature of herself.

As crime goes, the Kelly Gang was the only family to hold a greater place in Australian folklore than the Pettingills. More than fifty books would highlight their infamy. Newspaper crime reporters followed their every move; it was as if they had their own paparazzi. Just the name Pettingill stirred fear into even the worst of their underworld contemporaries. Acknowledged 'bad boy' of the family, Dennis doled out his own form of summary justice to anyone who tried to double-cross his family. The fact that this criminal was ever able to develop the status he did is an indelible stain on the Victoria Police.

Dennis worked with the police, embracing them when he needed to. Each time he was locked up, he'd trade off information on a lower crook to achieve bail. In his own villainous way, Dennis was as clever a criminal as this country has seen. He'd throw anyone to the wolves as he played the judicial system on a break, making a mockery of the courts. On one occasion he set off a bomb in front of the Coroner's Court, as a tactic to send fear into witnesses and the judicial system. Magistrates had come to loathe and dread him. There was no doubt some gave him bail just to rid their courtroom of his intimidation. With almost daily advice from his team of shoddy suited lawyers, he was able to show how a crook with bravado and blunt cunning could outsmart a hidebound legal system. And along his path, he also managed to place a few corrupt detectives in his pockets, to be played on a rainy day. It rained often in Dennis-ville.

Driving Dennis's legal team was his mouth of choice, Andrew Fraser. Dressed in Italian suits and whizzing around town in a green Porsche, partially paid for by Dennis, no doubt, he was a real contrast to the usual lawyer. Fraser and I locked horns weekly for a dozen years; never did we have anything to say other than a few words relating to the many cases he held for the Pettingill clan. I loathed him, yet tolerated him. Fraser would go on to build the biggest book of clients in Australia, yet none was more feared than Dennis: he and his family were at the top of their brutal game for more than a decade.

Although Dennis was the charcoal darling of the media, Victor Peirce, his younger half-brother, was equally bad. Only about 172 centimetres tall, he was fit, a non-drinker and held a constant fire of hatred in his belly. I came to know and work with, and against, the entire family for many years and always considered Victor the most calculating of the six men. He was the opposite of Dennis: no theatrics, no jewellery, no brash hard-arse attitude, just bad. If I had to choose facing either man in a Mexican stand-off, I would have preferred

Dennis. At least he would always have half a smile on his face, thinking about how he'd enjoy shooting you. With Victor, you just never knew. And he hated police like no other man I had ever known. I secretly harboured a belief that Victor had to have helped Dennis carry out many of his murders, though he was never a suspect. Victor was one of the worst criminals I ever met. I genuinely feared him.

For the last eighteen months of Dennis's life, Dennis was my informer.

Soon after starting at Richmond detectives, I made a point of visiting the Pettingill clan. Time and time again. My work in the secret squirrels had taught me the value of patience. I pulled up in front of Dennis's house and sat on the bonnet of my police car, making notes in my diary, writing down car rego numbers, anything to attract attention. I had a purpose: to annoy Dennis and to entice him out onto the street. His house was more heavily fortified than the national mint. I figured there was no use trying to lock him up; surely there was more value in using him to my advantage, making him an informer. What a wealth of information he could deliver. To win him over, I had to do something that would make him want to be an informer; he had to realise that I had the upper hand. Only then might his commercial brain tell him to give me what I wanted—names of crooks and stories of criminality—in exchange for his freedom.

Of course, I did other work in the shadows. After a few weeks I worked out one of Dennis's drug-dealing methods. The same dark Ford sedan appeared each night at exactly half past ten, parking at the front of his house for no more than half a minute. Dennis would walk to the car, lean into the driver and, within seconds, go back inside. This was obviously a drug transaction. A trusted colleague, Roger, and I hid out, just before drug time, waiting for the Ford to arrive. The eerie quiet of Dennis-ville enabled us to hear the hotted-up engine of the car in advance. We tucked ourselves into the shadows to watch the arrival. Like clockwork, Dennis walked to the awaiting Ford, and Roger and I stepped into the street light. The Ford accelerated before Dennis could lean into the driver.

'Dennis, nice evening, wouldn't you say?'

'Mr McLaren, Mr Puell, taking a walk, hey?'

'We didn't want to spoil your fun, send your friend away now, did we?'

'Don't know him, just came out to see what all the fuss was.'

Even in a situation like this Dennis had the confidence of a dog with two dicks. He stood openly and chatted, wearing his uniform sleeveless blue overalls and white sandshoes, minus laces. Like the rest of his family, he always prefaced a detective's name with 'Mr', a hang-over from the old school of criminals. I liked that; it made me feel like a headmaster.

'If we were betting men, reckon you'd be holding right now,' I said.

'Huh … there you go.' Dennis looked up and down the lonely street.

'Want to wager?'

'Want a win?'

'Not unless it's a million dollars … it ain't worth it Dennis.'

We emptied his pockets to find a bag of junk and a handgun. Not a bad night's work. We had the choice of enjoying instant headlines the following morning or receiving ongoing information about Melbourne's underworld. Roger and I weren't looking for our fifteen minutes of fame. We chose the latter option and Dennis became my informer.

He provided me with a mixed bag of information, from the highly valuable to the totally useless: that was how he played. He offered scraps of information that, if properly investigated, could lead to the arrest of a good crook. But for each gem there was the occasional stone, no doubt to allow him time to set up some other unfortunate canary. Overall, it was a worthwhile exercise. The two of us met every Thursday afternoon, inside one of his partially renovated houses. It was the same house each time, the one where he chainsawed the Hell's Angel into bits and emptied his pistol into another. The central room smelled of death.

Our meetings took only an hour. I walked into the empty house and waited, in silence, in the centre room, listening as intently as I could. Most of the solid plaster had been stripped from the walls, leaving a skeleton of horizontal timber framing. I guessed the replastering was waiting for funding from the next big drug deal. Dennis just appeared, always carrying his frosty can of Bundy and Coke. He had great stealth; I rarely heard his approach.

We each held back an ace. I was always wearing a secret tape and Dennis was always armed. Neither of us expected anything less, I guess. The more we met the more interesting the information became. It takes a while to relax a savage beast. The link that allowed us to bond was that we were both Richmond boys. My schoolboy boots had walked the same cobblestones as his sandshoes, and I fed him a few snippets of my childhood. Just enough: a few names he knew, a couple of happenings he knew of. I have little doubt my own upbringing helped me to garner favour with Dennis; it was my ticket to his world and he clipped it each week. The few times he asked about my past were mainly out of curiosity. Once, he raised his eyebrows and asked if I had made the right decision, following the straight and narrow. He answered it himself, in the affirmative. He later told Kath that I was 'okay'.

As the months rolled by, I sought the odd comment here and there on the many murders he was known to have committed, but never convicted of. Slowly I gained a bit more from him, words expanded to sentences, then to paragraphs. He walked through each room of the house, pointing out bullet holes: in walls, in the floor and in the ceiling. Some had been patched up and painted over. In the back room, he found three patched holes, placing a piece of wire through the plaster filler to prove their existence. He was obviously savvy to my tape as he always ended his comments by stating, 'Not that I had anything to do with that shooting.' Tape recorders can't pick up a sly wink though, nor a half-smile.

We locked up a few good crooks with Dennis's information; more importantly, we gained an extraordinary insight into the

Pettingill clan. Everything we spoke about I placed on information reports for other investigators. It was always our intention to use whatever evidence we could gather to prosecute Dennis. The homicide detectives were aware of our work and waited. Dennis was an out-of-control criminal who had enjoyed too long a run. Certainly, he didn't deserve any naive ideas of protection from us.

Fortunately for him, his devil got to him first. He died in 1987, aged thirty-seven, from a heart disease brought on by excessive injections of speed. And Richmond went quiet for a while. In dying, he beat a charge of murder that had been laid on him by honest homicide detectives, one of the alleged ten murders listed on his docket. Details of the other nine deaths went to the grave with a man who played the system, won in the short term, yet ultimately lost.

8

MASS MURDER

It was the start of summer, a hot afternoon shift a few months after Dennis Allen's death. I shared a car with a fellow detective, André; we were stuck to the clammy vinyl seats, wondering how much hotter it could get. It had to be thirty-five degrees outside. You could always tell when it was stinking hot: the tram wheels squeaked a little louder and the school kids took to dawdling.

Our patrol area went all the way across the centre of the city to the docklands. It was Tuesday and we knew it would be a quiet night. Nothing happened on Tuesdays. We had done one lap of our town; it was not yet four o'clock and the heat was still building. André and I parked under an expansive old oak tree in front of an East Melbourne house worth more than our combined superannuation packages, and tackled a couple of soft drinks.

'Richmond 503, Richmond 503'—our call sign came across the police radio.

'Yes, Richmond 503,' André answered.

'Richmond 503. Head to Queen Street, Melbourne, report of shots fired.'

'Roger, 503, on our way.'

We dropped our drinks into the gutter and headed into the city centre, only two minutes away. I slipped our portable blue light onto the roof and André took off along the empty tram tracks. The first call for any serious job is often taken with a grain of salt, mainly because witnesses or victims tend to overstate the emergency. The operator was working on getting a better update. We didn't need any confirmation; we could hear the sounds of what we thought were high-powered weapons. Shot after shot, it didn't let up. Despite what you see in the movies, this sort of crime scene only comes along once in a blue moon, maybe never in a career. Until this point, I had only ever shot at one crook, a fleeing drug dealer, and pointed my firearm with intent to use it two or three other times. What we had in Queen Street, by the sheer volley of bullets being fired, was a deadly serious crime scene.

André and I were the first detectives there. Everything I had ever learned at detective training school flashed before me in a jumbled mess. I pushed it aside, fast.

André abandoned the car one block away. As we ran to the nineteen-storey office block that was home to Australia Post, more shots splintered out from the windows and glass sprinkled to the footpath like snow. Frantic office workers ran madly in all directions; taxis swerved to the footpaths. Everyone was looking upwards with frowns of uncertainty. In the few minutes in which we donned our flak jackets, we reckoned there had been at least twenty shots. The police radio operator on our portable was screaming, filled with adrenalin, telling us there was a bank on an upper floor. In times like this, communication is everything.

From the street we could see the shots were coming from the eleventh floor. André took off, running to the rear down a back alley and I took the front door, the public entrance. A journalist friend scrambled past me on her away along Queen Street, notebook in hand, dropping her pen as she ran. Soon, the usually busy street lay empty. It was imperative we ascertained how many shooters there were; we had no information coming from the building. All the lifts were jammed and we quickly learned that most of the office workers were still inside, hiding under their desks. The police operator on my portable just kept screaming.

Bang! … Bang! … Bang!

The shots still rang out. I could see dozens of people watching the horror from the opposite building. They had a bird's-eye view, pointing to the eleventh floor and ducking behind desks at each shot. I believed the armed offenders might flee the building via the lift, so I used the edge of the building as immediate cover, expecting the lift doors to open at any time, sending hell my way.

Uniforms arrived and the area was shut down, with a show of flashing blue lights. We radioed for what we needed: 'Just send everything!' I was joined by a detective from St Kilda and we ticked off the shots, frantically trying to identify the number of weapons. We called for the SOG SWAT team and were told they were fifteen minutes away! 'Fifteen fuckin' minutes!' I yelled.

We thought there were at least two gunmen, based on the number of shots, perhaps a hundred by now. It sounded like a bank robbery gone wrong, with the crooks deciding to shoot it out, and no-one was telling us any different. We had decided to storm the building and were heading towards the lift door when it opened. A lone woman ran from the lift, screaming and waving her arms madly. Her hair appeared electrified and her eyes were exploding, lost in an image she must have seen seconds before. It was the wildest look I have ever seen. She was beyond supplying information, so we passed her on to some uniforms.

The shots stopped for perhaps a minute or two; the quiet was quizzical. Then, a shattering of glass, on the eleventh floor—someone was kicking out a glass panel. I ran back outside and looked up, squinting through the glaring sun at falling fragments of glass and debris. Some of it landed on my face. The entire panel of glass was flying outwards. A man's upper body could be seen, reaching out of the building, half in, half out, arms thrashing. Desperately, I tried to understand what I was seeing. Sweat was dripping all over me. Out of nowhere another person appeared, holding onto the first man; they were struggling. Fists flying, arms swinging—it lasted no more than a minute.

The first man seemed to free himself from the other's grip, thrusting himself further out of the building, as if clutching at straws, into the hot air. I couldn't fathom why. As I watched, he fell from the window, all the way to the ground. I watched his downward journey, falling heavily towards the footpath. I ducked under the line of the building as he got nearer to the ground, nearer to me.

The gliding man hit a metal pit cover on the footpath with a massive thud, bouncing a metre into the air. The second he hit the plate there was an inexplicable, cartoonish quality to seeing him bounce, to know that a body could do that. The noise was so ferocious; everyone watching jumped in fright. A fully loaded magazine fell from his pocket and some of the bullets rolled lazily towards the gutter and stopped. The brass casings glittered in the sun. He landed only metres from where I was standing.

'They're throwing them out,' I said, staring blankly at my fellow detective in near shock, believing the man had been thrown from the eleventh floor window by one or more offenders—though the magazine and bullets were telling me a different story. I kept thinking, 'Why does the victim have a magazine and bullets in his pocket? Why? Why? Why … for Chrissake, *think*!'

The answer came instantly: 'Because he's not a fuckin' victim, he's an offender, a fuckin' offender.'

And he had just jumped to his own death. But why? Despite the absurdity of the proposition, it was the only logical conclusion. Every available police officer ran into the building. We abandoned procedure, refusing to wait for the SWAT team. The lift opened again and emptied out a sea of raving people. Most of them were covered in blood; no-one was suffering any obvious injuries. We searched among the crush for a killer: none. The group was placed with a small army of uniforms who had now gathered. A few nervous detectives took the lift to the eleventh floor, firearms drawn; the stench of sweat hanging heavy. My entire body was damp by the time the bell dinged for our destination.

The doors slid open to a wall of injured, crazed victims jostling on the other side, surging forward, like a bloody tidal wave. It was horror in technicolour. We were scaring each other: they screamed at the sight of men with guns, their brains too traumatised to make the quick assessment that we were the good guys. We, in turn, reeled back at the graphic sight before us. 'In there, in there', they yelled, pointing to the office. We swapped positions, the victims taking the lift to the ground floor.

My first impression was that of a war zone but, of course, it wasn't war, just mass murder. Coagulated globs hindered my path. I moved slowly, stepping over carnage, here, there and everywhere. I prayed to be able to hold my focus as I moved towards the windows. The other detectives dealt with their demons as they too moved forward. Each desk presented more cowering victims, cringing timidly underneath as they held onto each other, their fingers biting into the arms of co-workers. They watched us move cautiously through the room. And as we walked, we looked for the odd man out, another offender, maybe one holding a gun, pointed at us.

I avoided the victims by stepping sideways, ticking them off, body after body. One woman was clutching a man, seeking support, comfort. He was dead, his chest blown wide open. Another woman sat in a corner cradling a dead female workmate; she looked at peace as she stroked the dead woman's hair. But still no gunman. I walked to a group of workers huddled in a corner, maybe six people, with shocked gazes. They had entwined themselves like a puzzle.

'Where's the gunman, where's the gunman?' I whispered.

They were silent, pointing to the window. There was no gunman.

'Where's the gunman, where's the gunman?' I raised my voice.

'There, there,' they insisted, still pointing at the window, deep in shock.

In my desperate need for information I leaned down to the victim, who kept repeating her nonsensical answer, her face zombie-like.

'You have to help me … where's the gunman now?' I yelled, jolting her back into the here and now. 'Where's the gunman *NOW*?'

'There … he went out the window … there, he went out the window.' She started to cry, pointing at the window. A distraught man, his clothes partially torn from his body, leaned into me. 'The gunman's gone, he jumped out, he's gone.'

As unbelievable as it was, a lone gunman had entered the building armed with a high-powered rifle and three magazines of bullets. He marched through a couple of office floors in search of an acquaintance he disliked—and shot anyone who dared get in his path. The gunman's rampage took him to the eleventh floor where he did most of his evil work, shooting, killing and injuring as many people as he could, until his gun jammed. As he attempted to reset his weapon a brave office worker charged at him, causing the rifle to fall to the floor.

A violent struggle ensued between the two, with the murderer kicking a window pane out in an attempt at suicide. As the struggle unfolded another office worker grabbed the rifle, hiding it in the staff fridge in the tearoom. The madman then jumped free of the hero's grip and fell to his death.

There was no other offender, just an office full of dead, injured and needy people. An odd sense of quiet eventually settled onto the office space. We holstered our weapons and methodically went from victim to victim, checking their conditions, offering our shaking calm.

Sitting four blocks away at headquarters, police command were listening to the event live. They'd set up a command post in the boardroom, despatching instructions. For reasons that I have never been able to fathom, the assistant commissioner gave the instruction not to allow paramedics to enter the crime scene. The ambulances were to park one office block away, until the building had been declared empty of suspects. Each detective in the bloodbath rang or radioed for ambulances, demanding they care for the injured. Despite our desperate pleas, we were unable to overrule the command decision.

We moved from deceased to injured, checking pulses and swabbing wounds. Brave office workers, many of them women, did just as much, and more. I found myself confronted with a horrific sight: a man, still alive, laying on the floor, his face half blown off. He was attempting to hold together the lower portions of his face, which dangled tenuously. I grabbed some towels from the tearoom and pressed them firmly under his chin, to stop the bloodflow; I guessed he had only minutes to live. I made another urgent call for a paramedic, '*NOW!*' My request was refused.

I saw the open lift and told the victim I'd be straight back; his eyes were losing me. I sprinted into the lift, taking it to the ground floor; frustratingly, it stopped at all stations. Outside I ran the full office block, only to be met by paramedics, eager to help, but without police command's authority. I pleaded for help until one brave paramedic stepped forward, asking me to guide him into the crime scene. He would follow behind with his MICA kit. As we got to the lift, the SOG SWAT team was entering the building and barring access. I told their leader of my plight and he quickly waved us on—but we were stuck with climbing the eleven flights of stairs. When we arrived back, the victim was slumped on the floor holding his chin. He was dead.

We moved on to a big man, well over 180 centimetres tall. He'd been shot badly in the buttocks. A quick decision was made with the paramedic that he'd stay and help the remaining victims. I asked the big man if he could make it to the lift. In hindsight, this may have been the wrong thing to do, considering his injuries and the possibility of paralysis, but we both agreed to take that chance. There were far too many other victims in need of the services of the sole paramedic. The big man bravely threw his arms around my shoulders and together we walked slowly out of the building and shuffled the entire block to the ambulances, blood streaming down his legs. The waiting paramedics' faces said it all; they were itching to help. At the sight of the man's bravery, all the ambulance units broke their embargo and ran for the office building as fast as they could with their kits. Common sense and decency overruled stupidity.

I followed them back in. The rest of the afternoon was more of the same: more injured, more dead and more blood. Seven people were murdered that day and one madman suicided. I don't give the killer a name, out of respect for those who died during his thirty minutes of terror.

As the sun set, there was so many cops, forensic experts and high-ranking police at the scene that it resembled a sticky doughnut covered in ants. I was glad to walk away after the last survivor was driven home. It was well after midnight and I reeked of death. I stopped at a late-night cafe on the way, sitting alone, drinking coffee and staring at the table. I spent a long time wondering how many victims might have been saved, had we been able to get the paramedics into the scene when first requested. A department where a commissioner in an office could overrule the lifesaving decisions of an experienced team of detectives on the scene was not a police department I wanted to be involved with. I tried a beer, but it didn't work, so I headed home to wash the night away.

I woke early the following morning; I was due back at the crime scene. As I was towelling myself off after a quick shower, I looked into the mirror at my tired eyes. I looked again, shocked to see every square centimetre of my body, head to toe, was spotted in pink. On the way to work I stopped by my doctor. My measles-like spots were a direct reaction to the level of fear I had experienced: stress was literally oozing out of my pores. The realities of being a detective soon outweighed any chance of taking time off, so, embarrassed by my affliction, I went to work over the next week with my face and hands covered in fake tan lotion. I don't think I really fooled anyone.

9

RICHMOND DETECTIVES

B y the time of the Queen Street shooting, I was sharing the terrace
house in Abbotsford with my old pal Jenny. Jenny and I were great
friends for many years, until she ran away to Queensland to chase her
beau. She gave me invaluable support in the days following Queen
Street, making sure I didn't withdraw or become consumed by the
sheer horror. She was a girl with a sharp wit and we often hung out
together, as she got a few laughs into me. We were like a family—
Jenny, Chelsea, who was now at Kew High School, Anzac and
me—happily ensconced in inner-suburban bliss.

It was a time when there was no-one special in my life. Since the
end of my relationship with Cindy, I'd been happy just going with the
flow, at home, at work and with a casual date here and there. Richmond
was blessed with some very attractive policewomen. There was one
female cop who occasionally got under my skin, always through sex.
On her designated 'bad' days, she wore stockings and suspenders and
would slink past me in my office. She had a way of staring at me, full
of study, offering a touch of promise, tongue in cheek, the one girl
who was able to make the otherwise drab police uniform look like a
pole-dancer's outfit. She often came upstairs to the detectives' office

late at night, if I was working alone. Sometimes she brought her baton and leant her back against the wall, watching me sorting exhibits or arranging paperwork. It was about power for her, trying to do outrageous things to distract me, like lifting her skirt and rubbing herself with her baton, eyes closed, drifting away, knowing that I was becoming more aroused by the second. The image she presented sent me to another place; driven by lust, I would pull her onto my desk, tossing files aside, knocking over papers, my handgun and holster landing on the floor, taking my trousers with them. She was magnificent, so provocative, and so risky to deal with.

Before long, there was something more serious, someone very special, buzzing on my radar. Annitia was a camera operator from the police audiovisual unit, and she had one of the most bizarre jobs around. She filmed crime scenes, mostly murders but also any other scene that was approved. In murder cases, when the detectives were done, Annitia would film the body, the exhibits and the scene, capturing it all for the jury to view at trial. It was a bit too much daily blood and guts for me, yet she had the ability to turn off, to shut down her senses. She was a stunning paradox at a nasty crime scene; good looks videoing gore as she moved about, usually dressed in something chic like a long slinky silk skirt, sandals and pretty cotton blouse.

We flirted a bit at first but she had a strict rule of not going out with cops; she didn't like their 'narrow mindedness', as she put it. I persisted. We dated on the sly for a while, just to avoid the gossip, just to see if I was 'different from the other 11 000 cops'.

I had purchased some land opposite a tiny park, 200 metres around the corner from our rented terrace, and I had a building permit. I intended to build a faux Victorian two-storey terrace using 100-year-old bricks. I had renovated two houses, in between all the cops and robbers business, and interior design had become my hobby, filling a great creative void. There is something unbelievably honest in being covered in plaster dust at the end of your day as you pull on a cold beer and survey the results of your day's work. I enjoyed this level of domesticity; a refuge is something every cop needs as even routine work can provide the stuff of nightmares.

Like the time I bumped into a victim's nightmare, working night shift with the Coca-Cola Kid—so named because he was addicted to the stuff, but he was good to work with, and had a fine analytical mind— and I were nearing the end of our night shift working 'day'. We knew we were in for a long slice of overtime when the operator said over the radio, 'Richmond 511, confirmed aggravated rape for your plate.' Anything that is 'confirmed' is trouble. You know it's going to be a hard one before you arrive at the scene, and whenever the word 'aggravated' is used (meaning a serious crime with violence), it is never good.

We pulled up at a smart villa with a neat backyard, part of a cluster of units. The outside was swarming with uniforms and crime reporters. We cleared them away. Our victim was a woman of about forty who had suffered a brutal rape. She was bleeding internally and her hands were tied, in the front. The paramedics and police surgeon were keen to get her off to the local hospital but we gained a short time with her. We cut the rope from her hands, keeping it for later analysis.

The woman was slowly drifting into shock but she managed to tell us that she had been home alone. Her daughter was at a sleepover; a man had forced his way through the back door adjacent to the garden. It was at about three in the morning and she had been asleep on the couch. The man tied her up, dumped her onto the bed and raped her viciously, cutting her across the face, arms and stomach with a kitchen knife. We had the knife.

When asked if she could recognise him, she blurted out that the rapist was her ex-husband. They had been divorced for years and he had a history of harassing her. He had visited the night before, then returned to rape her. The evidence at the scene appeared consistent with the victim's story and the surgeon was happy with the analysis. We had enough to work the case. The Coca-Cola Kid and I figured we had a lay-down misère; we'd photograph, fingerprint, video (with the lovely Annitia) and sketch the scene, then go hunt ourselves a rap-ing ex-husband.

The crime scene still got the full treatment; there is no value in taking short cuts. We moved through the unit ticking off the available evidence to confirm the victim's story. The surgeon sent word that the victim had fallen into deep shock, with severe blood loss; she was a mess. We asked other detectives to head into town and apply for a search warrant for the ex-husband's house. Things were progressing; we had a fine puzzle on our hands, just as detectives like it.

The backyard showed signs that an offender had been there. There were tool markings on the outside of the sliding door, tears in the flywire and the garden was up-ended. We were a little perturbed that we didn't find the offender's footprint, even though it had been rain-ing. But we also knew we couldn't expect to gather 100 per cent of the evidence at every scene.

The radio squawked a message to us, turning the temperature up on the former husband. Apparently he had left Melbourne a few min-utes earlier, flying to Brisbane on the early morning shuttle. He was on the run. 'Good', we thought; flight is a near admission of complic-ity in any crime. As we left the scene we mused briefly on the merits of flying to Brisbane, applying for the man's extradition, and lying on sun-drenched beaches for a few days, sipping umbrella-decorated Coca-Cola slurpies.

We snapped out of our dream and went to the hospital, after alerting detectives in Brisbane to arrest the ex-husband on the incom-ing flight. Our victim was sedated and the surgeon complained that the rapist must have worn a condom, as there was no evidence of semen. This news was a setback; without semen, we needed an admis-sion. So we headed into town to get authority to book our airline tickets. The game was on.

There's something wonderfully grand about being a detective, especially the moment when you've proven your case. That's a moment worth savouring. It's all about the matching of minds; the great chal-lenge, one story against another, truth against lies. And when that moment comes there's usually a pocket of time to bathe in the victory, to feel pleased with yourself, before you move onto the next puzzle, the next investigation. This elation isn't always reserved for moments when the suspect is finally charged, or convicted. Sometimes, although rare, the same feeling comes for an opposite result.

By the time we got back to our office the ex-husband had been arrested. He admitted seeing his ex-wife that night, but denied raping her or cutting her up.

The Coca-Cola Kid and I were sitting down to a coffee waiting for our flight approval. We were both exhausted and would no doubt rather have been somewhere else; Brisbane seemed eminently suitable. We waited in our state of comfortable drowsiness, the case ticking over in our sleep-deprived brains. Suddenly, we both looked at each other, and without uttering a single word, we each nodded and reached for a phone.

We called a 'what if' conference. Our first supposition: what if the rape had never taken place? The surgeon was perplexed, lost for comment. Our second supposition was even more disturbing: what if the victim was lying? We had the attention of our boss now. The third argument was the most riveting of all: what if the entire crime had been invented by a vengeful victim? The police surgeon went white and the boss looked out the window for an escape ladder. The stunned silence was swept aside by vigorous discussion, and our negative proposition gained legs. Minds were ticking and pens were flicking. Maybe, just maybe, those legs might start walking. The only obstacle was … why? Why would anyone ever do such a thing?

The absence of a footprint was the thing that gnawed away at us. There wasn't one in the rear yard. Yet the yard was surrounded by a brick wall 2 metres high; there was no way in or out. The ex-husband had to have jumped from the top of the wall to the dirt. There had been rain the day before, so where were the footprints? If our conclusion was correct, then what was the real story?

With our table of minds united, we cancelled the flights to sunny Queensland and postponed the umbrella drinks. We needed to catch the victim before she discharged herself from hospital. We arrived just in time and the surgeon undertook a broader, more probative examination of the woman's genitals. And the tearful truth came out.

She had seen her ex-husband that night and they had fought. While they had long been separated, she had never gotten over the failed marriage and wanted desperately to reconcile. The ex-husband had moved on; his only connection with her now was their teenage daughter, whom he had come to visit that night, only to learn of the planned sleepover. He had seen his daughter briefly as she went to her friend's home; the wife made sure the daughter witnessed her father's presence. The mother had also arranged the sleepover, as a convenient way to get rid of the child for the night. The husband held back and had a coffee with his ex-wife, leaving fingerprints and cigarette butts for us to collect. Then he left, explaining he had an early flight to Brisbane for a holiday, telling his wife the time of his departure, which she noted: six in the morning.

Once the man had left, the 'victim' sat at home planning her rape, designing her ex-husband's future. Her idea was that, if she couldn't have him, no-one would. She waited for the night to pass, calculating two hours before the early morning flight to Brisbane. Then she walked onto her stage. In the backyard, she quietly knocked over a couple of pots and disturbed a few plants before breaking a tree branch. Then, with an old screwdriver, once owned by her ex-husband, she scratched marks on the sliding door, making it appear as a break-in. Her next move was to tear the flywire screen, just enough to make it feasible, just enough to make it look as if the ex-husband had been stalking her. She ravaged her clothing, pulling so hard at her blouse that she caused the stitching to loosen. For good measure, she snapped off a few buttons and ripped some fabric.

Next, the real theatre: using a knife from her own kitchen, she repeatedly slashed herself across the upper arms, stomach and legs, consistent with the police surgeon's report. As if that wasn't enough, she stabbed herself repeatedly in the vagina, ensuring the wounds were deep and piercing, causing massive bloodloss. She sent out a few screams and she hurled a few pieces of furniture against the walls before calling the 000 operator for help. Her lines were perfectly delivered, like the talented actress she had become. As the sirens raced through the night to get to her aid, she tied her own hands, opened the front door, lay on the bed and waited, feigning unconsciousness.

As her story unfolded, I looked at a frail, pathetic woman and wondered if she was just a woman scorned or a very ill person. She finally made a full confession but not before she was faced with all the facts. I was so glad for our hunch and even happier the Coca-Cola Kid and I had our powder dry. She held out to the end, more than willing to send her husband to jail for twenty years. Immediately after her confession she lapsed into a deep depression and was unable to communicate at any level. It was a coma-like reaction. Just another performance, we figured. It worked; she was never charged. Even though we wanted to throw her before a jury, the psychiatric reports would have killed our case.

I went home after sixteen hours of unpaid overtime.

10

LOSS OF INNOCENCE

The three years I spent at Richmond were by far the most pleasing of my police career; we enjoyed a strong sense of camaraderie between the uniform section and the detectives. Some excellent police passed through Richmond, on their way to bigger careers, and we all shared a common goal—to look after our 'village' as we called it—and we got The Job done.

The spotlight often shone on Richmond, and much of that was due to the Pettingill clan and their tribe of bad-arse hangers-on. No real detective wants to work in a limp dick environment, where nothing much happens and where crooks toe the line. The very essence of being a detective is to 'detect', to solve crimes, to chase, to hunt and catch crooks. Richmond fulfilled all those criteria. I had also begun building the house I'd been planning. Annitia and I had become a serious item, so much so that we were almost inseparable. I had a couple of months leave owing and chose the sheer hard work of an owner-builder. I was home, at last, work-wise and domestically. But enough was enough; by the time I got back to my desk, I was looking for a change. I put in for vacancies for the major crime squad and my number was next on their list. I waited.

Since the death of Dennis Allen, his half-brother Victor Peirce had risen to the fore. It was as if he gained a sense of freedom with the passing of his more notorious brother; maybe he saw the door as now being wide open. There are only a few men you meet in the world of cops and robbers who are literally rotten, and Victor was one of them. He excelled in robbing banks but he was no ordinary bank robber. Not your stick-'em-up robber, wielding a note and a knife. Victor was the boss of the best team of bank robbers in Australia at that time and, by late 1988, he and his gang had become an epidemic. They hit bank after bank, each robbery, on average, netting about $200 000. His choice of co-offender, his best mate Graeme, was another career criminal who had spent half his life in and out of prisons. Along the way, Victor was using a few other scoundrels to help in the robberies, namely his pals Jedd and Bubble Head, two equally violent villains. Yet, for all Victor's cunning and smarts, he was unaware of one snippet of information that I knew. Graeme was having a sexual relationship with Victor's wife, Wendy. Had he known that, Victor would have killed them both.

There was a simple pattern in their robberies. Victor and Graeme would case a bank for weeks, watching for the ideal time to strike. Then they arranged to have a souped-up stolen car delivered, to be used as their getaway car. One stayed in the car as the driver and the gang would storm the bank, brandishing sawn-off pump-action shot-guns and revolvers. They jumped the counter, often racking off a few shots, grabbed the money and were gone.

They were so fast that witnesses didn't even have time to look up and see them properly. The getaway vehicle was always a V8 Holden, manual, stolen in the wee hours of the morning prior to the robbery. That way the car was fresh, not yet listed in the police data bank as sto-len. They wore similar bulky tracksuits and joggers, making witnesses confused as to who went where and who did what. They had started to embarrass the police department with their textbook cunning. One time Victor spent weeks watching a cash van, then made the tactical decision to abandon the stick-up as his surveillance showed there wasn't enough money. He was right; the van only delivered small amounts of change. The gang had certainly become masters of their craft.

The armed robbery squad worked around the clock, tracking the robberies, trying in vain for a breakthrough into the escalating number of stick-ups. Sadly, they made little or no impact. Every few months another bank was bowled over. Frustrations shadowed the squad. What prevailed was a stand-off of minds: Victor and his gang versus the collective investigative talent of the robbery squad. Thus far, the score was suffering a humiliating imbalance: Victor was streets ahead.

Unsurprisingly, Victor—given his violent history and his obvious family connections—dealt harshly with anyone who played informer. The secret squirrels were often thwarted as they tried to gain vital evidence, such as photographs of meetings between Victor, Graeme and others. At one point the investigation almost went into the 'too-hard' basket. Only professional responsibility to the community ensured the squad persevered. The media was almost serialising the exploits of the robbers as if they were comic-book characters. The robbery squad lacked a hook, the key ingredient necessary to lock the robbers up, and they were beginning to feel the pinch. Their trademark white short-sleeved shirts were losing their starch.

The robbery squad decided to raid some associates of Victor's, perhaps to stir the pot and see what jumped out. Informers are often gained this way. A bit of pressure is put on and maybe one of them will talk. Two of the raids were disasters: the suspects were shot dead.

The media went wild, screaming accusation after accusation, doubting the police claims that the suspects had weapons. Lawyers, family and friends all claimed the robbery squad had arranged to have the suspects killed. Solicitors representing the families of the dead robbers called for a public inquiry.

It seemed everyone had an opinion on the shootings, with criminals openly labelling police as 'assassins'. Pockets of the police department as well as criminals talked of fabricated evidence and shoddy police work. There was an uneasy, if not sour, taste in law enforcement, hanging in the public arena like a corpse.

Adding to this mess, a cash-van guard was busy picking up a hefty amount of cash from a Coles supermarket when, out of nowhere, a gunman stepped in with a firearm. There was a volley of shots and the guard was shot dead. He left a widow and small child. The robber was also shot but escaped, leaving blood at the scene. There was a strong belief the murder of the guard was the work of the same crew— Victor's crew. The gang simply had to be caught.

During this period, Victor was locked up in the cells at Richmond for a day, on a measly traffic warrant. It was an almost surreal situation: arguably the worst (or best, depending on your outlook) robber in the country being done on a 24-hour warrant. Victor came in snarling evil at everyone. He chose to sit it out without food or water, believing the cops would have pissed in it. After a few hours Wendy turned up with a sandwich. Wendy was a fireball, 70 kilograms of difficulty; at times she made Kath look like Mother Teresa. I can't recall anyone in the police station who had a good word for her.

Wendy was refused permission to see Victor and for her sandwich to be handed on to him. This was normal procedure, although it is usually no skin off anyone's nose to allow a brief visit. Wendy hit the roof, screaming and abusing the young constable on the desk. I was in earshot and walked out to lend a hand.

'Sorry, I just want Victor to eat something, he'll die in there.'

'You know the rules, Wendy; nothing gets passed into the cells.'

'The fuckin' dogs, sorry, the police shouldn't have locked him up.'

Wendy's sole purpose on that day was to give a lousy sandwich to her rotten husband.

'He'll starve, Mr McLaren,' she said, standing her ground.

A couple of more senior police walked past and out the front door.

'Fuck off Wendy.'

She looked livid.

'Give me your sandwich, I'll pass it on. Now go home and look after your kids.'

'You sure? Thanks, he'll be starving, I won't forget it.'

Wendy left the station and I gave Victor his silly sandwich. It was pointless to annoy every crook who came into our station, even the Pettingills. What possible victory could be had in denying someone a sandwich, especially as the food we were to serve him was indeed very likely to have been contaminated? I knew that, in the underworld, what goes around comes around.

Late one day I was at the office taking out a search warrant on a couple of lowlifes I wanted arrested. It was my last few days at Richmond as I was transferring to the major crime squad. I was typing away when I heard on the news that the robbery squad had attempted to arrest Victor's partner, Graeme, in a suburban car park. Graeme had attempted to flee in his car and had raised a gun at police. He had been shot dead. I flicked from channel to channel watching the footage, in disbelief at another death.

The police department thrives on scuttlebutt, the hotter the better. Telephones were running hot. At Richmond, we fielded call after call from fellow detectives seeking information that we simply didn't have. Like the rest of the community, we just watched the coverage and formed our own opinions.

Annitia missed out on filming the scene of Graeme's shooting, which was nice, as we were both glad to be out of that mess, preferring a quite dinner at home and a few glasses of shiraz. The house was finally built and it looked a treat. Chelsea would turn fourteen in a couple of days and she was having a ball, setting up her new bedroom with all her girly things.

I went to bed feeling uneasy that night, as I know many others did. I couldn't help thinking about what happened to Graeme, wondering what Victor was up to. As my head hit the pillow I remembered something I'd learned many years earlier as a kid in Clarkefield: 'Kick a dog for long enough and it'll bite back.'

My alarm went off well before five. I remember thinking I should stay in bed, turn the alarm off, go back to sleep, or make love to Annitia. Anything but get up at that ungodly hour. In hindsight, I definitely should have stayed where I was.

I couldn't hear the shots from my bed, just a kilometre or two away as the crow flies: Abbotsford to Walsh Street, South Yarra, nothing much in the way except 'Dennis-ville'. I stepped out of bed and hit the shower.

By the time I was fully absorbed in my morning ablutions, fifteen minutes had passed since two rookie cops first began investigating a stolen car, abandoned in the centre of Walsh Street, a narrow street in an affluent area offering quietly elegant homes to the wealthy, and chic apartments to the stockbroker set. Constables Steven Tynan and Damian Eyre had pulled up behind the stolen car, having been tipped off by an irate taxi driver unable to circumvent the vehicle. A few early risers also saw the car parked, doors open, side window smashed and lights on. It sat alone, under a street light, the perfect lure.

The young policemen went through the motions. There are a dozen different things you do with a stolen car: check the registration to see who owned it; survey the bodywork, in case it had been in a hit-and-run; check the interior. A couple of rookies could lose themselves for half an hour with a stolen car. Interestingly, this car was a V8 Holden, stolen only metres from where the boys found it. The steering column had been broken and the engine started with a screwdriver jemmied into the ignition.

It was still dark. The cops went about their pro forma tasks. At some point Constable Tynan was alerted by the damage to the ignition lock and he sat in the front seat, making notations in his patrol book. Constable Eyre joined him at the driver's door, possibly leaning into him. Two gunmen stepped out from the darkness, most likely from the driveway of a block of apartments adjacent to the car. At least one was carrying a shotgun. There was only time for Constable Tynan to be startled as he turned his head to face the shotgun, now only a metre away from his face. One shot killed him instantly. The wound was horrific. The shotgun was racked and another shot hit Constable Eyre in the back. Miraculously, Damian reacted by grabbing the shotgun, struggling with the murderer. Two more shots were fired into the night air, both impotent.

A second gunman grabbed the constable's service revolver and fired two rounds into Damian, hitting him once in the head and once in his back. Both gunmen ran from the scene, taking the shotgun and revolver, which was never seen again, leaving Damian on the roadway dying. The stolen car remained as it was found, headlights still burning, like the beacon it was.

The crack in the dam wall of criminal behaviour that had been the result of the Russell Street bombing was irreparably widened at 4.50 that morning in Walsh Street. There could be no stemming of the flow, no turning back. The streets of Melbourne had lost their innocence. Someone had kicked that dog once too often, and two innocent, dedicated, young men gave their lives. Their friends and families will grieve forever.

In police terms, when the shit hits the fan, you grab as many mates as you can and get on with the job. I dropped everything and headed to the crime scene, suited up, arriving as the two boys were leaving in ambulances. I parked a block away and walked into Dead Street: it was no longer Walsh Street. The atmosphere was cold, lonely and bleak.

The homicide call-out crew was also just arriving: Big John and his sidekick, Big Jim. Both were experienced men. They were joined by pals from their outfit, another John and Jim pair, along with a posse numbering dozens, including me. While checking the front yards of houses along the street, I watched them arrive, like ants to a picnic. Detectives and uniforms came from all directions, even country Victoria. Help was available in spades.

The trick with any crime scene of this magnitude is to gather the resources and put them to good use. It's important not to allow emotions to take over. Big John was a master at coordination; in minutes detectives were swarming the area, searching houses, apartments, streets, laneways, the Yarra River stormwater drains, parked cars, anything and everything in front of us. Information was coming in so fast it was clogging up the radio space, ideas after theories after hunches. There were a million thrown around in that first hour. The think tank grew by the minute, with dozens of detectives desperately searching for the answer to one simple question: why were these two boys targeted?

By mid-afternoon we'd searched every square millimetre of the ten streets surrounding the murder scene. We had spoken with every available resident. Many recalled seeing men fleeing the area. Some mentioned bandits wearing balaclavas, and men dressed identically. The critical mass of the witness statements gathered suggested between two and four men were involved and possibly two getaway cars, parked well away from the scene.

We didn't yet know the killers' names but we did have two unassailable facts: whoever shot these boys were long gone and they had been very, very professional. To get the jump on one cop is cool work for any executioner; to achieve the same result against two cops, and with such bloody, devastating results, is definitely professional. If we could only answer the question that haunted us all, there was a strong possibility we would find the culprits. It wasn't long before there were whispers about Graeme's death, linking the shootings.

We knew the killers wouldn't be found lurking, nor could we expect to be handed their names. We had to find them, and we were acutely aware, from the sheer thoroughness and audacity of the murders, how hard that task might be. All day, a team of detectives worked on the backgrounds of the two dead constables, in an effort to see if there was anything in their history that could prompt such brutal retaliation. Less than a fortnight earlier, Steven Tynan had attended an armed robbery in a TAB betting shop where two Asian students had held a knife to the manager's throat. Steven confronted the bandits, shooting one in the neck, and the other in the chest; both survived. The robbery was put down to a comedy of errors by two desperate and debt-ridden university students, although Steven's actions may have earned him a bravery award. The robbery was ruled out as a connection and there was nothing else that could conceivably have led to their murders. Both constables had exemplary backgrounds.

Kerbside conferences seemed to be taking place hourly as we desperately worked the scene. In a bid to stir up information, detectives began raiding select pockets of Melbourne's underworld. Across the city, house after house was done over, with some assistance offered interstate. The raids included houses occupied by the Pettingill clan. It was all designed to put pressure on the underworld and start a trickle of information. Someone had to know something, but crooks were holding firm; no-one offered a word.

Despite the raids, nothing was seen of Victor or Wendy. They had both gone to ground. Every available secret squirrel was swung onto possible targets, in the hope of finding a link that might give a lead. We prayed for divine intervention. There were so many targets that an extraordinary decision was made to call together every cop who had ever been attached to the secret squirrels and to get them back into plain clothes, shadowing the underworld. Crooks, gangsters, drug dealers, thieves, robbers, junkies, stand-overs, thugs, anyone with or without a reputation was being dragged in and questioned.

One of our kerbside conferences focused on the V8 Holden, stolen just before the killings, only metres away from where it was found. The car was the key. Not the owner of the car—he was just a square-head who lived locally—but the car itself. If we could understand the reasoning behind the car being there, we would know why the boys were killed, and then we could advance to working out who shot them. Everything pointed to the killers wanting the car to be found easily and quickly. Leaving the lights on, the doors open, smashing the side window, and parking it in the middle of the road: all pointed to it being bait. They may as well have placed a large flashing arrow on the car roof. It was a lure for two young policemen so they could be murdered. But who wanted two cops dead? And who was capable of such actions?

From the first moment I walked along Walsh Street I'd been thinking about Graeme's death the day before. I imagined Victor and what wild madness he would, could or might respond with. Victor was the logical one to be fingered for the crime, especially as Graeme had been gunned down in such controversial circumstances. Others in our group thought the same. Victor was the one criminal capable of committing a crime of this magnitude. He had proven himself to be a formidable foe and he had the firepower and guts to pursue such a ruthless vendetta.

By the end of the first day, a core group of detectives was forming. Within a few days that team became a task force. The homicide squad had the power to second detectives from any section of the department without question. Selection was based largely on experience or expertise. I was asked to join because of my experience as a detective in Richmond, my knowledge of the underworld, specifically the Pettingill clan, and my past work in the secret squirrels. Selfish desire and professional wants aside, I was glad to be selected in what was (and still is) the biggest police investigation ever mounted in this country. Every department in the country assisted the inquiry, offering staff, resources and as much time as was requested.

The task force started with twenty members and was scaled back to ten detectives, including two bosses, Big John and David. Having two equally ranked bosses defied logic and blurred the chain of command. Initially the task force had a chief inspector placed in charge, who would have created a balance between Big John and David. Trouble was, the CI took advantage of the hire-car budget allocated to the task force, hired a four-wheel drive, then disappeared to his hobby farm, sorting out sheep. On the occasions we detectives got to use the four-wheel drive, we first needed to hose out the sheep piss and hay from the back. After a short while, once the horticultural activities had been achieved, the good CI retired, and all of a sudden we had two equal bosses.

Big John was, as his name suggested, big: as big as a house and barrel chested, after years of pumping iron. He rarely smiled. David was his perfect opposite, lucky to be over the minimum height for a cop, oozing a softness in his build and personality. While they were both skilled men, David was the thinking detective's boss.

David was senior to Big John and had vast experience at all levels of the homicide squad; Big John had only been promoted a couple of days and had yet to prove himself as a leader at that level. As a fellow member of the male species, I sat back at times and observed two fascinatingly different examples: one akin to a tightly coiled spring, the other a loose lace ribbon.

I ventured home in those early days without any sense of elation. Annitia, Chelsea and I sat around flicking the late news, trying to get the public perspective on the investigation. As I watched the stories of the killings I often felt sickened. I kept seeing an image of the two constables' blood pooled on the roadway and the lonely Holden. I wondered if it was the smartest move in my career to work on this task force. I had no issue with the workload and envisaged I'd be working harder than ever before. But from the beginning I had a thought that the task force might ultimately have to question the past investigations of the robbery squad. Annitia and I spoke candidly about this concern.

In a masterfully played and unexpected move, Victor Peirce handed himself in to be interviewed for the cash-van robbery the day after the killings, the opening gambit in his cunning game. This slice of clever work was designed by his lawyer, Andrew Fraser, who feared that the next person on the robbery squad's hit list was his client. I remember seeing Fraser walk smugly from the building and sneering at his haute-couture figure as it got into his green Porsche, knowing his client was now safe.

Victor's offering of himself to police may have been the smartest move of his criminal career. By surrendering, he called our bluff, forcing us to charge him or let him go. Foolishly, the robbery squad charged him. His coup in being locked up was that he stopped the police being able to collect evidence against him. No listening devices, no witnesses, no secret squirrels, no anything! A future investigation would prove, by irrefutable DNA, that another, unrelated robber killed the cash-van guard; Victor was ultimately released on those charges.

After ten days we were presented with what was initially described as a breakthrough. I saw it as a disaster. Kath's only daughter, Vicki, had a son, 17-year-old Jason Ryan, who was by no means a typical teenager. He had lived in Dennis-ville for the previous four years, sometimes with Kath, sometimes with Dennis. Other times he had stayed with Victor and Wendy. I knew Jason well, having arrested him a few times. His head popped up at Kath's and Dennis's houses, and he was suspected of burning down a warehouse near his Uncle Victor's place. He was the very reason we have social welfare officers. This kid had been exposed to some of the most shocking crimes imaginable; he was the very essence of a juvenile delinquent. He had been present during a number of Dennis's murders—like the time Dennis gave a prostitute a 'hot shot' of heroin (a forced fatal overdose) at one of his brothels. He also witnessed his uncle bashing countless victims. Jason had always idolised his Dennis, although Victor considered him nothing but trouble.

Jason was no tough guy; in fact, he was the exact opposite. A weedy sycophantic kid, at best he could be called a hanger-on. His only ticket to the main event was being a full-blood Pettingill, otherwise he'd have been arse-kicked home long before. There are many who sympathise with young Jason, and perhaps rightly so. Any child born into that clan faced a tough life.

He was known to buckle easily in the hands of police and had, at one time, made a statement against his uncle, Trevor, implicating him in a crime. To fellow crooks, he was untrustworthy. He would sniff out a hard story and then run about town gaining notoriety from the tale. Jason had also made a statement some months earlier implicating Victor and Graeme in the shooting of the cash-van guard. The statement was made to the robbery squad and was one of the main justifications for the bungled attempt at arresting Graeme that resulted in his death.

The robbery squad also had been working away, trying their best to flush out information on the Walsh Street killings. They spoke to young Jason again, and subsequently he made a video interview with Big John. He claimed he was at his mother's house the night Graeme was shot dead. Jedd and Bubble Head were there also and during the night both men talked of taking revenge for Graeme's killing. Jason also alluded to guns owned by both men, and that they both left the house later that night. If this was evidence—as was being touted—it was flimsy, at best.

Great importance was placed on the statement, probably at a time when there was little or no other evidence coming into the task force. Many of us doubted the veracity of Jason's diatribe, yet it was decided that, in the absence of anything else, Jason was our man, or boy.

Big John placed him in witness protection. Jason's first statement was followed with another, and then another, and then another. As the weeks moved on, Jason added more lyrical detail to his original tale, in effect strengthening his claims on each occasion. A couple of times I was with Jason, back at the crime scene, assisting with re-enactments. Under the direction of the video unit, and with Big John alongside him, Jason took us through the crime as he knew it. He walked along Walsh Street, pointing out where the gunmen were, where Victor was, what happened next, where he stood, what he saw, who was where, and on it went.

In the end, Jason's re-enactment bore no resemblance to his original comments. He went on to make maybe five or six statements. The more he was asked about the killings, the grander his comments were and the more ornate was the tapestry he wove. Once he impli-cated his mates Manny and Anthony in the killings, then his Uncle Trevor. His stories became confused and were riddled with contradic-tions. At one re-enactment he indicated where the V8 Holden was parked on the night, yet the car was in fact parked in the opposite direction. Clearly he was struggling with his testimony. He even claimed to have stolen the car himself and arranged it in position; he later retracted that, saying it was wrong. I clearly remember watching Jason walk over the crime scene. I watched a confused boy walk, turn, look and think. He was trying his hardest, I'm sure. But I was seeing a kid who had never been to that area before. I saw a delinquent who, like so many times before in his short life, had probably sniffed out a hard story and was now running around Walsh Street with it.

Jason later denied even being at Walsh Street. It was getting a bit much for him. I voiced my private opinion, only to be brushed aside. It was early days and the task force needed something, someone to believe in. The entire police department needed someone to believe in. The national media needed a positive story to run with. It had been over two weeks since the killings. Jason filled that role, at least for one section of the task force. I never believed for even a split second that Jason had anything to do with the murders of those two policemen, nor did I believe anything he said had any credibility. He had become a dangerous liability.

I was more than pleased to lose myself in the mountain of information sheets I was facing and forget about Jason. His mate Anthony, however, would never forget about him. Three weeks after the killings, largely as a result of Jason's comments, Anthony was charged with the Walsh Street murders and remanded in custody. Another 'suspect' was now locked away, once again denying the task force any chance of gaining incriminating evidence. I began to wonder whether the mission statement of this task force should read 'competence' or 'bravado'. I believed Anthony had about as much to do with the Walsh Street murders as Jason. He was just a kid really, only twenty years old, and hardly the type Victor would use as an accomplice to kill two police. The other John and Jim also had concerns, and John urged the inquiry to move slowly. He said, 'If it takes a few years, it doesn't matter. We have to do this properly—go slowly, slowly.' It was great advice from a great detective but it flittered away as quickly as it was delivered.

Days later our attentions had moved to Jedd. Jason had also implicated him in the killings, only this time I had no issue believing it. Jedd was a hardened criminal, a man of violence and guns, and he was well regarded by Victor. Based on the information coming into the task force and the snippets from the underworld, I felt he was probably involved and could quite possibly have stood alongside Victor on the night of the killings. We needed to move 'slowly, slowly'.

The secret squirrels had been on Jedd and had him holed up in central Victoria. He was living between a caravan he rented on the outskirts of Bendigo and a rattly old house in town, owned by a friend. My old buddy Wayne was working with the squirrels, following Jedd. Along with half the task force, I went up to study the form.

Wayne's boys had installed listening devices, one in the house and the other in the caravan, allowing them to get a greater understanding of what Jedd's head space was like. He was brewing for a showdown. There was talk of him carrying a revolver and a pistol; we were still missing the police service revolver and the shotgun from the crime scene. Wayne gave us the interesting news that Jedd had a police scanner operating most of the time, obviously to keep a step ahead of the filth. Our prospects didn't look rosy.

Over a few days we watched Jedd's behaviour: he was like a caged tiger, often on the prowl, always on edge. It was perhaps with good reason; we sourced a friend of his who was starting to wonder what his old mate had been up to. The friend reckoned he had seen Jedd with four different handguns and ammunition, and added that Jedd had mentioned that he would shoot it out with police. We listened to conversations where Jedd talked about revenge for Graeme's shooting. Big John made the correct tactical decision to arrest Jedd sooner rather than later, due to his propensity for violence.

We sat in a farmhouse in Bendigo and waited for the ideal time to raid him. It was difficult to get Jedd alone, as he was often in the company of his girlfriend. We waited for a lucky break. The waiting meant bunking on the floor with at least twelve other task force people in the lounge room of Farmer Brown's pleasant but hardly five-star house.

Sometimes action is forced upon you. As we sat listening to our target rant and rave his hatred of police, we heard a series of crackling and screeching noises before the hidden microphone cut out. Jedd had been playing with a couple of handguns, occasionally looking out the window. He had discovered our listening device drilled into the window sill and went ballistic, screaming that he'd kill police. His buddy attempted in vain to calm him down, and for the first time we realised we had a fight on our hands.

Jedd left the house in a fury and rode his motorbike over to the caravan where his girlfriend was staying, deciding to settle there for the night, believing himself safe from prying police. They talked of heading for the warmer climes of Queensland. Jedd's girlfriend was a pretty young girl but, sadly, she believed in Jedd, and hated the police just as much. Despite her feelings, we needed to ensure she would be safe during Jedd's arrest. We didn't want any suggestion that we intended to harm her or her crazy boyfriend. There were already enough bodies.

I knew the inside layout of the van, having snuck in and taken a look one day when Jedd and his girl went shopping. If we were going to tackle him properly, we needed to be sure where the bed was in relation to the door, and so on. It was really just a small mobile home, with one large room containing a bedroom and kitchenette. When Jedd indicated he was going to sleep, we decided to do the raid immediately and called headquarters for the use of the SOG SWAT team. Police command refused our request, telling us to do the raid ourselves. 'Don't kill him!' they barked.

The four main detectives on the task force adjourned to a nearby yard to kit up, put on our bulletproof vests, and get our shotguns. We needed a few minutes to work out a plan. The first man to the door was to wield the sledgehammer and, with one strike, force the door open, then step aside. The next man in line was to be the first inside, the first to confront Jedd. The following man (me) was to follow and take the opposite position to the first man, and the number four man was to back up the first two inside. We went through the procedure over and over and got ourselves into the head zone—the space that's achieved minutes before a raid when you know exactly what is required. We drove to the caravan, only to be told to stop and abandon our mission. The SOG SWAT team were in the sky, on their way; command had rethought the earlier decision. Arr, you've got to love those dills!

The raid, when it did finally eventuate, couldn't have gone any worse. The SOG executed a textbook entry, as fast as lightning. Smash—the glass door went in and two men stormed inside, only to be confronted by a very alert, angry Jedd, sitting up in bed, holding a handgun aimed at the police. He refused to drop the weapon and was, in response, shot dead. His girlfriend was taken from the caravan screaming but unharmed.

Sitting with the other detectives in our car down the road, I heard the shots and realised we were in for bad news. When we arrived, the SOG had taped off the perimeter and we took over. Jedd lay dead on his bed. There were four handguns on and under his bed; it was obvious he went down fighting. Some of the weapons were later linked to robberies and shootings. I stood over his body, seeing entry wounds in his torso and darkness in his eyes. There was absolutely no doubt about his intentions.

I couldn't help thinking for the rest of the night that my raid team might not have been as quick or as efficient as the SOG and that, just maybe, one of us might have been shot. We returned to Melbourne to headlines across the country, 'Police kill another man'.

I spent a couple of days at home, enjoying the company of the more important people in my life. It was so good to be back after being away for several days. I was suffering the effects of being too close to an investigation resulting in too much death. We were carrying shotguns day and night. Work was no longer enjoyable. I thought many times of leaving the task force but leaving would mean turning my back on the murder of two innocent policemen.

I was struggling: wanting normality, wanting to be with Annitia and to allow our new and exciting relationship to take its course. I also needed to be able to see and experience Chelsea as a young lady growing up. My life had become totally absorbed with cops and robbers and intertwining dramas. Annitia was more understanding than anyone could expect, feeling my dilemma, but unselfishly compensating by supporting me every step of the way, and shielding Chelsea magnificently. I asked them both to give me a few more months and I would request to be the first off the inquiry.

The next week, for administrative reasons, we moved into a new office. There was an extraordinary amount of work building up and we needed more space. Detectives were assigned information reports every few minutes; we were making inquiries on the run. The media was demanding information on Jedd. The public was trying hard to assist and anything that might be considered important or relevant was being phoned in. Much of the stuff was rubbish but it all had to be investigated and we were grateful for the community's assistance.

On that first day in our newly created office, Big John and Big Jim began setting it up. It was the weekend and I thought I would help. The configuration of the area meant there was one space suitable for the officer-in-charge, his desk and chair. Big John assumed that space, moved his gym equipment into the office and his work was complete. David was allotted another space.

The second move that weekend proved to be one of the silliest decisions I've seen in any investigation. The other John and Jim pair had been working around the clock on the murders; they were old-school homicide detectives, and both enjoyed high levels of respect and praise. They had worked many homicides as a team. On the Walsh Street inquiry, they methodically worked through their information reports, making progress centimetre by centimetre, in typical thorough homicide squad fashion. I was in awe of their talent—the award for 'highest achievement' at the detective training school is named after John—and considered them the best two investigators on our team.

Ridiculously, they were removed from the task force over that weekend, a management decision that defied all logic. It was an indication of just what we could expect in the future. No position was safe.

11

LOST OPPORTUNITY

At least our journey wouldn't be as hard as the one being travelled by Wendy. She must have been struggling, having felt the effects of three or four raids on her house and seeing Victor locked up; her Christmas was getting light on. On Christmas Eve she got into a drunken brawl with a knockabout girl in a Richmond pub, stabbing her in the face, scarring her for life. The girl was just a barfly. She and her sister, Sissy, were part of an old family of crooks, safe-breakers mainly. Sissy was a good-natured woman, had once had a misguided affair with Victor but was now trying to get ahead in the back streets of Richmond. As far as her sister was concerned, the cat-fight was about Victor. Wendy was in typical form, abusive and vengeful. After Wendy was locked in the cells, I just happened to wander by; I had made a point of keeping on the right side of Wendy and she reacted well to a kindly gesture. I'd been brought up to know there is good in all people, even the so-called 'bad' ones. It all has to do with how you treat them.

Wendy was looking and feeling miserable in the cells. She reacted favourably to my visit, asking if I could arrange bail. I was trying to win her over, to see if she had the potential to become a crown witness. Being under enormous pressure and with Victor locked away for at least the next year before any trial, she just might break down and 'roll over'. Wendy was my long-term project.

This time I promised her nothing. She had been charged with attempted murder, a charge that would never stick but it was enough to scare her, to soften her, just a little. It was incredibly important that we bring Wendy into the witness protection program; she knew all Victor's secrets. When she was sent off to the women's prison for the next few months, I wished her well and she thanked me for helping Victor several months earlier with the sandwich. She asked me to visit her in prison; I told her I'd try, wishing her a merry Christmas.

Christmas came and went without incident. It was as if there was some sort of voluntary truce, like the days of World War I when the Allies and the Germans put down their weapons. The first Christmas in my new house was everything I had hoped for. Chelsea knew how I loved presents, a hangover from my childhood when gifts were a rarity. She often made hand-drawn cards in those days and I took great delight in receiving them. Annitia and I seemed to be getting stronger and stronger; she would be the love of my life. I sat back in my easy chair late in the day, after we had scoffed a grand dinner with Annitia's family and my Ma and Ray. I looked over the house, my life and my two girls. I watched them both fuss about in the kitchen, folding used Christmas wrapping, laughing, doing things together. 'They get on so well these two,' I thought. I drew back on my fat cigar and wondered what the poor people were doing.

I had long thought the key to solving the murder of the two constables was to work on the armed robberies we knew Victor and his gang had committed. We needed to focus on the getaway cars used; each one was strikingly similar. I voiced my thoughts many times at our weekly briefings, pushing the point, and David soon supported me. There was an obvious rift developing between David and Big John, the blame for which I laid entirely at the feet of the hierarchy. Both were good men; it was just that there was no room for two roosters in the one chook shed. David must have wondered at what an odd team we were, compared with the elite homicide squad he usually managed.

The task force seemed to have been locked into a silly tough-guy mentality. Lots of what we were doing was window dressing, showing off to the rank-and-file police that we were paying back the underworld for the shootings. While this may have had some merit as far as morale for the department, it wasn't getting the crimes solved. The words of the other John rang clear—'We have to do this properly, go slowly, slowly'—yet we were running like bulls at gates, often crashing into the gate, only to charge again.

In the New Year, everyone was summoned to a search of Victor and Wendy's house in Richmond. We systematically demolished the house, piece by piece, brick by brick, down to bare earth. This was the first time ever a house had been demolished as part of a police investigation. David made himself scarce, electing to hold the fort and take calls at the office. We didn't find anything useful to the Walsh Street murders during this exercise and I remember asking, 'What purpose has all this served in locking up the crooks who killed our two boys?' Was it task force members showing the rest of the police department that we had matters under control, that we were on top of things?

I was visiting Wendy regularly, in prison, trying to roll her over, so at least she and I had something to talk about: 'Hey, Wendy, we bulldozed your house!'

Wendy was getting to expect my visits and somehow she seemed to survive the fact that she and her children no longer had a home. As was often the way, we sat to one side in the prison exercise-yard and talked, about her younger years, her mother, early schooldays and what she'd have liked to have achieved, had she not married one of Australia's most notorious men. Bit by bit I gained her confidence and occasionally she'd even call me at my office, from the prison yard, and get me to run errands for her, all to do with her kids. I was happy to do so, especially as her children were now homeless and needed to be relocated. I always made sure that I noted every contact in my diary.

Big John didn't favour this line of inquiry, for mixed reasons, but mainly because Wendy was the sister-in-law of all the other clan members. David, on the other hand, felt this was a strong lead that should be encouraged at all costs. The task force was divided, and things between Big John and I were reaching a low point, which frustrated me.

A really valuable breakthrough became a great distraction from the tensions: we matched some ballistic evidence. The shotgun used at the murders and the spent cartridges that lay on the roadway near the dead constables matched cartridges used in the bank robberies. This evidence was damning. It had become simple: prove the robberies and you went to proving the murders. Follow the gun—and follow the getaway cars. The theory started to gather credence, and real enthusiasm hit our task force. The robbery squad, lingering in the background, demanded that they be able to reinvestigate their own crime scenes. When the issue was raised at our task force's weekly briefing, we all agreed that the robbery squad should be told to stay out of our investigation, totally. Big John toughed it out and told their squad leader that assistance was not required. Reluctantly they handed over their case reports.

We grouped together eight robberies that were obviously the same crew of bandits. The banks' security photos showed what appeared to be the same gang inside the banks, brandishing the same sawn-off shotgun, and possibly the same handguns. We called for every photograph taken by the banks' internal security cameras. Luck falls from trees sometimes. The bank photographs were all in perfect condition. We had images of every frame during the robberies, thousands of photographs. The story then started to unfold. The enlarged images showed a manufacturer's brand marking on the side of the shotgun: KTG. The images also showed the cut-down butt of the weapon, which was wrapped in black electrical tape, and the barrel of the KTG shotgun, sawn off in a rough jagged fashion, with the hacksaw markings clearly visible. At long last, the race was on; we had started to work like detectives. The squabbling stopped, if only for a short time.

Each detective was given a robbery to rework and some of us teamed up. This offered me the chance to work alongside Mark, a brilliant detective with a methodical mind. We would now collaborate for the rest of my time on the murders. As we worked away, visiting banks, reinterviewing witnesses, pulling the robbery files apart, it was clear that the original investigations were seriously flawed; the effort had been slapdash, at best. Every now and again you could hear someone in the task force yell out, 'What—what the fuck were those detectives doing?', so poor were the original investigations. Nonetheless, we went on to uncover important evidence, which was the main purpose of our work.

Our task force learned that the KTG shotgun had been very busy.

As we worked, I was forming an idea. Initially, I pushed the concept aside; it had to be naive, or even stupid. But it continued to fester, to niggle at me, until one day I blurted it out to Mark. In essence, my idea was simple, despite the massive size of the task. I'd once read in an investigative journal about a concept known as evidence by way of elimination. Where the existence of an object (any object) is crucial to a case, eliminate all other exact same objects, thereby proving, by way of elimination, that the object (under question) was the one used in a crime. The object in my concept was the KTG shotgun: the murder weapon.

I studied the limited historical data in English and American law text manuals and found three examples where attempts had been made. I sat in the Supreme Court law library for two nights reading the texts of the cases. It appeared each attempt had failed in the eyes of the court mainly because the key aspect wasn't ever achieved: *all* the objects were never located. This fascinating forensic concept played on my mind.

David saw merit in my 'elimination' theory and allowed me to investigate, warning, though, that I might hit a brick wall, especially if there were thousands of guns involved. One of the great things about David was his willingness to give anything a go, as long as it was conceptually sound. He always showed himself to be an articulate, competent man who passionately believed in thorough investigation. He had taken over my supervision.

My new line of hierarchal communication allowed me to open my mind more and I started my 'elimination' file. It sat heavily on my desk for ages as I contemplated the task. Inquiries with wholesalers and customs seemed to take forever. The shotguns were made in Japan and there were many different models, with more than a thousand imported. The sole importer had gone into receivership, making access to records almost impossible, yet, with persistence, the records were finally found. Parallel inquiries with gunshops that sold the shotguns also proved as difficult, as, naturally, many gunsmiths failed to appreciate what I was trying to do. A few of the more shonky ones were concerned they may have been under investigation themselves.

I waded through documents and then called for photographs of all models from Japan. I hoped to be able to make some progress, although I was starting to understand why 'evidence by way of elimination' had never been successful. The manufacturer eventually sent the material through and that same luck fell from that same tree, again.

The weapon used in our bank robberies was a particular model of KTG shotgun, imported into Australia for only a short period, and only forty-two ever left Japan. All I needed to do was find the other forty-one guns.

I got to it, knowing that it might take many months. Starting with the customs manifest, I confirmed the arrival of the weapons into the wholesalers, and then matched despatch papers with the purchase and invoice documents of gunshops across Australia. Once I gained the various gunsmiths' confidence, they went through their records to identify the purchasers. I helped some of them with this process, in case there were one or two less-than-honest gunsmiths.

Then I wrote to the police station in the area where the gun owner lived, asking for help. My request was simple: go to the address, sight the shotgun, verify the serial number and condition of the gun (making sure it wasn't sawn down), photograph the weapon, then send the information back, with an affidavit. The guns were spread across

Australia, including one that proved a worry; it was on a farm in the Northern Territory and had suffered damage to the butt and stock area. It had been attacked by white ants but, thankfully, the barrel was intact.

We discovered that two of the shotguns were sold to a gunshop in suburban Melbourne, which was subsequently burgled; both guns were stolen. These were the only two weapons not accounted for. The luck kept coming, and we discovered a criminal had been arrested with one of the missing shotguns a year earlier. He had been convicted and the shotgun destroyed, which is the usual practice with weapons after a court case. Two things fascinated me with this new information. Firstly, the weapon had been destroyed well before Victor's robberies, which meant it could not have been used to kill the two constables. Secondly, the crook arrested had received the gun from a docket-head named Gary. The gap was narrowing. The only gun now missing was obviously the murder weapon, but where was it, and who was Gary? Police records showed Gary was a close friend of Victor's.

While my head was busy in the KTG file, a gardener was busy working at the Royal Park Golf Course in inner-city Parkville. As he raked under a bush, he disturbed a sheet of black weed plastic. Under the plastic was a bag containing the last KTG shotgun, sawn-off barrel and cut-down butt wrapped in black electrical tape—our gun. Blow-up photographs from the bank cameras matched identically with the gun. The 'evidence by way of elimination' file was now complete. All KTG shotguns of that model were accounted for. The file took most of that year, along with many other investigations we were doing.

A detective can usually have ten or more files going at any one time, often twice that many. One of the other files I finally got off the ground was the 'car file', an effort to try to identify who had stolen the cars used in the robberies. Virtually the same type of car was used at each bank hold-up—a V8 Holden—and always stolen only hours before the stick-up, strongly suggesting that the car thief was procuring them to order; maybe, Victor's order?

For weeks, Mark and I researched old stolen-car reports, inspecting recovered cars, trying to get some insight into who the thief was. In time, we matched 'our' car thefts with many other car thefts in the western suburbs. I started profiling, digging into records on thieves caught for stealing identical cars. Soon, we tapped into a gang of crooks with dozens of convictions between them. Mark and I raided one thief after another, trying to work out who the right villain was. Thief number seven on our list pushed all our buttons. Theo was 'the world's best car thief', or so he'd tell television's *A Current Affair* years later, when demonstrating how easy it was to steal a car.

Theo had been charged by local police with stealing a V8 Holden sedan from a car yard. Coincidentally, the same car yard had another V8 Holden stolen weeks later. That latter car was used in a bank robbery where our KTG shotgun was photographed. I never did care too much for coincidences. Thieves often return to where they have had a previous win and Theo was a creature of habit; it had to be him.

We found Theo taking a well-earned break in Pentridge Prison. Initially he told us nothing: absolutely, totally nothing, except to 'fuck off!' He was too savvy to start giving us names straight off the bat. He needed to be won over and, for Theo, that meant we had to become his friend. 'Here we go again,' I thought, 'more jailhouse visits!' So, I added Theo to my list. Once I had let Theo whinge and carry on for a bit, he settled down, happy for the occasional visit, glad to sit and chat and take my packet of cigarettes each time.

For weeks on end, I listened to his domestic nonsense. He had a lot of personal issues to talk about before he opened up about the hard stuff. He was having trouble with his fiancée. They were due to be married when he was released, but she suspected him of screwing around with his old girlfriend again, so she was threatening to cancel the wedding. I spent hours dealing with this *Days of Our Lives* garbage, in an effort to get some truthful information from him. I even contacted his girlfriend and reassured her that Theo had turned over a new leaf. Slowly we mended his relationship, slowly Theo gave more and more information, and then, finally, he was released from prison, just days before his rescheduled wedding. I was even a guest: the things you have to do!

The point to all this soap opera is that Theo eventually did talk and kept talking, making many statements. He turned out to be a man with an extraordinarily fine memory, supplying information about every car on our files. His confidence won over, his tap kept flowing. Such is the way of crooks, at times; give a little, take a little. He told his story of being asked to steal Holden V8 cars for his 'boss' Stephen, a criminal we didn't even know about, who was the go-between to Victor and his gang. Theo identified some of the gang members, including Jedd.

The next logical step was to win over Stephen. Stephen could tell us all about the stolen cars, delivering them to Victor's boys, Jedd, and so much more. Winning Stephen over became the real turning point for the task force and everyone could sense it. Mark and I went on the hunt for him, but we may as well have stayed at the office and worked out in the gym for all the good it did. Stephen had fled the country. Seems that days after Jedd was shot dead he applied for a passport, hastily sold his house for a heavily discounted price and, packing up his family, took off to the goat country of his ancestry, Malta. Someone from the old Painters and Dockers union had helped with a safe passage through customs for his container of household goods. He was a man in a hell of a hurry.

David and I jumped on a plane to Europe. Interpol had responded quickly and found Stephen for us. We sent through a briefing paper to the Interpol representative, who facilitated our passage and meetings with local detectives. We made sure we stamped the file 'suspect not to be approached under any circumstances'; we needed the element of surprise when we arrived.

On the plane, David spoke at length about another task thrown on our plate. It appeared the robbery squad had a signed statement from another knockabout crook from Richmond—George—who claimed to have had a conversation with Victor before the Walsh Street murders. If taken on face value, his comments were hugely incriminating to Victor. The trouble was twofold. Firstly, like Stephen, this crook

had absconded just after the Walsh Street murders and was now resid-
ing in sunny Greece. Secondly, we were more than a little sceptical
about the statement, as the robbery squad had a string of similar statements that failed to get across the line. Were we poised for another
upset in chasing down the Greek? Greece was our first port of call and
Interpol Greece were fantastic people to work with.

Our plane touched down in 36 degree heat, nothing too difficult
for two Aussies in the throes of autumn. The Interpol boys were faithful to our request not to alert George; we didn't need a chase on our
hands. Yet, that is exactly what we had. He saw our car roll into his
street as we approached his house and away he went, over the back
fence and into the concrete maze of Athens. Interpol headed off after
him, holding their own, until neighbourhood knowledge got the better of them. George was gone. It was 'back to the office to hit the
phones', as we say in Australia—and they spoke the same language in
Greece, at least as far as detective work was concerned.

By early the next day the Interpol boys had a solid lead. George
had headed north, towards the Bulgarian border. If he crossed, he'd be
gone for good. David and I stuffed our suitcases and, with the two
Interpol boys, we raced to the airport, to a plane fuelled and waiting.

An hour and a half later we landed in the seaside village of
Kavalla, just 60 kilometres from the border. We crawled into town,
with the villagers' eyes following our car up the narrow streets. The
Interpol guys decided it was too risky to attract more attention, so
they dumped David and me at a hotel outside town to play tourists,
allowing them to do what they were good at, getting information. For
two days we paced the cold marble floors of our hotel, sweating on a
result, any result, to pass back home. Hours seemed to take days to
pass. Interpol had discovered George had been seen visiting an uncle,
seeking refuge. They had the whitewashed house staked out and
wanted to 'tap' on his door early the next morning, using the element
of surprise.

Happy to let them take control, David and I went back to pacing
the marble. Our Interpol boss could see we were riddled with anxiety

and declared, 'Tonight we eat!' There's one thing Greeks know how to do and that's eat. We enjoyed a magnificent feast of gyros, grilled octopus, garfish, stuffed peppers, souvlaki, Bulgarian feta and baklava, swished down with local ouzo and retsina.

At daylight, one of the Interpol secret squirrels woke us and dropped a bombshell. George had put on his running shoes and was headed for the Turkish border, last seen getting into a car just before daybreak. Luckily, there was only one road to Turkey. So, unshowered and still carrying our toothbrushes, we piled into a Fiat Uno, five men all with briefcases, and headed across the roof of Greece. As our tiny car flew along the dusty road, our Interpol guys telephoned ahead to the Turkish border in an attempt to stop George.

We figured we were only ten minutes behind our prey. David and I watched in fright as our Interpol driver tried to qualify for Formula One ranking. The border was three hours away. Fingernail marks became embedded in our briefcases as our driver swerved around every corner. He dodged goats, peasants with their donkeys and carts, and sheep grazing the roadside. Our road became so third world in appearance that we passed wild marijuana plants growing along the roadsides, enough to yield thousands of dollars in black-market sales. Finally, we passed through the sad, tired town of Alexandroupolis to the army post, just metres from the border. Our car's white duco could not be seen beneath its new thick coat of brown dust. We were lucky. George had been nabbed, and he was secure with an army lieutenant, awaiting his fate.

The Greeks are very proud people; they hate outsiders thinking poorly of them, and they deplore their own who engage in criminality. Once we arrived at the dusty tin-clad army base, our Interpol boss headed into a private briefing with the lieutenant and George, to help expedite matters. We heard one or two yelps from the room before we were politely ushered into our 'office': five chairs at a long, rough-cut timber bench. George was seated, with his head in his hands and tears streaming down his face. No more embarrassment, we thought, at least not for the Greeks. Our own fate was to be very different. David and

I had come a long, long way only to be made to look like idiots. Our George was just an immature, lowly docket-head, a scared little rabbit, a street punk more likely to have been mates with Jason than Victor.

George wasn't the type Victor would ever trust with his secrets. He sat meekly at the bench trembling. David and I sat at the same bench wondering what nonsense lay before us. Still, we were a long way from home, so we waded through our task and gave it our best shot, although we never doubted for a minute the honesty of his tearful words. It wasn't long before George told us everything, which, really, amounted to nothing much. It appeared he was forced into making his 'confession' in Australia. Once he signed his ticket to hell he was set free, allowed to go home. His parents, seeing his distraught condition, borrowed money for his ticket to Greece. George fled Australia only days after Graeme was shot dead.

Our Interpol boys and the army lieutenant looked perplexed at the revelations, as David and I shuffled our impressive-looking paperwork, feeling like fools. Somehow we managed to compose ourselves, at least long enough till we very humbly flew back to Athens, and crawled out of the country.

We hoped Malta would be a different story. At least we knew Stephen was definitely our man. Flight delays meant we had to stay overnight in Rome, en route to Malta. This gave us time to regroup after the Greek debacle and plan our attack. We found a typical osteria serving Lazio-style food, close to Vatican City. It was a balmy night, so seated at an outdoor table we shared a bottle of pinot grigio and a splendid meal. It was a night of talking, of reflection, with particular emphasis on the past eight months. As we enjoyed our *scampi di linguini* and *insalata mista*, and sipped our wine, we were lost in disappointment at the task force achievements, thus far. Being thousands of kilometres away from Australia helped us to see the stinking mess that had festered for nearly a year. We could only hope matters might improve.

Malta is really no more than one large rock, with barely enough room for an airport. As soon as the jet engines died out we knew something was terribly wrong. The Maltese police were there to greet us as the aircraft door was flung open, with their soft handshakes and smarmy smiles. It was obvious they were up to no good. They would prove to be the exact opposite of the Greek authorities. In short, while the Greeks bent over backwards to help, the Maltese offered nothing more then rhetoric. They had tipped off our suspect Stephen. The Interpol representative was the local commissioner. Stephen, full of attitude and smart-arse comments, was waiting in his office.

Stephen sat all smug, telling us to go home, that he had nothing to say. 'His' commissioner sat alongside him as Stephen admitted stealing cars, and boasted that, unless we had an extradition warrant, he was calling Malta home. He advised us that we should go back to Australia. David's patience wore thin. As the nonsense poured from Stephen's mouth, he hit the roof, challenging the commissioner for alerting our man. Yet the good commissioner sided with Stephen.

We persevered with Stephen for three more days, trying desperately to get him to return to Australia and help our inquiry. He boasted of relatives in the Maltese police department and of paying money to be told of our impending arrival. He feared that his life would be in danger if he returned to Australia, and demanded that we leave him alone, instructing 'his' commissioner to have us leave the country. Dutifully, the commissioner then booked our passage out of his country; he even escorted us onto the plane. We had been deported, and well and truly stooged.

The flight home felt twice as long as it really was. David and I just sat in silence most of the time, pondering the mess. We felt totally duped and at a loss as to how to improve matters back at the office. We knew we were coming home losers.

As we dragged our jet-lagged bodies into the task force office, we were met by looks of disappointment. In his kindly, decent way, Mark made a brave effort to cheer me up, and then a few others broke out of the doom and gloom that prevailed. We all listened to David's de-briefing, Big John staring out the window at the treetops. I placed my gifts of Toroni nougat on each desk and went home, in search of a friend.

Unbeknownst to me, while I had been wasting my time in Greece and Malta, Annitia had received a death threat. Victor had placed a jailhouse threat on my life, stating that he would kill me. He had heard of my regular meetings with Wendy and also that I was in Malta, speaking with Stephen. Obviously, we had hit a nerve.

Mark had liaised closely with Annitia and Chelsea and done whatever he could to step up patrols of our house and watch over my two girls while I was away. The SOG SWAT team had offered to stay overnight at our home but Annitia opted for normality, to keep matters as calm as she could, for Chelsea's sake. Bravely, Annitia kept most of the drama from Chelsea, allowing her to go about her life, as any schoolkid should be able to. And for a week, she suffered alone until I arrived home.

I held them both close, then hastily packed three suitcases and we disappeared to Tasmania for a week's break and a long, lazy time together, leaving the task force to defuse the threat. We went whitewater rafting, explored log-fire bed and breakfasts, anything, as long as it was away from the task force. It was nice to be away from the mess but my mind was still in Melbourne, with the threat Victor had made, with the Walsh Street killings eight months earlier.

This was a strange time for me. The pressures I felt were starting to chart their course, change my personality. I was depressed. I had become one-dimensional, living a life that consisted only of the task force. There was no head space available for anything else. I dwelled on the good old days as a detective at Richmond, when life had balance—times that were mere memories—and lost myself in daydreams. I had become concerned about my own family environment, scared for the safety of Chelsea and Annitia. Often the three of us would sit at home together at night, knowing that each of us was worried sick. Some nights were filled with silence and other nights were normal, happy and close. Our moods were becoming unpredictable; our family life was being seriously interfered with.

I walked into work and asked to be allowed to leave the task force and take my position at the major crime squad. David refused my request and we talked for ages about the dilemma. I learned that he, too, felt the same way and after discussing it at length I decided to stick it out. I felt as if I had a partner to fight the nonsense that prevailed in this most difficult investigation and drifted back into a steady work mode, which meant being almost buried under files and paperwork and kept busy by Wendy who virtually had me at her beck and call. We still held out great hope for her, but we also knew she had to be played carefully. In the meantime, Victor was pissed off at her and at me for having contact. I wasn't comfortable knowing a man like Victor was pissed off with me.

On bail and living in a rented house in the suburbs, Wendy was vulnerable. She had mulled over her life, studied her form guide for the future of herself and children and then asked for a secret meeting. It was a major step forward. We met in a nondescript hotel and she asked a million questions, yet she wasn't really seeking answers, not until she got to the one that really mattered. She asked about the workings of the witness protection program, dipping her toe in the water, sussing out whether she'd defect to our side.

Wendy was smart, playing the 'what ifs', mainly about her kids' schooling, maintaining her single-parent benefits, her lifestyle. As I batted her questions confidently back, scoring run after run, I sensed that we were only days away from snaring the biggest witness we could ever hope for. Her parting look sealed the deal; she had a smile from ear to ear.

Victor himself may have helped her make that decision. In prison, he'd been sharing a cell with a murderer, Timothy, who was up for early release. They were well suited, good buddies, both men of violence. Days after his parole, Timothy sauntered into Wendy's world. Victor had arranged for him to stay a few days, and a very sceptical Wendy reluctantly offered him a bed. One lazy Saturday he got the better of her, forcing her to inject a 'hot shot' of heroin, enough to kill her. Wendy was no match for a convicted murderer. For all her faults, Wendy had never taken drugs, so the effects of the heroin were catastrophic. Timothy left her slumped alone on the couch, with only minutes to live, staging a convincing suicide. I was sitting at home enjoying dinner, playing happy families and decided to give Wendy my daily catch-up call. Hearing the telephone ring, she conjured enough energy from her limp body to fall onto the telephone, pick up the handpiece and cry, 'Help'.

Paramedic units pulled into the driveway of her house about the same time as David and his posse arrived. Our timing was perfect; she pulled through. The effects of the drugs were eventually replaced by shock, as Wendy realised that Victor had had someone try to kill her. David took a fatherly line, advising her of options. I watched as her mind ticked over. She summed up her life, then she asked the question we had been waiting on: 'Where do I sign for witness protection?' That night Wendy disappeared off the face of the earth, as far as the underworld was concerned, and we took her three children as well, driving them to her new home, police headquarters. I admired her courage.

Once Kath heard of the coup with Wendy she hit the phones, claiming all manner of sinister workings by the task force. The media reported every word in large bold type. Our task force office was buzzing with excitement as David, Mark and I set about the mammoth task of obtaining evidence from our new, real, star witness; the wife of the man behind the murders of our two young boys. It was a great time for us all; gossip went spinning around the department and my spirits lifted.

The next few weeks were ridiculously busy. David pulled in a couple more detectives and away we went. Information just poured out of Wendy, as if the attempted 'hot shot' had burst her levee. Her information included the answers to seven unsolved murders that I had tinkered with when I was meeting Dennis in his house of death nearly three years earlier. Victor was woven through the stories, proving to be every bit as sinister as his brother. It's hard to forget Wendy's detailed account of seeing Victor after he and Dennis had chainsawed up the Hell's Angel's body, and how the brothers stopped for lunch, their faces and upper bodies peppered with fragments of flesh and blood.

To safeguard against any suggestion that Mark or I might have forced Wendy's admissions, we videotaped every one of her twenty-seven interviews, which would go on to become chronicles of the life and times of Dennis-ville, Australia's most macabre neighbourhood. The thing that impressed most was Wendy's unflappable memory. She spoke lucidly of the murder of one of Dennis's mates, Wayne. Victor had asked Wendy to accompany him to a state forest to act as nit-keeper, a lookout, so he and his brother could bury the body. In the witness protection program, four years after the murder, she drove us to the exact spot in the bush, as if she had been there just yesterday, and pointed to a clump of dirt. The body was no longer there—probably eaten by wild dogs—but what remained under a few centi-metres of soil was a rare tailored tweed jacket, once owned by the victim, a belt and buckle and a pair of his shoes.

Wendy moved on to telling us what we really ached to hear about: Walsh Street. 'Slowly, slowly'—we allowed her to set the pace. What a moment that was. She gave a vivid and detailed account of Victor's role in killing the two young policemen, a cowardly act of revenge for the robbery squad's shooting of his best mate, Graeme. Wendy opened her tale with a history of the two men, how they committed the robberies, what guns they used, the balaclavas and tracksuits they wore, how it was her job to shop for the clothing, sto-ries of Jedd's involvement, and on it went. All leading up to the early morning of the Walsh Street murders and how Victor snuck away to extract his revenge, then returned, to tell Wendy his darkest secret.

A feeling of tired elation enveloped the task force and exuberance was evident throughout the rest of the police department. To help buoy the elation among the rank and file, we deliberately allowed juicy snippets of scuttlebutt to filter out, to spread the message that we had a chance to convict Victor and that Wendy was the key to that chance. The buzz that came from her roll-over was exhilarating; cops were talking about it in bars, inside patrol vans—even the police radio operator broadcast the news. At long last, the media started writing positive stories.

Sadly, at this most important time, Big John and I still weren't speaking. The situation between Big John and David was now untenable. The task force split into two separate factions; in essence, 'David's team' and 'Big John's team'. Initially I saw this as ludicrous but before long I saw it as the perfect solution: at last we were all able to work in peaceful environments. I pondered the opposite teams. It was if we were kids in a school yard, in the middle of a squabble. I feared that the real objective might be lost, obscured by petty jealousies and spite. We were all to share a portion of blame, but most at fault were the commissioners, who had their heads in the sand hoping it would all go away.

Hankering for stimulation outside work, to take my mind off the ridiculous situation at the office, I started an exclusive breakfast club, for just four men. Each Saturday morning I'd meet the guys for a long breakfast, at the same table at the Fitz Cafe in Brunswick Street, Fitzroy. We had only two rules: each of us had to bring a different newspaper to the table, and no-one was ever allowed to talk police work. The club was such a success that it went for years; we laughed, argued and badgered each other every Saturday, and I don't think we ever missed a date.

It all started to feel too good to be true; something had to come along to stuff it up. Sissy, an ex-lover of Victor's, contacted the task force saying she had urgent information. She had been in a pub and overheard a gang of Victor's mates discussing a plan to blow up a house; they were in the throes of putting together a nail bomb. The bomb was to be planted and set to explode at night when the detective homeowner returned. The gang had been watching the detective's movements from a little park across the road, and they had even followed his daughter to and from Kew High School. I went white with fear; they were talking about my house.

David removed Annitia, Chelsea and me from our home instantly. Some of my old pals, detectives from Richmond, went into overdrive investigating the threat, trying to get on top of this latest setback. It appeared the coin barbecues in the park had been earning good revenue from the part-time chef-cum-bombmakers in the gang.

For two weeks we three lived in a hotel suite, with SOG SWAT guards for company, as the investigation continued. Chelsea had to be shielded from much of the information but she was now fifteen and it was hard to know exactly what to tell her and what to let through to the keeper. Each day, my remarkable daughter even took in her stride the oddity of being sneakily bundled into a taxi and driven to and from school. And it was odd; she was slipped into our hotel room and studied to the noise of police radios, briefings and debriefings, with a SWAT team standing around in their customary black pyjamas, shotguns and other heavy-duty hardware by the door. But not once during this time did my girl throw a tantrum, spit the dummy or retreat into herself. After two weeks, the gang of nail bombers was dealt with and life returned to normal, although our house was no longer our sanctuary.

During all of Wendy's statements, I don't think there was a time when she faltered. We, in turn, checked, rechecked and checked all the facts again. There were the makings of a trial and, for the first time in what was now two years, a few of us felt we might have a chance of winning the case.

On the opposite side of our fence, Big John's team had charged Bubble Head and Trevor, Victor's brother, on the strength of Jason's evidence. I never did understand why Trevor was charged. Gary, the burglar who originally stole the KTG shotgun, met a similar fate to Jedd; shot dead by non–task force detectives at his home, supposedly brandishing a handgun. I was so glad to be working on other duties.

All that remained was to keep liaising with the witnesses in protection: Wendy, Theo the car thief, and Sissy. It was paramount to keep our star witness happy. This was the difference between winning the case and having egg on our faces. Wendy and her kids seemed reasonably content in their new lives. I met her often, taking her and her children to dinner, usually a local bistro or pub, nothing too elaborate, as long as it got her out of the confines of her ever-changing safe houses. Sometimes she was hidden in a farmhouse, well out of Melbourne, and other times in a suburban home. Wherever it was, the accommodation was sparsely furnished and equal to the most basic of rental premises. It's a lifestyle that few people in our community would ever tolerate: moving from one location to another, sandwiched between eight or ten humourless cops and peering over your shoulder at every noise. She endured it for eighteen months as we worked on the many crimes she offered up. Somehow the queen of the underworld accepted the constant restrictions on her life. I don't know how, as the lifestyle was no party.

There was always something that needed fixing: schooling for the kids, new clothes, arranging visits to see her mother. I'd sneak her in to see my own doctor every now and again for a woman's check-up, that secret stuff that most men fail to understand. My doctor was a huge asset in times when confidentiality was crucial. The list of requests was endless, particularly as Wendy and the kids would take on new identities. She had shown interest in living in either San Diego, in the United States, or in the English countryside.

There was a whole new world ahead of her and she showed tinges of excitement. Her kids seemed to be coping well too; they were remarkable really. For all her faults, Wendy was a devoted mother, fiercely protective of her family, perhaps too protective. In between visits, we talked on the phone, usually every other day.

I had become too used to feeling the calm before the storm. When I felt things had been too quiet for too long, I started to get suspicious:

something had to be brewing. I was feeling drained and I rarely got more than five hours rest. So, one night, after a delicious meal in our 'castle', where Annitia, Chelsea and I shared the cooking chores, we decided to turn in early.

It must have been about four o'clock in the morning when Anzac sprinted upstairs and sat panting beside my bed. That meant only one thing: someone was on our property. Chelsea was asleep downstairs in her room, facing onto the verandah. I lay still for a moment, as did Anzac, and listened. I could hear faint footsteps creeping along the timber verandah, near the front door, along the side of the house. I felt my heart racing, thumping in my chest. As my mind followed the footsteps, I started breathing nervously, knowing that mischief was prowling around, downstairs. I had only just stopped bringing my shotgun home at night, thinking it was a stupid thing to do. Now I ached for it but had to reach for my handgun instead.

I slipped out of bed, telling Annitia to stay where she was and to telephone for help. Dressed in only my jocks, I took Anzac by his collar and led him down the stairs, taking my handgun. The dog did the perfect job, remaining silent, standing by my side. At the door I pulled back the curtain covering the glass side-panel and peeped out, to see a lone male peeping back. Thankfully, he couldn't see me; it appeared he was going along all the windows looking in. There was something in his hand; I couldn't quite make it out. He moved onto a long thin window, Chelsea's window. I watched him looking into that window and he must have made the decision to force his way in there. He tapped slightly on the glass a few times till it broke.

All I could think of was Victor, or one of his cronies. I kept thinking, 'Another one of Victor's mates, another one of Victor's mates', over and over.

Chelsea woke to the sound of the breaking glass and instinctively ran from the darkness of her room. I caught her in my arms as she headed to the staircase. She was shaking and petrified; her whole body trembled. I covered her mouth with my hand, silently telling her to be quiet, pointing her upstairs. Taking Anzac by the collar, she nervously crept upstairs to join Annitia. This left me downstairs, still in darkness; the assailant was tapping away, trying to remove the glass at the window.

Annitia whispered down the stairs, 'Police are coming.' I could have waited but I opted to open the front security door. The crook was still working on the window, possibly five paces away. All but naked, I sized him up; he was maybe my height and my build. I needed to confront this guy; I was fed up with all the cops-and-robbers bullshit. Taking comfort from my handgun, I yelled as loud as I could: 'What the fuckin' hell are you doing?' I yelled so loudly that my voicebox hurt.

Startled, he jumped, then turned to face me, still holding something. I couldn't make it out. I considered shooting him. It would have been so easy.

Then he charged me. I swapped my gun to my poor hand and landed the hardest punch I have ever thrown in the centre of his face. The bastard kept coming, crashing into me, and down we went. I held onto the firearm, worried about dropping it, and, once our bodies came apart, I swung another punch, then another, as he too threw the best he could, hitting me in the side of the head. Luckily my punches seemed to do the more immediate damage. As I kept hitting him, over and over, I could feel my fist burning hot. Pain ripped up my arm. He went down, lying flat on the verandah floor. I hit him again, his face unrecognisable as blood coloured his skin, until my hand could no longer hold a fist. My heart wanted to jump from my chest. I could hear the sirens in the background as I lifted myself off him. Staggering inside, I was met by Annitia, bravely shielding my daughter. He had been carrying a stick.

The next hour was a combination of uncertainty, twenty police of all ranks—uniforms and suits—and an ambulance that took the assailant away. By the time the sun came up, it was decided that the man was just a night burglar who, seeing the best house in the street, had decided to break in. Relief washed over Annitia and me, again. In a situation that would normally scare the hell out of most people, the fact that a common thief attempted a break-in was a far better proposition than it being any friend of Victor's. Chelsea went off to school with yet another story to tell of her most dysfunctional lifestyle.

In time, there was no more evidence to be had, and all that was left was to wait for the trial. Each week I either met Wendy or telephoned, reassuring her, and priming her before the big day. She had become content with her new life; her children were happy and life looked good. She was ready for her day in court, now only weeks away. We were on the final lap of what had been a two-year marathon when an instruction was delivered to David in writing: none of our team was to have any more contact with Wendy. She was to now be managed by the other team. Yet Wendy loathed the members of the other team. The instruction made no logical sense and was the worst possible news.

I sat in David's office staring blankly at the report, trying to find hidden words, rereading it over and over, unwilling to believe in its veracity. Why, on the eve of presenting the key to our prosecution, would her management team be taken away? It was akin to removing the scaffolding from a half-constructed building; surely the building would fall over? Surely Wendy wouldn't make it to the court room after this sudden hiatus? David and I pleaded for a reversal, yet the commissioner stood firm.

Wendy was making daily complaints about this new rule and was refusing to give evidence. Her protectors were calling, telling me Wendy might go hostile; her mood had slumped. Concerns ran through the department; rumours raced in all directions, as well as a lashing or two of gossip that Wendy was rolling back—back to the underworld. She managed to get several unauthorised messages to me, calling for 'help', messages that I was forbidden to respond to or act on. On the night before her court appearance she threw a tantrum and the boss of the SOG SWAT team contacted me at home. He pleaded that I break the instruction and see Wendy, to soothe her anger and disappointment. I couldn't; interference of this kind would have been the end of me in the eyes of senior management. I had been warned off.

On the morning of her court appearance, Wendy was placed in a room with her new team. Their differences were enough to cause major angst. The witness protection supervisor broke rank and rang me, begging that I help calm the situation; there was still time to speak to Wendy. She, in turn, demanded to see me or David, standing her ground, stating firmly that she would refuse to give evidence unless her requests were acquiesced to. We were denied access to her by senior management. Wendy's reaction was to have amnesia; she went adverse. She would not give any evidence. The 'Walsh Street Four'— Victor, Trevor, Bubble Head and Jason's mate Anthony—sat in the dock and smiled.

In the end, the jury was our judge, not the public, not the media, not the rest of the police department. 'Not guilty, not guilty, not guilty, not guilty,' was called out by the jury foreman, very loud and very clear. For me, Wendy's missing evidence was also heard loud and clear. She walked out of protection alone, gathered up her children and meagre possessions and went back to the underworld. I have not spoken to her since.

The jury system is the fairest assessment of any court proceeding. Obviously, as representatives of the community, the jury members were not willing to be hoodwinked by a poor prosecution case. Without Wendy, the evidence was appalling; a quaddie of 'not guilty' votes was inevitable. Jason was not credible and, sadly, the other witnesses amounted to little. In my opinion the jury got it right in offering up the 'not guilty' verdicts. The evidence just wasn't there to sustain any other verdict. It was inevitable; the Walsh Street Four could only have walked, and they did. The absurdity of the Walsh Street climax was that the police department then charged Wendy with perjury. She would serve nine months in prison due to her decision not to give evidence. It was a monumental management stuff-up that was overshadowed only by the media frenzy that followed Wendy's subsequent court case and incarceration. Madness had finally arrived at the tail end of the Walsh Street investigation. No individual was ever questioned over the reasons behind the ruination of the evidence of possibly the most important crown witness ever to enter the program. A few of us just walked home in shock.

At a time when the eyes of Australia were on us, watching from both sides of the fence, we had failed. We should have triumphed, good over evil; instead, our results were embarrassing. Solving the Walsh Street killings was crucial to law enforcement in this country. We had a chance to fix a complex set of wrongs and flunked.

I don't blame Wendy for not giving her evidence; I blame the system for destroying such a vital witness. I blame the hierarchy for moving Wendy's goal posts at the eleventh hour, for breaking an agreement that I brokered with her months before she came into witness protection. As far as the annals of criminality are concerned, the Walsh Street period, for some, provided little more than excessive Sunday paper reading and mild entertainment. To many who worked on the investigation, it provided years of heartache. To the families of the two boys, it left the door open, never to be closed.

Walsh Street was a time in our history that we must never forget, never colour, and never cover up. It was about situations getting out of control, about tough guys fighting tough guys, male testosterone, excessive force and bad behaviour. It was about poor investigations, shoddy judgement, intimidated witnesses, slapdash procedure and keeping fingers crossed that you'd get away with it. It was about bravado, easy access to guns and abysmal bank security, naivety, promise, youthful exuberance, and two handsome young boys in uniform. But, most of all, it was about the killing of Steven Tynan and Damian Eyre, the grief of mothers, and the unforgivable loss of innocence.

It should never be allowed to happen again. I'm sorry for the part I played in that whole tragic tale.

12

MR CRUEL

It is an understatement that I disliked the police department after the Walsh Street defeat. I simply couldn't fathom how one of the world's largest and supposedly most sophisticated police departments could fuck up so stupendously. For far too long, I lost myself to thoughts of ageing men too busy counting their superannuation points or tweaking their CVs to concern themselves with the real issues or the welfare of their rank and file. Any respect I had had for the robbery squad was well and truly gone; even though I had mates in that office, I couldn't face them, couldn't be in their company, and never was again.

Immediately after the acquittals, I found myself in social settings knowing that somewhere in the crowd, someone would be speaking about me: 'Look, he's one of the guys that fucked up Walsh Street.' I chose to become the guy with another tag: 'Look, he's the guy who never goes for a drink.' That suited me, and suited my mood. And so it was that, after the acquittals, I retreated from all aspects of police social life. Indeed, I went through the rest of my career without ever attending another police function; it was my way of coping.

My biggest dilemma was trying to rationalise what Chelsea and Annitia had suffered. Not once did they receive a kind word or a face-to-face comment from anyone, other than David. I assumed there must have been an expectation that they would just have accepted the relocation from our house, the bomb threat, death threats, the home invasion, the constant harassment and the relentless pressure.

Bad luck comes in threes, they say. The Walsh Street defeat was a hard enough hand to accept, yet the next joker that fell from the deck was far worse. Annitia had had enough. Realising that her dreams might not come true with me, she left one day, never to return. Both Chelsea and I were shattered by her leaving. She was the one who got away, and it would always be that way for me. She had it all: style, class, smarts, looks, poise and most of all, 'it', that magic ingredient that we all search for in a mate. But she wanted more than this obsessed detective could ever supply; she certainly didn't need to see shotguns sitting by her front door, handguns on the bedside table, or to be listening to her clock ticking away at night, wondering if I'd come home and, if so, in what condition. We would always stay close friends as she travelled through life, finding her nirvana: a charming husband and two beautiful kids. Just as importantly, she and Chelsea are lifelong mates.

The last blow that was dealt to me was selling the house. Chelsea and I could never live safely in our home after Walsh Street. There were far too many risks and skeletons, too many chances of another incident, too many bad memories. The house was sold in double-quick time. I could not take a trick.

We moved into another rattly old house, this time in Hawthorn, a single-fronted Victorian cottage that leaned to the right. It was sandwiched between other, far more impressive, residences and had a nice covert appeal; it was the type of house that no-one ever noticed. The best feature of our tired little home was that Jenny lived across the road. She had bought the best house in the street; Chelsea and I lived in the worst house. That was indicative of the friendship Jenny and I shared: two opposites who fitted nicely together. We picked up where we had left off—Jenny was still as mad as a hatter.

I rented that house for a few years, occasionally immersing myself in as much travel as I could. I had missed not carrying my passport, so over the next few years, I travelled extensively throughout Asia—at least twice a year—backpacking through most of its countries. Chelsea joined me on one or two trips and proved a resourceful traveller, moving through big cities without fuss, and handling our street-cart diet, which was half the fun.

It was 1991. Soon after settling into our new abode, Chelsea started Year 11 and her VCE study. She had developed into a gorgeous young woman with bumps in all the right places. Most parents would agree that they are most anxious about their children's welfare between fourteen and seventeen years. I have always believed that it is the time when they can run off the rails, turn feral, take the wrong path in life. No doubt Chelsea was presented with her fair share of temptations. Even so, she came through with ease, becoming school captain and an active member of her student council, helping younger kids with their own potential demons. As father and daughter, we'd always laugh about the oddity of the sex education 'talk', the stuff parents are supposed to pass onto their kids. I had no idea to what level Chelsea had been involved with boys. Although once she blissfully confessed to having hidden a boy somewhere in her room, I never was able to find him!

My breakfast club was still going strong, never missing a beat, and one of the regulars, Davo, teamed up with me to see France from the fastest Peugeot we could rent. For a month we zipped around every back street, country laneway and region of this stunning country. I don't think there was a major city we missed or an autoroute we failed to test-drive the car on. Davo can be an outstanding driver, given the chance, and on this trip he had too many chances. It was the scariest and most exhilarating trip I ever took, but sheer fun. When we arrived in Paris, a few days before I was due to catch my flight home, Davo continued on to see his cousin in Scotland. I went to visit the Australian embassy with a secret agenda.

I had applied for a job as head of security at the embassy, a job that I thought would be a dream. They were interesting times, with a few security scares and plenty happening, and the salary package was good. I imagined Chelsea and me living in gay Paris, someplace on the

Rue la Fayette near Montmartre, wearing berets and learning French. Perhaps not wearing berets. I went out of my way to keep the interview process a secret, wanting to just get the job and slip quietly back to Australia and out of the police department. I was given a deluxe tour of the embassy and had two interviews, both very encouraging. I spent a few days looking at real estate, running all over the lower arrondisements, climbing four and five flights of stairs at a time. The one-bedroom apartments were so tiny that some didn't even have proper amenities, just slapdash sinks, a couple of cupboards thrown together and nasty little cookers. There was even one kitchen with a handheld shower; I guessed you were supposed to take a shower over the sink. The two-bedroom apartments were even more disheartening, so much more expensive and not much bigger. I realised my desire to leave my detective's job and live in France was sadly just a dream. I declined the job and came home to take promotion to detective sergeant and to suffer my lot again.

A condition of my promotion was that I had to spend a year working in the fraud squad, catching white-collar criminals. I wasn't too sure about it but I gave it my best shot. I was given a team of young detectives and I thought we would have a go at testing new legislation that allowed us to take proceeds of crime—the assets of drug dealers. I liked that! We set about confiscating cars, boats, houses, investments, cash and bank balances from the best (or worst, it depends on your perspective) drug dealers in the country. It was fun for a while, especially as it was a nine-to-five job, a rarity in the police department. Before long I was tiring of emptying drug dealers' coffers and put my feelers out. I spent the occasional cup of bad coffee walking around the different squad rooms, seeing what investigations I might be able to wangle a secondment to.

One night, in April 1991, a shocking crime was committed. A 13-year-old girl, Karmein Chan, was kidnapped. She had been with her two sisters, playing in the bedroom of their family home in an affluent suburb. Both parents had been at work for the night. An intruder had broken into the house, tied up her sisters and grabbed the young girl. A car was heard roaring off into the black night.

While at the major crime squad the previous year, I had worked alongside a great mate of mine, Paul, as we hunted an offender in a similar kidnapping. In that case, the victim, Nicky, had just turned thirteen. She was stolen from her wealthy family's home where she had been watching television with her sister while both parents were out. Paul and I had worked around the clock to locate Nicky. The job turned into one of the largest media stories of the year. Kidnappings are one of the rarest of crimes and possibly the most frightening, especially when they involve kids. Despite the intensive search, Nicky was missing for three days before finally turning up; she was dumped in the wee hours of the morning, in a large plastic bag in a small inner-suburban park. She had been interfered with, but was still alive. Our perpetrator had a real awareness of forensic evidence, that *every contact leaves its trace*. Despite overwhelming efforts by eight detectives, we never located the offender, dubbed 'Mr Cruel' by the media.

There were some striking similarities between the kidnappings. The girls were the same age, went to private schools and were from wealthy families. They were home late at night with their siblings while their parents were out for the night, and on the list went. There was little doubt we were up against a serial kidnapper. As we went back through some cold-case files, we discovered three other similar crimes, all involving young girls, and the culprit always displayed that same quirky awareness of forensic evidence. The other thing that caused the hair to rise on the backs of our necks was that the culprit was otherwise kind and gentle to his victims. A wolf in sheep's clothing.

As Karmein was still missing, a task force was established rapidly. I was asked to run a team of four detectives and to help chart the direction of the inquiry. I jumped at the chance: anything to get me away from drug dealers and their assets.

From day one we raced at our work. We had to; there was a mad and very dangerous man on the loose. I watched as a group of fine detectives was pulled together. Having come out of the Walsh Street investigation with his reputation intact, as far as thinking detectives were concerned, David headed up this new task force. We all sensed that it was only a matter of time before one of the victims was killed. For that reason, it was important to have a homicide-squad mind running the show.

I was a logical choice because I'd worked on Nicky's kidnapping. There were three other teams recruited, all outstanding detectives, all worthy of their individual selection. We walked into the old Walsh Street task force office that had been sitting idle. Being back in this territory with such vivid memories, I had to overcome a bout of the shivers before I started organising my team.

My immediate second was my mate Paul, a detective of great calm and steady thought and with knowledge equal to my own of Nicky's kidnapping the previous year. He was a big man, with an equally big laugh, so infectiously funny that there were times when I laughed all day. He had dark skin—even in the depths of winter he might have passed for a burly Indian—and big floppy hands, which he waved in the air as he told his wild stories. I thought if I was going to be on another task force, I wanted to work alongside someone I could have an occasional laugh with.

Karmein remained missing as we worked around the clock, trying everything in our investigative book of tricks to locate her. Local detectives, uniform police and the media worked closely together. We stirred up dozens of names of paedophiles and sex offenders from the police data banks and criminal records section and banged on doors all day and all night long. We didn't give a damn what time it was. Pyjama-clad weirdos answered their dirty doors throughout the night to pushy detectives with one-track minds: Karmein. Desperation spurred us as we searched from room to room, upturning beds, cupboards and murky back sheds. All we wanted was to get her back home, alive, to her distraught parents and frightened sisters.

In cases involving innocent kids, police seem to find a little extra, a few per cent more. My mind went back to those early efforts of the many police at the Walsh Street killings, how hard they had searched for the killers. Now, we had another heart-stopping crime. The detectives on this latest atrocity were working just as hard, just as tirelessly. Many of them stayed in the same suit and shirt for days.

Time rolled on. With the dawning of each new day we knew we were getting a little further away from Karmein. Nicky had been released after three days, so at the end of the first week of Karmein's kidnapping, we were starting to feel the pinch. Many of the detectives were parents themselves and that seemed to drive the teams to work harder still. As we went from house to house, David handled the media with the child's parents, putting a heart-wrenching touch of reality to our search. We desperately needed to play to whatever decency might still be within the monster that had her. We needed to get through to this creep's conscience, to stir some good in him, or, perhaps, in someone who knew him. Someone had to know what this guy was up to. Someone out there had to be suspicious of his unusual behaviour. Someone must have noticed the odd ways of a neighbour, or friend or relative.

Everyone in the community wanted to lend a hand and dob in a pervert or weirdo, maybe a neighbour, perhaps that un-special someone at work whom they had always suspected. Everyone was sending in names and stories, many exaggerated, some malicious, and others very useful. We even had doctors and psychiatrists breaking their client confidentiality rules, passing on comments about oddballs who spoke of kidnapping little girls, or fantasised about having sex with schoolkids.

Each detective was throwing ideas into the ring, coming up with avenues of inquiry, but time ticked, and ticked and ticked away. We began to speculate that she had been killed, that we'd never see her alive again. Still, this premise didn't slow us down. We held on to the most optimistic proposition: that she was still alive and the kidnapper was holding her hostage, just waiting. But even the most fruitful investigative mind was dulling with the passing of a month or two. It became hard to think that a hostage could be held, fed and kept alive in a house somewhere in Australia, without some slip up, without someone seeing or sensing something. Notwithstanding, David still ran his emotional optimism through the media. I can see him sitting alongside Karmein's mother at a media conference, calmly asking the public for help and the mother sobbing hopelessly, clutching her daughter's toy, barely able to offer anything more than, 'Someone got my Karmein, someone got my Karmein.'

While we hadn't been able to find Karmein, we had amassed a very credible profile on what possibly happened to her, mainly through Nicky's help. She proved to be the finest witness I ever met; a smart, bright kid who, after having been held for three days in the most harrowing of circumstances, was still able to calmly and very efficiently go though her ordeal, step by step, with our task force team. More importantly, we now had the resources to chase up every lead she was able to give us.

Nicky had been forced to travel in her kidnapper's car, bundled up on the front passenger-side floor, forced under the dashboard. She remembered that they didn't seem to drive far, although there were a few stops and starts, indicating traffic lights. She spoke of driving continuously (indicating that they had travelled on a freeway) and felt that the whole journey only took ten to fifteen minutes. Once they arrived at their location, she was walked, blindfolded, to a house. They took only ten steps in a straight line; they never stepped sideways or around anything (indicating that the car was parked down a driveway that was on the right-hand side of the house block). She was barefoot and could feel concrete underneath. At the end of her walk, she stepped up three steps to a door (indicating a footpath coming off the driveway leading to two to four steps to the door).

Even though Nicky had been blindfolded throughout her three-day ordeal, she was still able to pick up valuable information. Often she was led around the house by her captor, to the bathroom and toilet in particular. Through her recollections, we believed the toilet was separate from the bathroom. The toilet door opened from left to right and inwards. The toilet-roll holder was mounted on the left-hand side, if you were sitting on the toilet, and there was a dual-flush cistern. The bathroom had a full-length bath-tub and a separate handbasin and cupboard; all the taps had star-shaped handles. She had her own belief that the bathroom was old fashioned. Seeing she had done so well with her other comments, we decided her perception of an old bath-room was worth keeping in the description.

Nicky explained that almost all of her time was spent in a bed. She was chained by her ankle to the foot of the bed, unable to move. On the bedside table was a clock radio that her kidnapper left on the entire time. She listened to the radio and heard the news updates and her name mentioned often. On her first morning, she heard the ten o'clock news. The next news she listened to was at eleven, mentioning her name again. For the hour in between she quietly lay alone, believ-ing the kidnapper was in another part of the house. She then amazed us by revealing that, during this hour, she heard and counted eleven aircraft flying overheard. She believed nine of them were jets and the other two aircraft were smaller. Because she had travelled extensively with her parents and was interested in planes, she could tell the differ-ence in aircraft engine noises. She said the aircraft were all flying from the same direction, at varying times in the hour, descending, on a flight path that moved across her body. But the aircraft eventually changed course, banking ninety degrees, then flying in a line from her head to her toe, before fading away.

What we now had was a firm belief that the 'safe house' where Nicky had been held was near an airport flight path, but which one? Melbourne had two large airports and two other significant airports handling a number of planes. We turned to the head air traffic control-ler at Tullamarine International Airport, who arrived promptly at our office armed with reams of flight records, runway drawings and aero-nautical maps. Apparently there was a host of different approach air-lanes into Melbourne. Our day of interest was a Wednesday. The two busiest days of the week for airport arrivals were Sunday and

Wednesday. We were getting a bit swamped with the complexity of it all, and Paul, in his best keep-it-simple tone, waved his big hands and asked the question.

'On the Wednesday mate, what lanes were open?'

'That's easy; we only had one aircraft approach laneway open that morning.'

'Well, which one?'

'Laneway No. 2, approaching from the north-east towards Tullamarine.'

'Does it run straight?'

We stood there holding our breath as he tossed his chart onto the table, his finger following the approach lane.

'It does for a while … then banks hard left, then into Tullamarine.'

Everyone in the room looked at each other, stunned. Paul continued.

'Tell us the number of aircraft and type of aircraft on that approach between ten and eleven that morning.'

The air traffic controller flicked through his records, sheet after sheet, making calculations, feeding our edge-of-seat curiosity. He could tell we were a bunch of anxious detectives, only interested in facts, nothing but facts. He took his pencil from his mouth and read his answer from his calculations.

'For that hour there were only approach aircraft, not departures. We did nine jets and two smaller aircraft, it was a busy day.'

'It certainly was, and we're getting busier,' Paul offered, looking gob-smacked.

What Nicky had done with her calm logic and outstanding recall was to open up a whole new world of inquiries. She had given us facts we would never have been able to gain by any other means. Her recall and tenacity as a witness sent us down a path that just might help us to find our villain. When the air traffic controller left our office, an extraordinary brainstorming session started.

Every house in the suburbs underneath the No. 2 flight path had to be inspected from the outside. We had maps copied and composite drawings made of the comments offered by Nicky, each drawing outlining what the exterior of the house might look like: the concrete footpath, left-hand driveway, two to four steps to a door and other snippets. Inside the house we were looking for a separate toilet with a left-hand opening door, toilet-roll holder on the left-hand side and a dual-flush cistern. The bathroom also had a full-size bath, separate handbasin and star-shaped taps. We had a lot of other information noted on the drawings, such as possible floor surfaces, light switches, a description of the bed and so on.

The more we pored over the flight path maps, the more we realised the vastness of our search. It centred on the suburbs of Essendon and Keilor, more than 10 000 houses. Many could be eliminated by a quick drive-by, checking which side of the house block the driveway was located, while others could also be scratched using sheer common sense: those built on steep blocks, or where there were many steps leading to a front door.

We realised that if we sent in a dozen detectives to scour the area, it wouldn't be too long before the neighbourhood twigged and the game would be up. It was imperative that each search be done without anyone knowing; if our kidnapper became aware, he could easily just burn down his house and we'd be left with nothing. And, of course, if there was the remotest possibility that Karmein was still alive, we didn't want to see her further harmed. It was time to put the secret squirrels' hats back on.

Hastily, we arranged to meet as many of our government and supply contacts as we could. Useful and valuable names from electricity supply companies, local council offices, the water and sewerage authorities and the like. We needed to come up with a covert way to get inside the thousands of houses that matched Nicky's description.

The scam we invented was easy; in conjunction with the local council, the sewerage authorities were going to replace certain pipes in the area, depending on their condition. Of course, as plumbers or sewerage workers, we needed to make quick inspections of the toilets, thereby getting us into thousands of homes without search warrants. Something that was very unlawful! We borrowed a few uniforms, overalls, jackets and shirts, as well as working drawings of the streets, sewerage systems and pipelines, and then we got schooled up on the jargon. We set up a system where two detectives went down each side of the street, dressed like sewerage workers, plumbers and council workers. Armed with a fistful of drawings, they knocked on doors and talked toilet talk.

For a fortnight, with unshaven faces and dressed in overalls, we swarmed over the area, tapping on doors, checking leaky pipes, crawling under houses, loosening off or tightening pipes and taps, showing uninterested owners the proposed sewerage system, helping grannies with their chores, taking cups of tea, talking over the fences and, eventually, getting into every single house. And, of course, every toilet and every bathroom of every house that found its way onto our enormous list. We were akin to a hive of bees buzzing around a bloom of roses. But, by the end of our massive effort, we had nothing to show for ourselves, nothing but a boot-load of dirty overalls and way too much useless information on the condition of the sewerage system in Melbourne's north-western suburbs. What started off with such optimism ended with sheer bloody despondency.

Sure, there was a handful of houses that looked red hot, matching Nicky's description. With that many houses, there were bound to be some interesting prospects: I remember at least twenty. We had a long checklist that each 'suspect' needed to clear before they could be crossed off our list, not just the basic alibi stuff. But, as we burrowed into the background of the owners or occupiers, one by one they were all eventually eliminated. We were left with zip.

It amazed everyone to discover the number of weirdos who lived in our city of three and a half million people, not to mention those in rural areas and other capital cities. Our investigation went Australia-wide. There were literally thousands of sex offenders, too many with a profile or propensity to undertake a kidnapping. Some of the rock spiders had records going back years. More worrying, there were others who had hardly been spoken to by police, living quietly in our community, befriending the neighbourhood and its children. It was a revelation.

Any who had the slightest history got a look in. Of course, pae- dophiles were our first priority and the scum that got our highest level of attention but, when you lift the lid off a sewer, it's funny what crawls out and scuttles off into the night. There was one parasite, Porter, who had been advertising for sexual partners in the underground sex mag- azines, usually available on the counter at sex shops. In a broad-minded community, as we tend to be these days, there mightn't appear to be anything wrong with advertising for a like-minded partner in a monthly sex magazine. But Porter did something very weird. Porter portrayed himself as a young, very attractive girl called 'Leonie'. For two years he answered letters to his advertisements, writing to 179 girls, all seeking a fling; many of them had boyfriends or husbands who were happy to participate. The biggest problem for 'Leonie' was how to manage his/her popularity. There were thousands of photographs and hundreds of homemade videos coming into his slimy post office box in Mentone. In amongst his sordid lot, he was also selling child pornography, which was the reason we took an interest in him.

We soon saw that Porter had nothing to do with our kidnapping and all the child pornography he was peddling was manufactured in Europe. Yet there had been a large number of frauds committed on a lot of otherwise normal, yet randy, young women. Their naked frolick- ing on the videotapes was never intended to be viewed by a smelly, obese fifty-two year old in a raincoat. We needed a small truck to transport all the material back to our office, and one of my detectives had to contact all the 'victims' to return their personal photos and videos. I found it difficult to understand how so many articulate and attractive women could be so magnificently conned. We ended up charging Porter with fraud, closing down his seedy little operation; he was given an 8-month jail sentence and immediately appealed.

While Porter was on bail—on the morning of his appeal— I received a ten-page letter from him, ranting about his treatment by my team and offering facile advice on how to catch paedophiles. Silly stuff really, nothing we hadn't already tried a dozen times over. The document contained the ravings of a very disturbed pervert. Curiously, he sent a copy of the letter to Derryn Hinch, a prominent radio talk-back host of the time, and also to his sentencing judge and to the police complaints ombudsman.

On the day his letters arrived, Porter lay down on the track of the 5.30 a.m. express train from Frankston to Melbourne. The train came around a bend and decapitated him. I was blissfully asleep at home. The first police on the scene noticed a handwritten note in the top pocket of Porter's shirt, which read, 'If you want to know who I am, contact Detective Sergeant Colin McLaren at the task force.' He had graciously included my telephone number. Just after six that morning, I was called in to view the body, and the head that had rolled 20 metres away. Naturally, Derryn Hinch savaged Porter on his morning talk show; I filed him away in the waste-paper basket. It was my thirty-sixth birthday, so Paul, the crew and I toasted the odd, departed Porter over a few wines on the way home late that night. One of those dills at police headquarters still chose to formally interview me over Porter's death, suggesting I might have put too much pressure on him, causing his suicide. Bless him!

It was around this time I started up another club to run parallel to my still-popular breakfast club. This time around it was a 'bar-stool club': I guess I'd been reading too many pulp-fiction novels about detectives and bar-room antics. But I liked the idea of sitting at a smoky bar with great mates each Wednesday night, sipping aperitifs or imported beers and talking absolute drivel. So, each Wednesday for many years, a group of diehards wore out stools at Virgona's Wine Bar in Brunswick Street, Fitzroy. The publicans slapped down an endless mix of elixirs as an assortment of mates came and went; seven or eight lost souls, journalists, cops and do-gooders. Again, the only subject taboo was the exhausting and sometimes boring subject of cops and robbers—and weirdos and perverts, and any other creature that belonged wedged under a bluestone, at the back end of a dark alley.

The Porter nonsense was typical of the many distractions we suffered trying to locate the real offender. None of us would have ever believed the number of strange people we encountered.

Many highly regarded people were peddling sex or images of sex, some child pornography. One dark road we followed took us to the door of the University of Melbourne; one of the administrative staff there became the largest distributor of child pornography uncovered by our efforts. Not satisfied with his well-placed, lucrative job, this parasite took to selling child porn, doing much of his trade while sitting in his day-job chair until we sent him away for a long holiday.

Almost a year from the date of Karmein's disappearance, a construction crew was levelling a parcel of land in the northern part of Melbourne, an otherwise built-up area, full of low-value real estate and light industry. Earthmoving equipment had been working away, shifting soil and preparing the site. As one of the bulldozers skimmed the soil from the crusty surface, the remains of a little girl became exposed. She'd obviously been buried many months. An autopsy showed she had been shot in the back of the head. At last, we had found Karmein.

The news hit the task force hard. Even though we all suspected that she was dead, we still held onto a miniscule twinkle of hope. Hope that she might be found alive one day. We all knew such hope was absurd, but it was this hope that got us out of bed each morning. Just in case she might turn up. The sadness of the day was most visible in the distraught face of her mother during the media conference. A newspaper photograph of the hurt in the mother's face would later be awarded the Press Photo of the Year. We all shared a small quota of her pain.

The site of Karmein's rough burial yielded a few extra clues but there was nothing there to take us any closer to our prey. It seemed every weirdo, every deviant, had been raided, searched, spoken to and eliminated. During the previous months, a dozen men had fallen into the category of red-hot suspect—the type who could easily be charged with our kidnapping—only to be efficiently eliminated. Thousands of others were placed onto a special database, a list of society's worst, as well as society's twaddle. About a hundred of those were charged with sex crimes, many receiving imprisonment. But still we didn't have Mr Cruel.

Due to the rarity of his crimes, Mr Cruel became known around the globe. The FBI heard of our man Cruel and asked to be kept up to date. The FBI's behavioural science unit was fascinated by his deeds. Initially we sent a full briefing paper to the unit, detailing as much about the crimes as we could, offering copies of statements, crime scene reports and anything else we considered relevant. The notorious Hannibal Lecter movie, *Silence of the Lambs*, had just been released, sensationalising the unit's work. We thought we would offer the real boys anything they wanted in return for assistance. Once they had time to analyse our case reports, they requested a 4-day conference in their office in Chicago. I blew the dust off my passport and jumped on a flight.

The unit head, Greg, had the worldly pressure of being the guy who had inspired the Lecter movies. I was optimistic. He was serious. An overly officious sort of guy, Greg convened a series of highly professional briefings where we performed an investigative autopsy on each of the crimes. The process was deeply probing, enlightening and a little cathartic. For days we studied comments by each victim, witnesses and neighbours, often labouring over single words. We postulated the flight-path theory, delved into our street maps for possible exit paths, and basically bashed our heads around day after day, trying to flush out any new or untried avenues. By the time I was due to head home, it was obvious our task force had done everything the FBI could think of. There weren't any secrets I could bring back to the office.

I stayed on the task force for a few months after Karmein's body was uncovered. My team continued knocking on doors, pulling weirdos in, checking and double-checking alibis. But the trail was ice cold and the list had dwindled to the also-rans. Most of the serious contenders had been worked and reworked. We had a system where the dozen best suspects were reinvestigated by a different team, hoping to flush out fresh information. Then we reworked them again, and again, until finally, we put the files down.

While the task force would go down as failing in its endeavour, it was still extraordinarily successful in gathering highly accurate information on the seediest of our world.

I won't forget one oddity, which highlighted the darkness we rubbed shoulders with. The manager of a dodgy sex shop was feeding me information about a network of men who were trying to coax boys into a sex-slave network. The intended victims were only thirteen and fourteen years old. The manager knew of one family where the parents had volunteered their son for the group. We tried to set something up, to get the parents recorded, talking about their parental guidance, when the manager was attacked, late at night, in his back laneway. He was held down and had his right leg nearly severed at the knee with a Bowie knife. Melbourne's a big city, full of some bad and very sad stories.

After the question I am most often asked—'Who killed the two policemen at Walsh Street?'—the next-most-asked question I've fielded over my years as a detective is: 'Who was Mr Cruel?' I wish I could answer that, not just for Karmein's mother, but for selfish reasons. The truth is that I have no idea who Mr Cruel is, or was. I do know he was the one that got away. I can answer, with considerable certainty, who killed the two constables at Walsh Street: Victor and Jedd, both now dead. But I still can't say who Mr Cruel actually was. There was a time when it haunted me. But haunting is for ghosts and I don't believe in them, so I stopped letting him get to me.

What I do know is information I gleaned from four brave young girls. Each of them was a victim of the enigma the media called Mr Cruel. I know, or at least firmly believe, he was a man then between the ages of thirty-five and forty-eight years, not too tall, soft in build, possibly carrying a little weight, lacking excessive body hair, clean-shaven and kindly spoken. There is a possibility that he didn't smoke, then, nor was he anything other than calm and confident, which goes against his media-given name, 'Mr Cruel'. I also have a sound belief that he may have a background in medicine, whether as a doctor, medico or paramedic. He had an uncanny awareness of forensics. The rest is left to professional hunch. It would not surprise me if he had connections to New Zealand, or a remote pocket of Australia, such as Tasmania. Nor would it surprise me if he's already dead.

To understand Mr Cruel is to understand the ways of sexual deviants. Mr Cruel was a man driven by the strongest of sexual urges, which resulted in the assaults on many young girls, often in the presence of their own family. The urges increased to the point where he resorted to kidnapping. The act of breaking into a house, confronting people, taking calm control, tying them up and then making off with a victim shows a mind that is certainly driven. The execution of crimes like that is no walk in the park. And he did this many times over. If you follow his run of assaults, the intensity and daring increased after each attack. He was becoming uncontrollable until he surrendered to the ultimate of his urges, killing his final victim.

It's difficult to accept that he then just stopped acting this way, snapped out of it, and ended his behaviour. Based on all that he did, I find it impossible to accept that he 'retired' from his deeds, hung up his breaker's kit and ignored his sexual demons.

So where is he? The task force investigated every male suicide in Australia for the twelve months from the date of Karmein's kidnapping, particularly in the favoured age span. We didn't find him. The task force did lots of probing, the likes of which hadn't been seen in this country before. But he failed to surface. One important thing did come about as a direct result of the task force effort. Mr Cruel has never offended again. And maybe that's not a bad result, for some.

Meanwhile, I know of an extremely competent detective, Chris O'Connor, who sits at his desk, sometimes glancing at a picture of Karmein that hangs on his pinboard, waiting for a cruel man to pop up again. For my money, I reckon he's long gone.

13

LAW OF THE LAND

During the latter part of my time on the Mr Cruel investigation, I came to understand a problem that was causing worry within the investigative team and hampering our ability to catch some of the weirdos we faced. There was a massive legislative inadequacy glaring at us. Remarkably, there was no actual offence of possessing child pornography. The world of modern policing was without the necessary tool to seize child pornography and charge the offenders.

We were required to rely on an antiquated federal law requiring the tapes, photographs or images to be declared 'abhorrent'. The act of declaring them abhorrent was long-winded and cumbersome, often taking months, and done by a boffin sitting on a chair in Canberra. Even more of a worry was that the law required the material to be declared within ten working days. What nonsense!

Once tapes were seized, they had to (of course) be viewed by a detective to ensure that they weren't sending tapes of *Mary Poppins* to Canberra. Sex offenders usually souvenir something from their victims, like underwear or jewellery or, at times, they video their victims, hiding the footage in the middle of an innocuous tape. Many hours could be wasted viewing the stuff, just to make sure there weren't any images of our victims spliced onto a tape. Should we seize hundreds of tapes, as we were doing every week, the existing law became unworkable. No one man at a little desk in the nation's capital could possibly view such an amount of material in so short a time. We needed a new state law, without time constraints. Running parallel to the many other inquiries facing my team—hunting paedophiles, chasing weirdo accountants and beheaded peddlers of child porn, and while still searching Karmein's whereabouts—I set about preparing a research paper.

Our task force was going to make sure that child pornography was one hot potato that wasn't going to go cold. I wrote to all manner of people, seeking their comments, ideas and input: to all the chief commissioners' offices in the country, the attorneys-general, offices of public prosecutions, and many of the investigative bodies. Within a few months I had gathered enough data, facts, figures and anecdotal evidence—in fact, I had a file about 15 centimetres high—to put before a parliamentary committee. I admit I had no appreciation of the size of the task, of the sheer time and effort that goes into creating a new law, although I was warned by our legal office that it could take forever to draft new legislation.

A short time later, the Victorian Parliament reconvened for its spring session. If there was any chance of getting this law in, it had to be now. I briefed the police minister's staff officer, Gary, a most helpful and decent man. I hoped he could get our file in the door and possibly read. He tried, but the government of the day was busy with other agendas. I sniffed around the contacts I'd made from my research and hit slabs of negativity. Apparently, the government was not up for creating new laws. So I tinkered with a new strategy.

I went down to Annitia's office. We had a pleasant catch-up before I suggested she go home for the night, leaving me with some time I had booked in one of the audiovisual suites. I had brought along a couple of boxes of child pornography tapes, which she didn't need to see. Making sure I had the most atrocious material we had ever seized, and throwing in a few other sordid tapes—stuff involving sado-masochism, bestiality and necrophilia, just to pepper the collection—the booth operator, Greg, and I sat together for one very long night editing a tape of horrors, complete with a soundtrack of crying and screaming.

The resulting spliced segments, 10-second snapshots of the most shocking material, would cause genuine horror in most people. It defied any description. At the end of the night, Greg went straight to the beer fridge and pulled out a couple of drinks, very glad to see the end of the job. I took the tape and hid it in my office, making sure no-one could see it.

A few days later I delighted in receiving a message to attend parliament. The minister's secretary wanted to speak about my proposed new law. The office was sceptical, but we thought we should give it our best shot. I fussed about and made sure that I had on my best suit and tie, grabbed my colossal file and my tape of horrors, and arrived for my appointment. I had been allocated ten minutes to speak on the shortfall in the existing legislations. As I sat alone in the briefing room, I noticed a television and video player on a trolley. As quickly as I could, I plugged all the leads in and gave it a test drive; it worked. I cued my tape and sat back to wait.

To my amazement I was handed a bonus. The premier, John Cain, the police minister, Mal Sandon, and the deputy premier walked in right behind the secretary, along with two other Labor heavyweights. The secretary made a few opening comments about how full their book was and how there would be no chance of debating any new laws that year. The premier looked me up and down with his puppy-dog eyes, and then stared out the window, drifting off to places unknown. The deputy premier, Steve Crabb—who was a former police minister—chipped in, with his fine Scottish accent.

'Ye have to know detective, it ain't an easy thing to git a new law home.'

'But, Mr Crabb, we need this law, we can't do our job without this law.'

'Our books er full this year. Ney other state has the law?'

'No, and that's the problem. Our laws are inadequate: we need to take the lead.'

The premier still wasn't showing a scrap of interest. I continued throwing facts and figures at them, to little effect. They had been sitting in parliament since late the night before and were clearly exhausted. I was getting frustrated, wanting to reach over and grab hold of the premier, pull him away from his window view and sit him upright. Mr Crabb continued.

'I'd be worried, detective, to be bringing in a new law that no-one else has.'

'The current situation is allowing peddlers of child pornography to go free.'

'Maybe—we canna look at it till next year,' he said.

My ten minutes was now up and I had failed to make any impact. I had just one slim chance at getting them on board, to come round to my way of seeing things.

'Let me show you an example of the material we are talking about.'

I turned on the video and, on cue, one of the cronies quipped 'kiddie porn, hey'. The tape started to roll and four sets of eyes looked at the screen; the premier still stared out his window. I had deliberately set up the tape so that the first few scenes were of toddlers being forced to have sex with old men. Each of the victims was crying, some were screaming, and the tears were obvious to any viewer. Greg and I had enhanced the volume of the crying children.

'Gentlemen, many people just dismiss this horrid material as "kiddie porn", when what it really is is a documented account of the rape of innocent children. These children are Australians.'

The cries and screams of a child filled the room. The premier's eyes were now locked on the screen; he straightened his chair, now sitting like a student. The moving images rolled on, horror after horror. I sat quietly, head down, deliberately reading my file, ignoring the tape. Not a soul moved. After about five minutes, when I had counted down twenty short scenes on the tape, I looked up. There was utter shock on the faces of the five transfixed men; not a single word was uttered. Mr Crabb looked extremely emotional.

We would watch only another three or four minutes, as no normal human being could stomach much more, and then I turned it off. Still the silence hung heavy. One of the cronies left the room. The premier pushed his chair back and returned to staring out his window; the tiredness had been replaced by a look of deep concentration.

'You can see what we're up against gentlemen.'

'How long's ye tape go fer?' asked Mr Crabb.

'An hour.'

The premier kept thinking. Mr Crabb made some additions with his pen on paper.

'Ye mus be jokin, en hour.' He shook his head in disbelief.

'I took the material from thousands of hours of tapes. We need the legislation.'

'We can push it through in two days, by the end of this week. We'll do it. Yes, if we do nothing else, we'll do this,' came from the premier.

He turned his chair back to the table and repeated his instruction, looking determined and as committed as any man I've seen. For the next hour the table became a think tank on how to draft the new legislation, how to make the new law an absolute priority of the government. It was a wonderful table to sit at, an inspirational exercise to be a part of. I went back to my office, a little pleased with myself, knowing I had changed the law of the land.

A couple of days after the parliamentary victory, I bought myself a slice of real estate, a most beautiful art deco apartment overlooking the city skyline in East Melbourne, full of stunning gardens and period homes. Complete with the finest interiors, walls, cornices and ceilings imaginable, my apartment was big and lofty. The downside was that it was a protected tenancy: I was unable to kick the tenant out. Another recently proclaimed law forbade owners from evicting tenants who had been living continuously in the same address since before 1956. The old lady renting my wonderfully fantastic, best-in-the-world apartment was eighty-eight years old and had been a tenant since she was married, in 1930. To make matters worse, her protected tenancy meant her rent was fixed at $100 per month.

She was entitled to stay in my apartment until the day she died— I hoped that wouldn't happen in the main bedroom. I figured I'd either poison her daily milk delivery or wait it out till she passed away.

III
UNDERCOVER WITH THE N'DRANGHETA

14

HOME-GROWN MAFIA

I had met Connie in the hallway of the apartment that I owned but wasn't allowed to live in; she owned the one opposite, and now she lay on her back, on the bonnet of my car, a tantalising porcelain nymph, gloriously stunning: not just her nakedness, but her eyes, staring deep into my arousal. She held on tightly to both my wrists and pulled me hungrily towards her. Her elegant little black dress lay beside the car just where she'd stepped out of it, along with her lace knickers. Two bottles of wine had freed all her inhibitions and she had me locked tightly between her legs; we found the perfect rhythm. Every now and again she'd arch too far and I'd pull her back onto me watching her breasts sway as she rolled her back, relishing the cold metal on her bare skin on our steamy night.

We were oblivious to passing cars only a few metres away through the bushes. The freeway traffic was steady, as was our movement. I held her hips tightly, one hand on each, enjoying the cushioning of her firm flesh. A wave of lust washed over me, heat flushed my cheeks, flowed through my shoulders, down my arms and tingled up my legs, to resonate at my most vulnerable place. We held tight, locked together, eyes closed, opened and closed again, finally spent. Our hunger satiated, the sounds of the passing cars became way too obvious and our vulnerability returned. She lifted her head, squinting at the headlights. I searched, like a gentleman, for her dress through hazy eyes and we made a rushed attempt at modesty, putting things on inside out and backwards, before scurrying into the privacy of the car. And away we went again, climbing to another dizzy height, 100 kilometres per hour.

Connie had an abundance of sexual daring and a desire for us to make love in as many public places as we could, without getting busted. Sometimes her desire battled with her common sense; sometimes she just didn't care, going with lust, enjoying her freedom. She could be way too dangerous for any sane man. I liked her.

In the meantime, I was sharing my rattly old Hawthorn house with an old mate, Thomas. His wife Sally had tossed him out, suggesting that he choose between his two great loves: football replays or her. He chose football. He and Sally had been together for ages and it was odd not to have them playing pigeon pair anymore, but it was nice sharing with Thomas. We had done it for a short time once before, towards the end of my nappy phase, before he and Sally got hitched.

Thomas had moved in when Chelsea moved out. Her best friend, Vanessa, had become a part our family, as Chelsea was a part of hers. Chelsea often stayed over at Vanessa's, studying and having her 'Dad-free zone', where they discussed boys and solved the world's more important teenage problems. As Chelsea had never had the advantage of brothers or sisters, Vanessa seemed to fill that gap nicely. Chelsea was now coming to the end of her VCE final-year exams and was set on securing a university place. She needed a more suitable permanent study environment. It seemed our cold old house just didn't cut it, and she felt some time at Vanessa's might improve her chances. I was sad to see her leave but, true to her own special way, she handed me a beautiful, handwritten note that said, 'Hey, Dad, I'm leaving you!'

Of course, it said much more than that. I remember sitting down on the lounge chair, reading her two heartfelt pages of why she needed to 'do this'. I still read that note every blue moon. Such a well-delivered sacking! My life was, and always would be, topsy-turvy. My work wasn't conducive to waiting by the front door after school, having dinner in the oven, and fussing over the household. We had led a somewhat bohemian life, Chelsea and I: cooking when we wanted to, seeing movies often, eating out a lot, hanging out with friends. What Chelsea needed now was routine; I became her Thursday night boy.

Thomas had glided into the vacant bedroom, bringing with him his French cooking videos and giant television. We cooked potato and garlic soup so often that our friends constantly complained that we reeked of garlic. Perhaps we got the French translation wrong; we used six potatoes and twenty cloves of garlic in the recipe. I'm sure there was a garlic haze hovering above our house. Identifying quickly with the plight of poor Sally, I attempted to throw a house rule at Thomas: football replays were officially banned. It wasn't passed by our committee of two and I suffered the endless drones of '... and-he's-got-the-ball-and-is-taking-a-run-and-he's-bounced-it-and-is-about-to-kick-for-goal-and ... it's ... a ... *goal*!!'

Thomas and I had become a modern odd couple. He was the neat one, as organised as a mother hen. He got home and put on the roast, did a load of washing, cleaned up and had the old joint humming. I, on the other hand, wandered in at any ungodly hour, threw my shirt and tie off before I got to the bathroom, landed on the couch, pulled the cork on a Heathcote shiraz, put on a CD, usually with the volume loud enough to have the neighbours threaten death, and sat around thinking about dinner.

Thomas would tell you that he enjoyed having me as a mate, I hope. He should have: he accumulated so many frequent-flyer points from me that he could have almost travelled the world for free. He didn't know but, for years, I had used his name for my undercover work. When I was buying drugs or meeting crooks in earlier years and needed an identity, I called on Thomas's name. It seemed logical; after all, it was an easy name to remember, which is important when you're facing a crook with a gun who says, 'What's your name, dude?'

'Well, I'm Tommy the drug dealer.'

I sat Thomas down one day and confessed.

'Tommy … mate. I need to tell you something, I hope you understand.'

'This better be good.'

'Oh … you might say it's good … you've been a dirty rotten drug dealer for years!'

'What the fuck!'

'But, Tommy, you've been a very talented drug dealer.'

'What's the catch, there's usually a catch.'

'Yeah, but look on the bright side. I've got 200 000 frequent-flyer points you can use … take a holiday!'

And, after the initial shock, he did. He and Sally flew to Italy to enjoy a little romance and some Italian football.

While they were sampling pasta and sangiovese, I was stuck at my drug squad desk, in charge of a crew of fiery detectives. I had long moved on from the fraud squad and was now lucky enough to have scored a dream team of keen young wallopers, all focused on their careers. More lambs to the slaughter, I thought. We had been running pretty hot, locking up a swag of crooks. We had just closed down a gang of Romanians who were bringing in buckets of heroin from overseas, leaving the bosses bragging to the media that a 'major ring of importers' had been arrested. My team went off into the night to celebrate, chasing tasty morsels of Japanese sushi and sashimi, swished down with far too much sake.

I was asked to hang back and chat with Rodney, a section head in charge of a task force hunting the Mafia. I had no interest in talking about dagos. Most of the ones I knew were my friends. I was more concerned with missing out on the sushi and sake. Rodney opened with his worst possible line.

'We want you to come upstairs here next week, take over.'

'No thanks, happy where I am.'

'We need you up here; it's a good opportunity, good targets.'

'Good … I'm happy that you have good targets … so do I.'

Rodney was a career administrator, and a fair one at that. One of those guys who enjoyed the success of others. He reckoned he had a bullet to the top job one day; he just needed a victory to make his CV glisten.

'Just sit down and we'll talk it over.'

'Can't … my sake's getting cold.'

'What? You're shifting here Monday, to take over, get a win up here.'

'No, I'm not. They'll call me the Task Force Junkie!'

Rodney sensed a battle. He had squeezed his chubby body into his exhausted office chair and was desperately trying to get comfortable. Dressed in a cheap suit, with a collar that was way too tight, he leaned forward—his chair was pinching.

'You'll have a dozen detectives, and squirrels. You get to work on the Mafia.'

'What Mafia?' I raised my voice. 'There's no Mafia, that's all movie bullshit!'

Rodney stood and, sucking in his fair share of air, he dropped his pen, shouting, 'Eight o'clock Monday morning, that's an instruction … be here!'

I turned and walked out of his office, ungraciously ruminating on my loss. Mafia stories interfered with the warm and cosy vision I had of Italians, homely people with whom I had enjoyed some of the happier times of my life. I wasn't feeling like changing that perspective, no sir, not for anyone. I suffered my instruction and went looking for sushi and my detectives.

Reluctantly, I fronted for work at my new office to have my love of Italians tested. The task force office was where I had worked eight or nine years before as a secret squirrel. I plonked my carton full of useful and useless odds and sods onto an empty desk and got an insipid hello from an uninterested bunch. I had heard rumours that the task force hadn't seen much action for months. They had become a room full of ineffective detectives lacking direction. Among them, Rodney had recruited half-a-dozen internal affairs cops, the guys you don't ever want to see. Why they were on a real task force had me baffled; there's no space for internal spies where real detectives work.

The first victory I had with Rodney was the immediate removal of these spies, swapped for my own guys: Sandra, Leigh, Tony and Rob. I figured my four were equal to six of them any day. By the start of our second week together we had the beginnings of a brand-spanking new task force on the Australian Mafia; ten detectives, a team of secret squirrels, two analysts and half-a-dozen whiteboards waiting to be filled.

Our first briefing wasn't much to speak of. We all sat blankly looking at the empty whiteboards, wondering if they'd fill themselves; a bit like a team of artists with blank canvases. We hadn't been given any particular crime to work on or any targets; we had to find our own. The federal government had set up a parliamentary committee to investigate whether there were any Mafia in Australia. The committee asked one simple question: 'Does the Mafia exist in Australia, and if so, indicate to what extent.'

I had read all the crime reports over the years and I had a quick answer for them already. 'No, they don't. Italians are good people, they grow fabulous tomatoes and olives and have delicious Sunday lunches. Now let's all go back to what we were doing and get us out of here!'

I knew I was on a professional loser with that line.

The question raised by the committee was directed to the National Crime Authority, and our task force was the investigative arm of the NCA in Victoria. There were similar arms in each state, all due to report back to the parliament in a collective report. We had two years before our report was due. I had to manufacture a complete shift in my attitude and get on with what I was supposed to be good at: investigating or, in this case, leading a team of sixteen investigators. I took a deep breath. 'Okay, it's time to bounce the ball and get this show on the road … again,' I thought.

My senior analyst, Squid, was Maltese; he was a fascinating guy, bright and full of ideas, with a keen mind. He was aware of my utter disdain for his people, at least for the Maltese police, as I had told him my yarn about being sold out in Malta years earlier. The quintessential criminal analyst, he just raised his eyebrows in a gesture of mild disgust. Squid had the knack of being able to research hundreds of names and could sift through the chaff to get to the wheat. He enjoyed the game of linking names to addresses, to car details, to bank accounts, to girl-friends, to airline flights, to just about anything. Thus far in the task force, he'd been wasted, chasing old rabbits down even older burrows. He had hankered to be a part of a real team, to have a win. I had asked him a week earlier to come up with his 'dirty dozen'.

Squid had the floor; looking confident, he handed me a dozen folders and then placed the same number of photographs on a white-board. We listened; we wrote notes. Squid had articulated a well-prepared brief on each of the faces, none of whom looked familiar, although their family names were well known, part of police history. I was in strange new waters. Squid wrote down their dates of birth, the various addresses for each suspect and their links to other Italians, and on it went, reams of information on his 'dozen'. Before long we had a canvas starting to form. Arrows were drawn linking names, then more arrows, and then more names; different coloured arrows for dif-ferent reasons. It was police art in the making.

Leigh, an old homicide squad man, a detective who had been with me a while, was concerned by the credibility of the links. He wanted the facts that proved one villain was associated with another—like squirrel reports that showed the same two suspects photographed getting out of the same car—real stuff, not superfluous crap. Leigh pushed Squid for more facts, told him not to use words like 'I think' or 'I reckon'. We had a saying, based on the 1950s television series *Dragnet*, that we used often, in jest: 'Just the facts ma'am, just the facts'. Leigh pushed all morning for 'just the facts' and Squid obliged won-derfully, filling our whiteboards with fact after fact.

Our think tank was coming to a consensus on the dozen names: all Italian, all linked, all up to no good. Some of them had prior con-victions or prior police reports for serious drug dealing. They were all involved in cultivating large marijuana plantations in the Australian outback. Some even had links to drug-related murders; the air was ripe with investigative interest. Possibly the smartest of my detectives, Sandra was racing through volumes of telephone records as we worked through our list, confirming telephone activity between the targets.

The man in charge of the squirrels, Nico, followed Sandra with his surveillance reports. Most of the targets had been seen and photographed in Little Italy—Lygon Street, Carlton—where they met for coffee, huddled together in whispers, shook hands and talked sideways. Something was obviously cooking, but what?

By the end of the day we had over-analysed almost everything. Collectively, we had unravelled a serious network. We had established a group of targets, some with bank balances way above their means. Many of them lived in what we called 'grass castles', huge homes erected in various parts of the country and obviously financed by drug money. By the time we all stepped exhausted from the office late that night, we were a task force. Unfortunately, most of our targets lived in another state, New South Wales, and especially in the country town of Griffith.

Griffith, which had a population of 25 000, was established in the early nineteenth century and had long been considered the stronghold of Italian organised crime in Australia—the home of the Mafia. It is more than a 6-hour drive west of Sydney, and about the same distance north of Melbourne. The adventurer Charles Sturt summed up the area in his original report: 'the dreariness of view ... the plains are open to its horizon, but here and there a stunted gum tree or a gloomy cypress is placed by nature as mourners over the surrounding desolation. Neither bird nor beast inhabits the lonely and inhospitable region.' It was desert, and it appeared all that could survive there were the local Aboriginal people, the Wiradjuri, and the proliferation of acacia scrub.

At the turn of the century, renowned architect Walter Burley Griffin placed his civil design on the town, as he had done for Canberra. In time, tree-lined streets and parks appeared, all requiring water. This need helped establish the Murrumbidgee Irrigation Area in the early twentieth century, harnessing waters from the nearby rivers,

canals and weirs. As the water catchment improved, so did the yield of
the soil and postwar Australians started farming the area. With settlement came advancement. Apart from returned servicemen, the ideal
people to work the lands were the Italian immigrants entering
Australia by the boatload from poverty-stricken southern Italy.

It could be said that Italians are the finest market gardeners in the
world, if not the hardest working. Griffith welcomed their skills and
offered land to immigrant families willing to work. The Australian
immigration policy of the postwar era favoured Italians from Calabria,
Campania and Sicily, the most southerly regions of Italy and the most
destitute. Coincidentally, these were the three regions that gave rise to
the three most notorious arms of the Mafia.

Although Italy had enjoyed unification in the late nineteenth century, its wealth was not evenly distributed. Large industry, championed
by the automotive factories of Fiat, Alfa Romeo, Vespa, Ducati and
specialist car-builders like Ferrari and Maserati, built its factories in
northern Italy. The same can be said for a great part of the leather
industry, with the affluent northern regions gaining the lion's share.
With wealth came fine schools, universities and academia. The southerners, who had always been considered peasants, were left to fend for
themselves. Illiteracy was widespread; of every ten people in Calabria,
only three could read and write. Their only exposure to riches was
when their wealthy northern 'cousins' travelled south to enjoy the
beauty of the Amalfi coast, or the prosperous seaside towns of Taormina
and Palermo in Sicily, or the cliff-top haven of Tropea in Calabria.

What developed from this inequality, the constant and ongoing
suppression of southerners, was La Cosa Nostra, a Sicilian dialect term
which loosely means a secret society or family group; in other words,
the Mafia. A band of people who drifted into criminal activity, originally out of necessity, the Mafia was first recognised in and around
Palermo more than a hundred years ago and flourished between both
world wars. La Cosa Nostra preyed on the well-fed tourist families
of Milano, Bologna and Firenze. They stole from their seaside villas

and raided the truckloads of cigarettes and alcohol that were delivered to the region to meet the appetites of the wealthy. And they introduced their own 'tax' on almost every shopkeeper and business in Sicily. Across the Messina Strait—the narrow run of water that divides Sicily from Calabria—the Calabrese people established their own Mafia, originally hilltop bandits, known as the N'Drangheta, which translates as the 'honoured society'. They lay in wait for passing holidaymakers, occasionally moving to a northern region to ransack towns. In Naples (Campania), the Camorra was formed. Its specialty was gangs of pickpockets and petty thieves who toured the major cities of Italy, relieving travellers of their cash and suitcases.

Each Mafiosi operated independently but, as they were immediate neighbours, they would sometimes share their scams and spoils. With the arrival of the swinging 1960s and 1970s, each of the Mafia groups branched out into illegal drugs and eventually took control of most of the upper-echelon drug trafficking worldwide, dropping the petty crimes that had once been their bread and butter. By the 1990s, the Mafiosi had taken ownership of many of the ocean ferry companies, 'Made-in-Italy' designer clothing sweat-shops, toxic and industrial waste disposal and most of the concrete construction businesses across Italy. They were now a truly multifaceted criminal conglomerate, beyond ever being eradicated.

While Hollywood has allocated the name Mafia to the Sicilians, should you visit the region, you will discover it is merely a newspaper term, popularising the local crime gangs, whose names are often too hard for non-Italians to pronounce. Simply, the word Mafia could relate to any cell of Italian organised crime—whether in Calabria, Campania or Sicily.

A significant proportion of the immigrants to Australia were Calabrese, from the major town of Reggio di Calabria. It is a region with a very ordinary coastline; its main beauty lies in the stunning Aspromonte and Sila mountains, the hard-to-access foothills, and pretty, sleepy towns built of local stone. Most of the towns have at least one osteria, offering some of Italy's finest antipasto and splendidly made wines. There are, however, a few sad towns without the slightest hint of style, towns that are home to generations of N'Drangheta. One such town is Plati, a hovel of only 2000 inhabitants. Like its neighbour San Luca, it is a town you just don't ever want to visit. Gangs there prey on the nearby autostradas, kidnapping wealthy folk and offering them one of two options: a quick ransom or a faster throat-cut. At one point in its near-death 1950s history, much of the town fled for brighter days on boats to Australia. They disembarked at either Sydney Harbour or Port Melbourne, and from there it was only a 6-hour bus trip to the New World: Griffith, a town that was growing as fast as the asphalt could be poured.

Of course, the majority of Calabrese immigrants who found their way to Australia, and in particular to Griffith, were hard-working people, steeped in tradition. Many of them turned to market gardening, growing wine and table grapes and planting groves of oranges; others became bakers, restaurateurs, agricultural agents and even cafe owners on the main streets. But some desperate, hard-done-by peasants, with chequered pasts and an inclination towards the bad, became many of Australia's future gangsters.

By the late 1970s Griffith had become the centre of N'Drangheta— 'Mafia'—activity in Australia. While highway crime, kidnapping and grand theft were not options in the New World, there was another lucrative way to make a fast buck—in fact, millions of fast bucks: growing marijuana. The N'Drangheta learned that marijuana is merely a noxious weed and that, once the seeds were down, the weed can usually look after itself. What better terrain to plant a massive hard-to-detect crop than the vast red earth plains of central New South Wales, where nothing exists but scrub, king brown snakes and a few Aboriginal people?

Throughout the 1970s and 1980s, king crops were cultivated in outback New South Wales and across the border in Queensland. Each year there were at least two such crops harvested. Criminal labour was cheap; there were plenty of lowly hangers-on more than happy to keep the kangaroos and rabbits at bay for a few dollars and as much choof as they could carry.

Some crops had tens of thousands of plants, the value of which, even at a wholesale level, was many millions of dollars; one crop was reported to have yielded $30 million. Much of the money was spent in the township, and vast houses began appearing on the landscape. It wasn't long before the former Italian peasant farmers were accumulating vast wealth. The risks for these endeavours were low, as lone police officers rarely ventured far off the beaten track to snoop for marijuana. Every now and then, a caretaker docket-head would be found shot dead, often because they had tried their hand at a little unauthorised trading. Underworld killings flourished with greater frequency.

In fewer than ten years, the N'Drangheta had taken over most of the cultivation and distribution of marijuana nationwide. Fears gripped the non-Italian criminal element, and most were happy to concede that any large quantities of marijuana grown would be the sole business of the 'wogs from Griffith'. Such was the way of organised crime; such were the ways of self-preservation. The Aussie knockabout crooks were satisfied to take their slice of the pie, selling the drugs in the pubs and clubs across the land.

Logically, it was only a matter of time before a royal commission was announced to investigate the goings-on in and around Griffith, and that came in the 1980s. Preceding the commission, and possibly prompting its setting up, was the disappearance of Donald Mackay, an outspoken local councillor and anti-drug crusader. He was the voice for the honest Italians and locals, a voice of the majority, a man of immense character. He simply vanished one night in 1977 after locking up at work. Everyone suspected that he was shot and dumped in a local river, never to be seen again. With the formation of the National Crime Authority in the mid-1980s there finally came wide-ranging powers to outlaw organised crime. A royal commission found the murder of politician Donald Mackay was ordered by a syndicate of Griffith Italians, headed by locals with Calabrian surnames, some from the township of Plati. At the top of the list was 'Aussie Bob' Trimbole.

By the time my crew and I were shanghaied to the task force, marijuana cultivation was slowing down, just a smidgeon. Improved funding had given the Federal Police satellite surveillance of suspected drug crops; outer-space cameras were detecting crops, which were destroyed, and the lowly docket-head caretakers were charged. The N'Drangheta were pulled, screaming, into the later part of the twentieth century; they were forced to diversify, forced to get smarter, and they did. In later years, members of the N'Drangheta were behind some of the largest illicit drug busts, involving cocaine and ecstasy, the world has seen.

It wasn't long before our task force built up a sizeable file of data on our 'dirty dozen', all with direct lineage to the N'Drangheta. Some were cousins, nephews or sons-in-law of the older, now retired, family members who were believed to have instigated the murder of Donald Mackay.

We had worked out the pecking order and identified who was who in their zoo. The main players were Antonio Romeo, the newly appointed leader, the so-called godfather of Italian organised crime in Griffith. He scored the top job after marrying the previous godfather's eldest daughter. Antonio was a charismatic man, blessed with good looks and charm, as well as a few more centimetres in height than most Calabrese. He was considered ruthless and behind many unsolved drug murders and shootings. We allocated the number-two position to Rosario Trimbole, nephew to 'Aussie Bob', who was the typical peasant type, a classic number-two fiddle. He was stocky; his legs looked as if they were 15 centimetres too short for the rest of his body. He wore a very bad range of clothing, especially his loud shirts, but he too was dangerous.

Both men were nudging forty and ran the cover of being farmers of large orange groves around Griffith. They certainly were growing oranges but not at the levels to enable them to afford their lifestyles and grass castles. The secret squirrels were packed off to Griffith for weeks on end to gather as much up-to-date information as they could, and each week they would come back with valuable information that they fed to Squid and his overloaded brain. I often wished I could have gone with them, just to have some fun snooping around. By now the Calabrians fascinated me and I missed the squirrels and all their secret ways.

It didn't take long for us to realise that we had problems with our phone taps on Antonio, Rosario and others. They almost always spoke in a Calabrese dialect, which no-one at the office could fathom. I secured the services of an elite translator, Vito, who had done a life-time of covert work for agencies throughout Australia and Italy. He was a wizard with the many Italian dialects and a fabulously decent man. We became extremely close mates during the next two years, as I pestered him, often on an hourly basis, demanding to know what our targets were saying. Vito responded without fuss and often burned the midnight oil deciphering comments that could literally change the course of our investigations. He was indispensable.

It was Vito who unravelled a series of mobile phone calls between the main players that told us that they were on their way to Melbourne to meet their N'Drangheta group. They were learning to diversify.

Vito also told of a meeting scheduled at the Old Melbourne Hotel on the edge of the city. It was their hotel of choice and Antonio was calling all his Calabrian buddies. We raced ahead of them, linked up with a friendly hotel manager and quickly wired the rooms allo-cated to Antonio, who was said to be travelling with the retired god-father. We had about an hour before the N'Drangheta were due to arrive in their big new Ford sedans and figured it must have been a very important meeting to dust off Giovanni, the old boy, one of the men fingered for Donald Mackay's murder. The squirrels followed behind, calling them into the hotel. Everything ran like clockwork. Antonio and his gang were photographed walking into and from the rooms and our listening device taped the rest.

Vito was sitting next to me in my office with his headphones on. He whispered enough for me to know we had hit the jackpot. The two godfathers told their people everything we had suspected: the police were getting too smart, too many crops had been busted, it was time for the 'family' to find new ways to grow marijuana. They had a friendly farmer outside Melbourne whom they had leaned on so they could build a massive shed, which could house two indoor crops of marijuana per year, on his property.

Antonio and Giovanni left the meeting in true Mafia fashion, shaking hands and waving their arms in the air like peasant generals. Everyone got kisses to their cheeks and into the cars they went. Nico's crew followed them to a miserable little dirt farm; fairly obviously, the Calabrian farmer was having no success with his fruit and veg venture, hence his new business plan with the N'Drangheta. Godfather-elect and godfather-retired disappeared into the farmhouse for ten minutes to deliver their ultimatum.

We now had enough evidence to get a Supreme Court judge to allow us to tap six mobile phones, and the task force launched into full flight. One of the key Italians in the hotel meeting gathered a few trusted hard-noses and construction of the shed began. The squirrels were kept busy around the clock following the underlings: visiting hardware stores, timber yards, metal-cladding factories and concreters. For two months it was a watching brief as the working bee continued. In the meantime Vito was flat out, translating every word.

To get a better handle on the efforts of the men building the shed, I sought help from an undercover dude, giving him the oddest role of his career. We borrowed a clapped-out utility, an old paddock bomb. Then we scrounged up a chainsaw, axe and some work boots, and I handed it all across to Hargy, suggesting he get some practice cutting firewood.

Squid had done some sticky-nosing and found a hobby farm next door to our shed. It was owned by a female schoolteacher; she was not travelling well financially and could do with a bit of extra income. Her farm was full of fallen trees, so Hargy knocked on her door one day explaining that he was a local woodcutter and would pay very well to cut up and take away her fallen timber. Delighted with the cash offer, she allowed Hargy to get to work. He parked his old ute against the rear fence, only metres from the shed construction, which by now was looking like an aircraft hanger. Of course, the squirrels had fitted the ute with a few hidden cameras; we filmed the entire construction, stage by stage.

Though we had excellent coverage of one side of the shed, we were lacking footage from the opposite direction. I took an old mate from the SOG SWAT team for a beer and asked a special favour. Initially he looked at me as if I'd been smoking all the choof we'd been investigating. But after a while he agreed, 'only because it's the Mafia, mate, otherwise no way!'

Well after midnight, the SOG boys crawled onto the farm, across a kilometre of paddock, to within 10 metres of the shed wall. Bit by bit, they dug a foxhole, large enough to hide a man and camera, and of course his gun and lunch box. Then before dawn, every day for the next month, a SWAT man crawled into the foxhole, covered himself with a timber panel camouflaged with grass and, from a peephole only a couple of centimetres square, he filmed the construction of the shed and all the busy little Mafiosi as they worked from dawn till dusk. After dark, the SWAT man crawled out of his hole, back across the paddock, into a hidden car and straight to the nearest toilet—but only after he had dropped the film off with Hargy, who was waiting nearby with blistered palms and a ute full of firewood.

To complete the evidence I persuaded yet another of my detectives to sit up a giant pine tree opposite the driveway to the farm, every day for a month in the winter rain. He matched the hours of the others, photographing the hardware deliveries and the cars that came and went, bringing the N'Drangheta workers to and from their shed activities.

As the shed's roof went on and construction seemed only weeks away from completion, the squirrels presented us with a magnificent bonus. One of the main men in the syndicate had been followed late at night to what appeared to be a derelict factory in an industrial part of Melbourne. Leigh and I snuck a look at the factory in the wee hours one night. A creative electrician had been at work and had diverted the factory's electricity supply so that it bypassed the meter, which indicated only enough power being used to run a couple of lights. 'Hmm,' we thought, 'someone's up to no good.' We made our way into the empty factory to take a closer look and discovered a real treasure trove. The factory had a series of false walls, making up rooms within rooms. None of them had any doors or windows, just fixed panels, one after the other. And the walls were warm to touch. With painstaking care, we unscrewed a couple of the air-tight panels. As they came away, beams of the brightest light shone from the cracks; inside each room was an elaborate hydroponic marijuana plantation growing thousands of seedlings. Collectively, there must have been 20000, and all being cultivated for the nearly completed big shed. We whispered 'happy growing' to the seedlings, screwed the panels back into place and, after tidying up our sock-prints, we quietly left the factory as we had found it.

In fewer than three months we had gathered enough evidence to lock up most of our dirty dozen for conspiracy to grow marijuana. But cops aren't usually too crazy about conspiracies, opting for the actual offence most of the time. So we sat it out, waiting for the shed to be finished. The pressure on the ground crew escalated, especially the man in the foxhole and our man in the pine tree. And, of course, Hargy was getting well and truly sick to death of chopping wood, although his wife did appreciate the firewood over the winter.

All we needed was for the N'Drangheta to transfer the seedlings to the big shed, turn on the lights, and their world would come crashing down.

Don't you hate it when things go wrong? Just as the shed was completed, just as we were talking about getting ready to raid everyone, the peasant farmer who owned the land got himself all nervous and decided he wanted to back out of the deal. Vito hated translating the telephone call where the farmer was overheard pleading to the godfather to end all works immediately. The N'Drangheta decided to allow the farmer a year to think about the shed usage and everything was put on hold.

We all sat at an extraordinary briefing, totally dejected. Squid, Vito, Sandra and I spent a good week or two looking into the direction of the task force, mulling over whether we should just arrest our Italian targets now or keep running with them, keep investigating. We agreed we'd never get another chance to know what this group of crooks was up to. The godfather had been overheard to say that the 'family' had other ways to make money. There was talk of importing cocaine that fascinated us and, besides, the Italians still seemed to have access to huge quantities of marijuana.

We needed to test the quality of the marijuana being shipped out of Griffith, so we arranged to bust a delivery into Melbourne. The squirrels followed a ute onto Antonio's orange grove and watched it being loaded. When it was halfway back to Melbourne, a local traffic cop on the Hume Highway pulled the ute over for a routine licence check and, lo and behold, the cop discovered a car full of drugs. The biggest bust of his career! Apart from locking up the courier, we ascertained that the marijuana was the highest-grade 'skunk weed', the most potent of all choof, worth half-a-million dollars. The bust would have hurt Antonio badly.

With the ease of this success, we felt confident to risk one more, just to confirm the original result. Our very best friend by now, Vito, was hot on the phone taps and picked up a similar run, again organised by Antonio. The squirrels lay in wait, alongside the highway, and coordinated the traffic cops to pull the vehicle over. We found another car full of drugs, and another half-a-million dollars that wouldn't be going to Antonio. This was becoming fun, plus there was a large bag of cocaine and a .38 revolver in the car. This was intelligence that was vital to us. Our Mafia targets apparently had an endless supply of excellent quality marijuana, as well as cocaine. It was time to work out a new strategy, one that could get us closer to Antonio and arrest the upper echelon of the N'Drangheta.

It was time for me to visit the legendary town of Griffith, a town to which I had never been; time to run away from the task force office for a few days and hang out with my old mates from the squirrels. I knew they could get me in and out of town without anyone knowing. We hit the long road to Little Calabria, leaving Sandra to mind the store.

By mid-afternoon we were driving into Griffith, a classically dusty Australian town with essentially one main street, buildings on the left and on the right till the road ran out. I was travelling in Jude's car; she'd been in the squirrels a few years and had no intention of ever wearing her silly uniform again, enjoying her covert role. I understood her sentiment. Jude had been up close and personal with dozens of bad-arse crooks over the years, yet none of them had ever seen her. She could handle a car like no-one else and always carried a few changes of clothes, often swapping the look of her long blonde hair or the clothes she wore as she walked, following her targets, and dumping clothes on the run.

Jude gave me the budget tour of the town, showing me the homes of our rich and famous. Like the massive brand-new faux Tuscan villa owned by Antonio Romeo, 700 square metres in size, costing over a million dollars to build. And the faux Calabrian farmhouse of the old godfather, or the faux Federation-style cottage of Rosario Trimbole. I had decided that the whole town was fake, yet the potential for violence, and even a disappearing act, was very, very real.

We pulled into one of the three hotels in town and parked our bags, agreeing to meet for dinner. I had taken the liberty of booking a table at La Scala Restaurant, famous for being the venue of choice of the old godfather the night Donald Mackay had disappeared. It offered him and his cronies the perfect alibi: 'Oh, no, royal commissioner, I was at La Scala having dinner with three other blokes, it couldn't have been me!' he swore. It wasn't a bad choice; the food was outstanding. By the second bottle of Italian wine I was getting toey, itching to visit the Working Man's Club; the squirrels had often spotted the big boys from the N'Drangheta sitting at their side tables, sipping a beer or two, and chatting to the desperate and dateless, a well-known Italian pastime.

We wandered in on a busier than usual night to the sounds of poker machines and the rancid stench of cigarette smoke. We secured a table and began to suck in the atmosphere and play 'Spot'. The place was full of Italians and they all had attitude; young ones, not-so-young ones, middle-aged ones and even old ones, all doing high fives, all wearing their worst jewellery and best smiles. Such a surreal level of crassness. Jude nudged me.

'There's your man.' She pointed to Antonio Romeo, walking to a table.

'The only smartly dressed dude in the joint,' I quipped.

'It's your night, there's the old boy,' she replied, indicating the old godfather.

'Son-in-law, father-in-law.'

'And Rosario too.'

'That's luck falling from trees again, hey Jude,' I said.

I left my gang sitting inconspicuously at their table, doing what they knew best, blending in. I strolled over to the large bank of pokies, making out I was in gambling heaven and taking in some passive smoking. I moved slowly around until I found the perfect machine. I started feeding coins into the wretched one-arm bandit, which offered an uninterrupted view of the table where our guests of honour were seated: my two-armed bandits.

As I watched our jackpots, my mind scanned every possible trick in the book; how to get close to these guys, the so-called main event in the Mafia stakes. I studied Antonio Romeo: the way he sat, the way he dominated the room with his presence. He was smooth, oozing confidence. Rosario Trimbole seemed more interested in the girls than business; his eyes darted all over the young flesh in the room. The few underlings looked like they had been decked out by some of the cheaper discount menswear stores. Finally, my eyes rested on Giovanni, the old man who had moulded the group for more than twenty years. He sat alongside Antonio, dressed in a customary white open neck business shirt, full of old age and wispy white hair, every bit the Francis Ford Coppola image of a godfather.

I liked watching these two; as they leaned conspiratorially into one another, their talk appeared serious. The others studied the girls, giving their testosterone a run for the night. Some of the girls flirted, others just giggled, too young to know, too young to understand. I wondered what their parents might have thought, before deciding to stop acting like a parent and to concentrate.

My interest was diverted almost immediately. There was an older woman hovering, maybe she was in her late thirties, much older than the teeny-bopper blowflies. She was running beers, visiting the bar and returning a couple of times until all the drinks had landed. She kept the change, which gave me a clue as to her character. She sat confidently down on the old man's knee and took herself a free squeeze and tickle. The old godfather looked pleased with the attention. I watched the show repeat itself a little later. The woman was given a fistful of coins and off she went to play the machines. And off I went, working my way around to her. She had had a few too many drinks, I hadn't; I was working, and it was time to keep working.

Then she moved to a machine near to where Jude had started to play and they both swapped a line or two, gambler small talk. I then moved in as Jude moved away, temporarily. We had her nicely covered by now.

'Can't take a trick, can't win anything.' My best line for the time being.

'You can never win off these,' she said, feeding coins in at double-quick pace.

As we had broken the ice, talk soon took over from gambling. I learned her name was Sara. Originally from Sydney, Sara had lived in Griffith for a couple of years. She wanted to know what I did.

'I'm an art dealer. I buy and sell art; my business is in Melbourne.'

'Wow, I love art, I simply love art.' She was genuinely excited.

And so we talked non-stop about Australian art for the next hour. She knew more than I would have liked, as she had studied art at university. Our conversation was on a roll, and maybe I was flirting with her, just a bit. I deliberately steered the conversation to the edge of being too familiar. She enjoyed it; we talked of Griffith and her plans to find work. At one point she darted off to fix the drinks again and for another tickle and squeeze. When she returned, I let her know that I had noticed her Italian mates.

'They're my friends, they're all good guys,' she offered, with a tinge of boasting. Clearly, at least one of them was a 'good guy', I thought.

We kept talking, not sweating anything too serious; as long as I could keep in the good books with her, I hoped we might become mates, very useful mates.

Near to closing time our guests of honour started strolling out, passing by Sara, who gave a few kisses and another little squeeze to the old man. They looked me up and down, and I nodded. They didn't. Sara walked the godfather to the front door and I turned and winked at Jude. I had ignored her for a time, ensconced in what I was trying to achieve. It wouldn't have worried her; she was well aware of what I was up to. Responding to my wink, Jude came over, just seconds before Sara returned. I embraced her and kissed her firmly on the mouth; she responded perfectly—perhaps a little too perfectly. I whispered in her ear.

'I'm an art dealer from Melbourne, you're my girlfriend, you've been playing the pokies all night, and we're off to Broken Hill tomorrow, to buy art.'

I backed away from her kiss, smiling, and faced Sara, who was now standing beside me, also smiling. I formally introduced the two girls, hoping my earlier flirting hadn't been taken too seriously. Thankfully, all was well; in fact, Sara and Jude got on like a house on fire, and before long the art dealer and his cute girl were taking her off to a Griffith nightclub and pizza bar till dawn.

By the time Jude and I had taken the very merry Sara home, we had discussed the whys and wherefores of Australian art, my favourite painters, Sara's favourite painters, my art consultancy, Jude, our plans to get married in a year or two, our pending visit to Pro Hart's gallery in Broken Hill, our dislike for cops, and our love of making lots of money. Oh, and how we didn't mind the many ways there were to make money. Sara, bless her soul, seemed to be assessing us and later that night she informed us that her Italian gentlemen friends were 'the Mafia'. On cue, Jude looked at her puzzled, explaining we didn't know anything about that sort of stuff.

Jude and I drove out of Griffith the next morning drained, slightly hung-over and full of anxiety, knowing that we had just spent most of the previous night in the company of a Mafia dirty girl. I wondered if I was perhaps being naive, thinking we might meet some of our targets through Sara. It was a delicious mixture of doubt and excitement with no thought to what dangers might lie before us; my head was caught up in the moment. We high-tailed it back to Melbourne and called an extraordinary meeting, believing we had a realistic shot at infiltrating the Mafia. I was now an art dealer. I had someone visit the Pro Hart gallery and get me some postcards and key rings while I wondered if I could pull off the biggest sting of my career.

15

INFILTRATION

A fortnight after meeting the artless Sara in Griffith, Jude and I were rehearsed, studied, polished and ready to go, and driving our new car, a snappy two-door coupé, befitting a successful art dealer with a very fluid cash flow. We had spent every moment of the past weeks backstopping our cover stories, creating a history for an art connoisseur and his sexy girlfriend. Inside the glovebox was a mess of brochures and invoice pads and my wallet was full of calling cards. We had opened personal and business bank accounts, all tied to a well-known national banking group, and with healthy balances dating back years. My name was Cole Goodwin. Often the best first names to use are variants of your own, and Goodwin had a distant tie to my family.

Back-catalogues from most of the art auction houses in Melbourne were scattered in the car. We also had a few oil paintings in the boot, just in case an orange grower wanted to invest in art. Jude had her cover story sorted; she was a child-care worker. Our rationale was that the Italians wouldn't care to visit a crèche full of screaming kids. And for anyone who asked, we planned to announce our engagement at a party in twelve months' time, having been together now for three years. This was an important element to our cover story, as one thing we knew well, especially from Vito's translations, was that even though the Italians were married men, they had a string of girlfriends. We hoped an engagement would deter any unwanted smooth talk from our targets. Jude and I had taken a swanky Georgian apartment in East Melbourne, overlooking a quaint little park, and managed to backdate the lease for over a year. We had no pets, our families lived in Sydney, and we did most things together: the perfect couple, really. The rest we could wing—once, that is, I had madly studied up on Australian art.

I thanked my lucky stars for my ongoing love of art, triggered by my time in Europe twenty years earlier. I embarked on two weeks of pure research, often sitting in the reference library at the National Gallery, reading volume after volume of material. The night before Jude and I hit the road, a friendly mature-age arts student in her final year of a degree majoring in Australian art and good looks fired question after question at me, testing my knowledge for hours. By the end of the evening, she gave me her best smiling 'pass' mark, fascinated as to what I might be up to. I knew then that I was ready to infiltrate the Mafia.

On the long drive the next morning, while Jude gave me my final art quiz, I marvelled at the latest gadget from the technical whiz-kids. I have always held that undercover work is only as good as the cover stories you invent and the equipment you use during the sting. We had a wonderful bunch of technicians who delighted in inventing gadgets to beat the crooks. Their latest show-off piece was my mobile phone. It looked like an everyday phone—and it was—but when you wanted it to be a voice transmitter, you just pressed 51 on the key pad and it became a listening device, capable of transmitting back to my office in Melbourne. Upon reflection, a portable wire that enabled Vito to listen to our every conversation may not have been the perfect toy to have strapped to my hip.

After six hours of art questions and answers, Jude and I rolled into the lonely streets of Griffith, overdosing on the unknown. As I drove down the main street, looking for a hotel room, my mind wandered back to my younger years in undercover work, the ideal apprentice- ship for what I was now about to begin.

Soon after settling into our hotel room, we ventured over to the Working Man's Club in search of Sara. The previous week we had sent her a cheery postcard from Pro Hart's gallery in Broken Hill, just the sort of thing new friends do for each other. As we walked through the automatic glass doors of the club, a ferocious blast of air conditioning instantly chilled the desert heat. I was as nervous as I ever had felt in my 14-year career chasing crooks. Jude grabbed my hand and threw her gorgeous smile into the room. We headed for the pokies and the sounds of a familiar voice.

'Guys, oh you're back, I've missed you two so much.'

Sara wrapped her fleshy arms around us both, kissing cheek to cheek, and we responded in the same enthusiastic manner. Jude gave Sara a Pro Hart key ring, which prompted a small tear; our Sara was in need of a friend. We spent the night chatting and sometimes laughing, knowing the squirrels were filming our performance. Sara was the perfect target, really; she was lonely and vulnerable, and had a direct 'in' to the Mafia. To compensate for her loneliness and to balance her own lack of interesting stories, she skited of her association with her Mafia mates and talked of Antonio and Rosario and their activities. We played back a cautious curiosity, careful not to seem overly keen. As more drinks were consumed, she got cavalier.

'Do you want to meet the Don?' she offered.

For an elongated second, I couldn't believe what she had asked. I wanted to pinch myself. I wanted to stick a sharp pin into my eyeball to make sure I was well and truly awake, not dreaming. I simply couldn't believe our luck. I had just won the jackpot and I hadn't used a coin.

'The Don, who's Don?' I asked casually, taking little notice.

'The Don—the godfather,' she uttered, looking as if half the wind had dropped from her sail.

'Oh yeah, I suppose.' We tried to look uninterested but mildly willing.

Sara walked us over to a large round table in the main room where Giovanni, Antonio and Rosario were seated, along with a gang of other lesser villains. She introduced us, one by one, in the pecking order we'd expect. I shook the hand of the old godfather, Giovanni, and the surreal nature of the moment made the hair on the back of my neck tingle. I rubbed my neck vigorously with my left hand while shaking with my right. Then I met Antonio and Rosario and the others. Antonio looked as handsome as a movie star, as a Romeo should. He offered us a chair and we sat in their company for over two hours. Small talk was all that was on offer, of course; the Italians weren't as stupid as Sara.

Rosario Trimbole spoke of his love of Melbourne and his many visits to the city, as did Antonio. Our cover stories got a thorough going over, piece by piece, question by question. Jude and I worked the table as hard as we could, oozing smiles and charm, while making sure not to overstep the level of friendliness. We acted aloof yet interested in our new acquaintances. The laughter flowed. The key to our acceptance was Jude and her sexuality; she was a mixture of the classic girl-next-door with lashings of temptress. And she was dressed to kill that night, in a cream pantsuit and black low-cut satin top, carefully designed to play to the ego of our targets, especially Rosario, who had a one-track mind. Jude deliberately leaned into Rosario as she spoke, putting herself into his space, enough to ensure that he never wanted to leave the table, and the others enjoyed her repartee. I worked on Antonio, playing our cover stories, hoping to stir his interest for another social get-together.

By the end of that first night with the N'Drangheta bosses, Cole Goodwin had convinced Rosario and Antonio that there was a lot of money to be made buying and selling art. Antonio took my calling card. Jude had worked Rosario beautifully, suggesting that he was a very handsome Italian man and that all of us should catch up in Melbourne in the future, for drinks. I sensed that night that Jude would be my ticket to the Mafia, as long as I could hold up my end of the sting.

Jude and I were welcomed back to our Melbourne office like rock stars. I don't think I had ever worked in an environment that could sniff such promise. These were exciting times but that initial rush was soon hosed down by the naivety of our management, who were more interested in trying to chart time-lines for when we'd be buying drugs from the Italians. Yeesh! They had simply no appreciation of the complexity of an undercover infiltration. And that was precisely what we had just started; an infiltration of the Mafia that may or may not succeed. It was far too early to get carried away with anything else.

I insisted that we be allowed just to befriend our targets at this stage and leave the issue of drugs completely alone. After all, our cover story was that of an art dealer and sexy girlfriend, not desperate drug dealers looking to buy from the Mafia. We needed to move 'slowly, slowly' with our new mates. I requested six months to infiltrate. It should be the Italians who made the first move, who first raised the issue of drugs. This premise caused issue with some, whom I sensed were itching to sprint around the hierarchy corridors, touting success.

A couple of weeks later when Rosario arrived in Melbourne, the squirrels were onto him. He rang my mobile phone and left a message for Jude, wanting to know if we wanted to have dinner with him and his two cousins later that night at his favourite Lygon Street eatery. We agreed by return message and swung into action, racing off to our East Melbourne apartment for showers. At the restaurant it was obvious that Rosario had taken a fancy to Jude; the Latin lover was coming out in him. We had half-expected this, as she had turned on a considerable level of charm the first time they met, so on this encounter we made sure she stamped her feelings all over me, just enough to cool him down but not to ruin our achievements. I enjoyed her ear playing, frequent kisses over dinner and roaming hands.

The night ran like many future nights, full of laughter, stories of Italy, comments about food, and having a rollicking good time. I have no doubt my history with my Italian mates from my younger years helped me to befriend my targets. Rosario was relaxed, and by the end of the night he confided that he was able to pass on the names of horses in fixed race meetings. He paid the tab for dinner, telling the restaurateur to look after us each time we dined there, that he'd pick up our tab for any future visits.

Each time Rosario came to Melbourne we caught up for dinner or drinks, often with his cousin, little Rocco. He showed up in his red Porsche 911, which he kept hidden on one of the orange groves. It almost got to be a constant for him: dinner with Cole and Jude. Likewise, we were finding reasons to visit Griffith, mostly under the guise of buying or selling art works in Broken Hill or Canberra, and always available for a catch up with our friends.

We stopped overnight in Griffith, staying at the same hotel each time. Every now and again Rosario helped with our luggage, in gentlemanly fashion. I believe that he was actually sussing out the details we had left at the hotel register, as well as checking what might have been in our bags. We were prepared for both and just rolled with whatever punches he had. Jude and I noticed one morning that someone had ransacked our car overnight. While nothing had been taken, we had carefully set up the glovebox to alert us to any snooping; the car had been relocked and to all intents and purposes looked exactly as it had done the night before, except that the documents in the glovebox had been replaced the wrong way around.

Antonio owned a restaurant in the main street of Griffith, a tidy little side investment, probably to hide a portion of his wealth. He invited us to dine; it was a long night of fabulous food and wine in the upstairs room. Antonio joined our table of Italians, sitting opposite my mobile phone. It was comforting to know that Vito was listening in the event that it all went sour, as we were a long way from home with no back up and no gun. The main topic of conversation that night was art and how easy it was to launder money by investing in art works. Antonio's questions were probative; he was visibly stirred by this money and art thing.

Whenever we ventured into Griffith we were showered with gifts—cases of oranges, boxes of wine and bags of mandarins—all from the farms of our new-found best friends. Our new godfather and his number-two man were obviously greasing us up for something, but what? The plan was going beautifully but it was still a waiting game; the trouble was that time was never our friend. With the constant demands for results from the hierarchy, we were concerned that soon we might be pre-emptively forced to find an opportunity to raise the subject of drugs in our conversations. While Jude and I were under-cover, it was decided there couldn't be any drug-related arrests; we couldn't afford to have the N'Drangheta getting paranoid, thinking their new skippy friends might have tipped off the cops.

Back at the office, everyone was running at a now familiar fast pace. Each social occasion that Jude and I attended increased the workload for my crew: confirming facts from our meetings, telephone checks and translations of their calls to each other, especially after our dinner dates, to hear what they thought about us. Vito was moving like an Italian sports car. My commitment to the infiltration side of the investigation meant that I had less and less time to devote to managing the entire team, so I started scaling back on that aspect.

The most angst Jude and I encountered was in keeping up with our paperwork. We had to make handwritten notes in our court books, as well as transcribe the many tapes from our conversations, all important stuff for a later trail. In between our meetings we sat around in our swanky apartment; we were living there now, like a happy little soon-to-be-married couple, with our headphones on and our note-books out.

The Italians had taken to visiting our pad when in town, so we had to be there, just in case of a knock on the door. The solitude from the mayhem at the office at least allowed us to keep the transcripts going. As the months ticked by, our only release was sipping bottles of wine and Antonio kept us well stocked in that department. It's so odd playing lovers when you're not. I found it difficult being cooped up with such a cute woman every day. Despite the delicious attraction that was forming between us, we worked hard at not letting it get too far advanced. Jude needed to be there, to keep things natural. We cooked and lazed about. Jude had a penchant for fine lingerie, and there were times when the spare pillow found its way to the centre of the bed, as a moderator to the obvious tensions that built up. It would have been crazy to allow too many shenanigans anyway, as each room in the apartment was wired for sound and there were half-a-dozen secret cameras, all operated by the flick of a switch from our office. It was enough to make Jude very nervous before her shower.

It was nearing Christmas; Jude and I had been running with the Italians for six months and we could honestly say we had well and truly infiltrated the Mafia. We kept ahead of their questions; we made sure our stories withstood their scrutiny and endured the long days and nights of socialising. We had become spies, more so than under-cover cops, the most difficult of all grey professions to sustain.

I thought the world of Jude; I admired her integrity, which was above and beyond that of most people I had dealt with in the police department, if not in all my life's journeys. She was resilient. I was an experienced undercover operative and task force manager; Jude was just a squirrel, with no actual undercover experience. Yet she had the tenacity and dash to match the very best operatives; her natural charm had lured the Italians to us. We both felt it was only a matter of time before I'd be swamped with offers of drugs. I could sense it, but the constant whingeing by our hierarchy to 'buy drugs, for Chrissake, buy drugs!' was beginning to wear me out.

Just in case we had forgotten how serious these men really were, an incident occurred to sober us all. A few large drug deals that had gone down in Queensland prompted the NCA to raid some Italians, believ-ing it wouldn't affect Jude and me. Antonio became worried, cagey, suspecting a worm in the organisation. He vowed to find the snitch.

A detective friend of mine, Big Bird, worked in the Sydney arm of the NCA and I trusted him completely. He was a giant of a man, a touch under 2 metres tall with long sandy hair and blue eyes. In another life he would have passed for a Viking. He was the only non-Melbourne office investigator who was aware that Jude and I were undercover—or so I thought! The lid had to be kept tight, or Jude and I would end up feeding the fishes, like Donald Mackay. My Sydney confidante promised to keep his ears open, to monitor what sort of information Antonio was able to find on the snitches.

Big Bird rang. I wished he hadn't, as I knew he'd only call with bad news.

'A dago's been killed overnight mate, eight rounds into him,' Bird told me.

'Where?'

'On a road that leads to Griffith.'

'Fuck. Who's responsible?' I asked the obvious.

'Your best mate Antonio, he ordered the hit. He believes there's a snitch.'

'Was he the snitch though?'

'No Cole, of course he wasn't. You know who the snitch is.'

Jude was seated on the lounge chair. She didn't know who was on the phone and I made sure that she didn't hear my conversation.

'How long have you got?' he asked, sounding worried.

'I want six more months; it'd be nice to get them all cold.'

'If I were you, I'd get out now, just disappear mate.'

'Can't … thanks, been on too many losers up till now.'

'Watch your bosses. They've been up here, bragging about their undercovers—there are too many loose lips.'

'We both know that Bird, can't put brains in monuments.'

'You're mad. I'll keep my ears peeled for you, stay safe.'

It was obvious that some of our own managers were getting ahead of themselves, so keen to blabber to their border counterparts, instead of maintaining confidentiality. I guess I had expected nothing less but, with Big Bird on side, we might at least stand a chance of keeping half a step ahead. Our friendship became even closer after that phone call.

The following evening we had a dinner arranged with Rosario and Rocco at our usual Lygon Street restaurant. The only catch was that Rosario had been bleating again about his poor cousin Rocco, a very old-fashioned quiet guy in his early forties. Months earlier, Rosario had asked Jude to find a girlfriend for Rocco. Strategically, we thought it important to have Rocco content when visiting Melbourne. It would have ruined our investigation at this crucial point should Rocco drift away from us, taking Rosario in search of female company elsewhere. So on this night we had Liz, our friend, come along to flutter her eyelids at Rocco and make him all gooey. Little did the Italians know, but Liz was also a policewoman, attached to the undercover unit.

Rocco enjoyed the vivacious company of the good Constable Liz. He believed she was unemployed, recently separated from her husband and needed to go 'slowly, slowly' with any dating. Meanwhile, on my end of the table, I got into some heavy chit-chat with Rosario. Something serious was on his mind. After a few wines, he blurted it out: there'd been a discussion in the 'family' as to whether Jude and I might be cops; they'd completed checks into our background, among their own contacts, and we had passed. He went on to reassure me that the 'family' had to make sure we were okay.

We already knew that someone had been snooping around behind our backs as only a few days earlier the Griffith branch of our bank had tapped into the Cole Goodwin accounts, not knowing that head office had a covert watch on. Squid told us immediately. Things were hotting up.

Big Bird's team of squirrels had been busy tracing Antonio, who had spent a fair time in Queensland staying at Jupiter's Casino, no doubt fixing his own security issues, over and above gambling. Whatever concerns or worries the N'Drangheta might have had, they now seemed to be satisfied with the authenticity of Jude and Cole. Antonio spoke of using the Cole Goodwin art bank accounts to hide some of the 'family' money, for a fee of course. Rosario relaxed too, talking freely about buying a Ferrari, some land, and of wanting to build a new home, though one not quite as large as Antonio's. Squid had figured Antonio must have ploughed more than a million dollars into his castle, so heaven knows what sort of money Rosario planned to throw at his own ranch.

Jude and I celebrated Christmas with our Italian *compadres* in true style, taken to their most favoured restaurant, again in Carlton, near

Lygon Street. We enjoyed a feast as honoured guests; there was little doubt of our esteemed friendship. After seeing so much of each other, it was only natural that we would form a close bond. In long-term infiltration work, this is an accepted phenomenon. Jude and I struggled daily, making sure we didn't lose sight of who our targets really were. Our job was to report back to the federal parliamentary committee on the goings-on of Italian organised crime and our role, as two undercover operatives playing in the most elevated cell of the N'Drangheta, was crucial to the committee's final report. There would be no Stockholm syndrome for us!

Spread out along our Christmas table were Antonio, Rosario, Rocco, Jude, myself and, of course, Liz, who was working harder than any of us, in her own way, deflecting the constant romantic attentions of Rocco. Liz was a great operative, totally understanding her importance in the entire operation. I had promised her that the second we hit pay dirt on drugs, I'd phase her out of the job somehow.

Poor Liz; we used to tease her a lot, at our strategic planning meetings in the basement of an old factory in Collingwood. We met weekly, plotting and planning, exchanging the facts and information that we had gleaned about money laundering, drug sales, assets accumulated by the Mafia, violence and a whole lot more. Liz could only offer the number of times Rocco had tried to kiss her, or how far his Roman hands went the previous night. But her role was crucial; I reiterated that when the timing was right we might have her squashed by a truck, or die at the Infectious Diseases Centre, anything that would stop Rocco from ever seeing her again. She liked that and monitored my promise daily.

Meanwhile, she suffered Rocco's gentlemanly soft chatter and occasional hand touching. I had no fears or nightmarish thoughts that Rocco would ever try to harm Liz, despite the sheer violence that the N'Drangheta was known for. He was from the old school of Italians, happy to be chaperoned with Liz till the time was right. Sadly, no time would ever be right for Rocco.

A most beautiful 19-year-old girl was also at our Christmas dinner party. Kim was a local Griffith girl who worked in Antonio's restaurant. I was taken by her stunning looks; she hung on Antonio's arm all night. We learned that she often accompanied him to Melbourne on his drug-dealing missions, spending a few days in the finest hotels the city could offer. It was a lifestyle completely foreign to what she had known in Griffith. Kim appeared completely besotted by her beau. He, in turn, appeared very ... Armani.

We all clinked glasses and wished everyone a '*buon Natale*' and '*buon anno*' throughout the evening. Later that same night, back at our apartment, Jude and I gifted three matching paintings to Rocco, Rosario and Antonio. Each was by the artist Michael McCartney. I had purchased the three under my paddle at Sotheby's a few weeks earlier, and Jude made a song and dance about wrapping them in pretty ribbon and tinsel paper. They went down a treat; the three boys were over the moon, probably thinking they were worth a small fortune, which they were. I gave up trying to get reimbursed by the department, which had trouble reconciling the fact that the art works were a necessary operational expense.

It was that same night that all the hens came home to roost for Jude and me, when all the sheer bloody hard work of the previous six months paid off. Sitting in our lounge room at East Melbourne, sipping after-dinner drinks, Rosario offered me an opportunity to buy drugs—lots and lots of drugs. To open my account I could buy 'pure' cocaine, in vast amounts, and also car-loads of marijuana. Ho, ho, ho, Santa Claus was coming to town. The moment Rosario put his offer, I just wanted to scream, jump a metre in the air and embrace my pseudo-girlfriend but, of course, I couldn't. I stayed cool and acted nonchalant. Besides, there was a lot of work ahead.

Together, Rosario and I hatched a plan that worked for us, bearing in mind we were crooks, or at least one of us was. We schemed on how to move some serious weights of cocaine. And, should we need to talk to each other in the future, we drafted a code. All drug dealers use codes and we were no different. We decided to call the cocaine 'Picasso'; this would work well because I was an art dealer and if I rang Rosario seeking a 'Picasso', a prying ear might believe we were just talking about art. One 'Picasso' equalled one kilogram of pure cocaine, sealed fresh from Colombia.

Rosario offered to get me a sample in the New Year. He thought I could sell the cocaine in my whizzy art world and to people I knew in the music industry, whom I had casually mentioned earlier. He later offered me large quantities of marijuana 'heads': the tip of the plant and the most potent part. He spoke of recently selling 600 pounds of 'heads'—around 240 kilograms; drug dealers never really took to the metric system—at $3500 per pound, a total of $2 million. In the most matter-of-fact way, like a baker offering his warm loaves of bread, he took me through his price list: heads in 10-pound lots and the price could vary from $3500 to $4000 a pound, and so on. He spoke freely to a man he thought was able to sell his wares, and confirmed everything we had learnt through our phone taps and Vito's painstaking translations.

As I listened to Rosario prattling off his price list, I stared keenly at a spot of cotton on the knee of my trousers and began to fidget with it as the prices kept coming. The money ticked in my head: millions of dollars, tonnes of drugs.

I pulled at the cotton, wanting to yank it out, as my mind's eye saw newspaper headlines: 'Mafia arrested for drugs'. I wanted to turn the page to the cartoons. I was despondent, wanting it all to go away. I had lost interest in the game and the police department. I just wanted to take my bat and ball and go home. It was a massive anti-climax. But Rosario was on a roll, seamlessly moving his price list from heads to cocaine and back again. I nodded, like a bobbing dog on a parcel shelf.

The cotton piece that had so taken my attention was getting longer, more annoying, as was the information I was receiving on drugs. 'Too much information!' I wanted to yell. 'Stop telling me all your secrets!' I wanted to scream.

But I couldn't; it was my job to infiltrate. To worm my way into the lives of these people, the N'Drangheta, to pry into their crimes. And now here I was, I had been so successful, so clever, that the talking head in front of me wouldn't stop. I wished he'd just go back to

Calabria, and maybe I could disappear someplace peaceful and idyllic, with the patient and long-suffering Connie—somewhere with a palm tree or two and no cops-and-robbers nonsense.

I experienced the most vivid image; like a slow-motion slide-show it seemed to last for many minutes yet it could have only lasted seconds. That first meeting with Rosario and Antonio and their gang, at the Working Man's Club floated past, then the dozens of other meetings, the many smiles, the laughs and the many dinner parties, all leading to this moment. I wanted them all to be erased. I wondered why I was such a driven person, so in need of success, so unable to accept failure. As my internal slide-show rolled, Rosario punched the inside of one hand with the fist of another, doling out instructions: be careful, and wait for a sample of cocaine. I kept nodding. I was one of his men now, he thought. But of course, I was not; I was a detective, gathering crucial evidence on the Griffith Mafia. I was doing my job, on a detective's paltry salary of twenty-eight dollars an hour. I only hoped that I never saw the bad side of Antonio.

The cotton broke away from my trousers just as Rosario finished his price list routine. I held the thread between my fingers, twirling it into a fine tight spear of fibre. Rosario looked at me. As I dropped it to the floor, I realised that I had ruined a good pair of trousers, just as I was also about to ruin the lives of Rosario and Antonio, as well as many others. Success wasn't in me. I carried a can that represented the invisible faces of maybe fifteen people, my broader team all hovering in cyberspace listening to my conversation with an Italian drug dealer, and the hierarchy sitting in their timber-panelled offices punching the air with each of Rosario's precise comments, my mobile phone listening device transmitting his every word.

I mentioned to Rosario that I had a young brother who was a bit dodgy, a young surfie type who was a builder. He might want to take five or ten kilos of the heads. This was small change to Rosario. While I knew it was a mere drop in his bucket, I also knew how tight the police department was. I had enough experience to know that I would battle a hard war to get the department to spend money for us to gather the evidence we needed to put these Italians away. Away for a long, long time, so they could never get back at me or sweet-faced Jude.

As soon as our Italian friends left for the night and we were alone, Jude and I pulled a bottle of French champagne from our fridge and quietly toasted our success. After a few bubbles tickled the tips of our noses, the smiles dropped from our faces and we sat on the sofa together in silence. We had drifted into the same thought at the same time, wondering what the fuck we had gotten ourselves into. Should we survive the next year or so, we would always be looking over our shoulder, always wondering who might be walking behind us, especially on cold, dark nights. Our wine and celebration went flat.

They say necessity is the mother of invention. That's what happened with my creation of my brother. Rodney had decided that Jude had to be phased out of the investigation; he believed it was getting too dangerous for a woman. Jude was devastated at being removed at the most crucial point, when drugs were finally starting to run freely. I couldn't for the life of me see how I'd be able to explain her absence to my new best friends, Antonio, Rosario and Rocco. None of it was making any sense. Luckily, over the New Year period our targets were busy with other commitments, which allowed me valuable time to renegotiate Jude's exit. She remained adamant that she wanted to stay till the end, to stand by me—to corroborate the vital evidence. We had only just removed Liz from the operation. Seeing that drugs were on our agenda, Liz had dropped a few tears on Rocco, telling him that she wanted to make another go of it with her ex-husband. The perfect drug-dealing gentleman, Rocco fully understood her decision and wished her well. Liz promised not to keep in touch as she felt it would be too sad to meet again, what with feelings and all.

Now, no amount of my version of logic could change Rodney's mind; Jude was out too.

I worked out a story that should appease our targets: Jude was caught up in family illness, nursing her dying mother in Sydney. We planned a cosy lunch together for her final day. Jude and I felt relaxed in being able to sit around our swanky apartment and just shoot the breeze, nibbling on antipasto and sipping a glass of Heathcote shiraz. It was a sad day for both of us; we had become so attached to each other that it felt more like breaking up an old married couple. There were sparks still hovering but we were both professionals, just doing our jobs. I made sure she knew the importance of her work, not only in the early days of our infiltration, but through all the telephone calls she had with the Italians, as well as all the dinners she livened up. Whatever success the task force might ultimately have, I would always attribute it to the special ways of Jude.

Jude and I mopped up our artichokes and olives, knowing that the inevitable would follow the last olive leaving the plate. She took a slow walk around the apartment, glancing at the bathroom, then the bedroom, stopping for a moment, with her hand on her face, looking at the secret panel that held the twenty or more notebooks of all our dealings with our targets, the evidence to send them to jail. She looked at the hidden cameras that she had dodged in getting dressed each day and smiled. Finally, she came back into 'her' lounge room, the room that she had prettied up and socialised in.

She grabbed her bag and reached for the front door. As she opened it I handed her a bunch of twenty-six long-stemmed red roses, one for each week she had bravely and so deliciously wrapped our targets around her cute little finger. We looked at each other, aware of tears waiting to break, and we kissed, ever so softly. We held our kiss long enough to know we had reached a line; reached a point where it was time to stop and walk away. And she did. She walked off and I went to the kitchen window, following her with my eyes until she disappeared from my view. I would miss her every day over the next six months. She was an extraordinarily brave woman.

16

OUT OF OUR LEAGUE

The Italians were now dominating my life, with many frequent trips to Griffith and swanning around Carlton restaurants and bars, negotiating drug buys. But I still had to satisfy the craving for my drug of choice: Chelsea. She was still my little blonde-haired girl, even though she was now nineteen with long, flowing brown hair. Memories of her younger years occupied my thoughts more than ever, maybe because of her absence. Her last few months at school were more defining than she imagined. She achieved excellent grades in her final exams, clearing the way for her university entry, but she elected instead to take on a chef's apprenticeship. Over the years, we'd fantasised about going into business one day, but I didn't expect her to become a chef. Just the same, I was immensely proud, remembering the countless restaurant nights we'd shared. She started working at a local seafood restaurant owned by Jenny's newest squeeze.

Thomas had moved out of my house, eventually succumbing to the harsh reality that he and Sally were truly finished, although they would remain the closest and dearest of mates, which everyone in our group thought was a fair consolation. Chelsea was now living in a studio apartment perched high on a rock, with the wildest views of the Melbourne skyline. As it was just two minutes away from my old dump in Hawthorn, Chelsea had been happy to move in. Over the next few years I'd lap up some fabulous dinner parties there, with Chelsea and her young chef mates all cooking. Up to a dozen of them could drop in and I would hang out with the kids, trying desperately to shave a few years off my age!

My 88-year-old tenant was now older and still enjoying her life in art deco heaven, at $100 a month. I had decided not to poison her milk delivery, although I did consider engaging the SOG SWAT team to extricate her. I started drawing up a floor plan, making notes on the type and strength of the front door, and suggested ways to force entry into the place. Reason won in the end and I decided to let nature take its course, but I still didn't want her to die in the main bedroom.

Connie was still just as wild and adventurous, and by now we had found a nice even path on our 'part-time' relationship. But Connie was keen to start a family. She was the classic still-waters-run-deep girl, offering almost nothing in the emotional stakes, just enough to keep the intrigue ticking. Her finest quality was that she never asked questions, never pried into what I was up to, why I was away in Griffith for days on end. My feelings for Connie were one thing that made me glad to return to Melbourne after my visits to the desert.

I still missed my covert partner Jude far too much—her level head and great input—but with her exit came Cody's entrance. My old buddy from the drug squad days, when we were buying from the bikies. I welcomed his common sense to my cunning game. He still looked like Clint Eastwood, although, like the rest of us, he had aged a few years. It was good to have him back in the saddle.

I had given up running the investigation at the task force. I had to step aside; the intense undercover work was now centre stage, and I couldn't be seen sneaking in and out of the task force office any longer, hiding my face as I ran through a back door in time for an urgent meeting, then scampering out the same way. To underpin the integrity of the covert investigation, it was time for a controller to come on board, to help me plan the future strategies and to move the investigation to a proper and safe conclusion. By now, far too many people had come to know of my achievements. It's part of a controller's role to keep a lid on the job, to maintain confidentiality and try to ensure smooth sailing. I had specifically requested Cody, as he was the finest in the country. We both knew how the other worked. Day by day over the next six months, we sweated the small stuff and planned the bigger, more important moves in our game of drug chess. Each move was designed to protect our King (me) and to make sure we'd clean the board of all the Italians in our game. Once planned, Cody would disappear into la-la land (headquarters) to make it happen, while I stayed tucked away, dealing with Antonio and Rosario.

I had already placed an order for a kilo of 'pure' cocaine that the Italians didn't hesitate to accept, offering a 'wholesale' price of $185 000. As it was pure, the street value could be up to a million dollars. Not bad work for a shifty art dealer.

Our biggest problem was extricating money from the police coffers to pay for the cocaine. It appeared that every Tom, Dick and Harry needed to stick his two cents' worth into our investigation and debate whether we needed to spend that sort of money. Were there cheaper options? Could we run with a conspiracy brief of evidence, saving the expense? On and on the bullshit ran.

The more it was discussed, the more people knew that 'an undercover cop had infiltrated that Griffith Mafia'. The juicy gossip bounced high above the usual dull crap; it was a nerve-wracking month or more, waiting for approval. Every few days the Italians made contact, wondering what I was doing, what the worry was. Whenever we met, well before the caffe lattes were ordered, Rosario or Antonio would query the delays.

The Italians weren't some Johnnies-come-latelys who had just happened onto some coke or grass. I argued that it was important to prove to the parliamentary committee and the courts that these guys were able to do just what they claimed: supply pure cocaine and truckloads of marijuana. In the seedy world of drug trafficking, anybody can talk highfalutin nonsense about the drugs they can supply and how much they have access to. We needed to place some serious drug weights onto the parliamentary table!

Apart from this, my long-term security and that of Jude needed to be considered. By purchasing drugs, we would be able to secure serious jail-time, thereby alleviating the stress and worry of our constantly wondering if our Italians were coming after us. This logic didn't seem to be up there in the hierarchy's concerns, as all the reports had the bosses squarely focused on trying to save money.

By late February, the department announced we could only spend $50 000 on drug buys. It was an utter embarrassment; it seemed that our goal posts were moving daily. We knew from Squid and Sandra's constant probing that the Italians were the top of the tree, dealing in heavy weights. The sum of $50 000 was not credible, considering I had put myself out there as a big-time art dealer capable of moving large amounts. The Italians let it slip that they had a shipment coming into the country in a month or so, and that each kilo was sealed and uncut. They simply wouldn't break up a kilo for a smaller deal. I was losing face; all that was saving me was our long-term friendship.

There was a new crop of marijuana ready to be harvested at the end of the month and they offered me as much as I wanted. I had a price list and now it was up to me to come good with the orders. I was left in a Mexican stand-off, and it was my move. Put up or shut up. Cody was busier than a one-armed waiter, arguing our case with management, while I kept socialising with my Italian friends and eating very good homemade pasta.

One of the Italians I was introduced to was very well known to the task force. He was about the same age as the old godfather, Giovanni, and his name had been mentioned in past royal commissions as being in the upper echelons of the Mafia since the early days. I had read pages of information on him. His name was Pasqueli and I found myself sitting opposite him in a hotel room in Carlton. I had my measly $50 000 in my bag. I felt like an Aussie pimp. He and I were waiting for an underling to bring a sample of cocaine to our hotel room; we started some idle chit-chat. Rosario was sitting with us, talking about his plan to buy into a Melbourne brothel, when out of the blue Pasqueli dropped his plan on the table: he wanted to import a plane-load of marijuana.

Rosario turned the volume up on the television to drown out our voices as they leaned into each other, welcoming my opinion on the subject. I pushed my mobile phone closer, transmitting every juicy word to Vito.

Rosario initially stirred the pot by vouching for me, and Pasqueli said he had already been told that I was 'okay'. Pasqueli explained that they could bring in any amount of marijuana, or cocaine: up to 100 kilos at a time. I sat looking at Pasqueli, feeling a little giddy at the numbers involved, $50 to $100 million worth of cocaine! My mind boggled, amazed at the straightforward way these guys spoke about such high-level criminality, as if they were talking of planting this season's crop of tomatoes. Pasqueli detailed a plan that had obviously been on their drawing board for some time, where they would fly vast amounts of drugs into Australia. There was mention of a partnership of up to six shares, with one share being reserved for the person who could arrange the pilot and plane. Why were they telling me this? My world started to reel; I wasn't sure I wanted to play this game any more. They kept talking, detail after detail.

'Point of no return' fears kept shooting their pangs at me. I tried hard to deflect them, one at a time. As I listened to the start of this grand conspiracy, I felt like leaning into both Pasqueli and Rosario and whispering, 'Sorry guys, I promise not to tell anyone, just fuck off out of here and I won't say anything. The cops can't afford to play in your game; they won't give me any money.'

Of course, my imagined moment came and went as quickly as Rosario drew on his cigarette. The conversation thickened to a conspiracy, with Pasqueli confiding that being Italians and Mafia, they had been unsuccessful in finding a pilot. They desperately needed a pilot. Both men stopped talking for a second, a sort of pregnant pause. Their silence had left the gate in the conversation open; I was standing in front of it, alone, looking at Pasqueli and Rosario.

I looked down at my mobile phone, knowing my audience back at the office would all be urging, 'Come on art dealer, go for it, it's staring at you, grab it … we want it.' I wrestled with myself. Did I walk through their gate or did I turn and walk away? With all the problems we had faced in getting police money authorised to buy drugs, another avenue had just presented itself that could achieve the desired result: serious jail-time for our targets. Why not enter into as large a conspiracy as possible with the Italians? It wasn't a bad compromise. I had but a few seconds to consider my comment.

'I know a dodgy pilot with a small plane,' I said. Rosario and Pasqueli inched closer to me.

Less than an hour later, I was briefing Cody in the basement of our secret warehouse; he was beaming, as were the others. The first thing Sandra said was, 'Thanks mate, another thing we have to work on, you dirty rotten drug dealer.' But they saw my logic.

I was seeing less and less of my crew by now. Obviously we couldn't just catch up for drinks or coffees, so most of our communications were via quick phone calls. There was a fair amount of missing going on, as we'd always been such a tight team. As she was an extremely capable detective, Sandra had been elevated to run the show, and Leigh offered a special friendship during those times. My alienation from my workmates was something that played on my mind at times, sitting every day in my groovy apartment, suffering the sounds of my own voice, and those of Antonio and Rosario, on my transcription machine. It could be enough to drive a man to lone drinking. Leigh had the smarts to sense this isolation, and every now and then he called me in to some quiet little cafe or bar, tucked away in the back streets, and we just sat and chewed the fat.

Cody used this time to discuss finding an undercover operative to play my brother. We agreed we needed someone highly disciplined, able to comprehend the complexity of our investigation—certainly the most difficult undercover operation Australia law enforcement had ever attempted and, potentially, the most dangerous. Sadly, our choices were limited. Some operatives had ongoing workloads; others had already been exposed to Italian organised crime. In the end, we were forced to settle for a young guy with way too big an ego. We hoped that, with input from Cody and me, he might come into our long-term game plan. We named him Ben, and the three of us spent days going over his cover story, prepping him for the moment he walked onto our stage at Griffith. Apart from the long hours of briefing, Ben was swamped with reading the many notebooks and transcripts we had amassed. He had to develop his cover: that of a small-time house renovator and weekend surfie with connections to rock bands. After a couple of weeks, Cody and I looked at each other and gave a silent prayer that my 'brother' would do the right thing by his adopted family, the task force.

Although the Italians hadn't seen Jude since Christmas, they so far accepted the many excuses for her absence. I wanted to see how Ben would perform away from the mirror he kept staring into, so I set up a get-together with Rosario and Rocco at our apartment, to have them meet and break the ice over a wine or two.

The meeting went well. Ben was a little shy, possibly overawed by the occasion. His past investigations had only been nickel-and-dime jobs, but he seemed to take the elevation into the big league okay, throwing in a line here and there and getting a laugh. On the quiet, Rosario asked me how I was going with my pilot mate, I explained that I hadn't had time to work it all out yet, but I'd get back to him, possibly in Griffith the following week. I sensed that Rosario might have been sounding Ben out, trying to spook him, to test his resolve, as he mentioned selling more than 100 kilos of marijuana the previous year in one deal alone. It didn't seem to faze Ben and I thought Rosario started to relax.

The fiasco with the department dragging its heels on finance had actually worked in our favour. Antonio and his men were fairly locked into getting their one tonne of marijuana into the country. They had their minds on bigger fish and forgot that their art dealer mate hadn't come up with the cash required to buy kilo weights of cocaine. It was a peculiar position for an undercover operative to be in, yet one that actually helped, in an odd way.

Twelve months earlier the squirrels had followed Antonio when, like an Italian general, he had travelled south with his band of N'Drangheta in big Ford sedans, a convoy of hardened criminals. They had cut a swathe through the reception crowd at the Old Melbourne Hotel, bee-lining for their room, focused on their meeting to build a massive shed to grow vast quantities of drugs. Now, I was asked to join an identical meeting, with the same players at the same hotel room. It seemed the only difference was that the calendar had moved one year on. I stood in the reception lobby and watched the dusty convoy of Ford sedans swing into the car park and the many soldiers step from the cars. Despite his journey, Antonio looked fresh and alert. The gang, again, cut a swathe through the reception crowd, shook my hand, and moved down the corridor to a waiting room, where we gathered a mass of chairs and sat, and talked, and planned.

'Cole, we have all arranged, our army man in New Guinea is ready in a few months, we need your plane.' Antonio was putting it firmly on my shoulders.

'I'll have it sorted next week.'

'This is our future. We need a good pilot, one to trust,' Antonio stressed.

'He'll be good, this guy's the best.'

'You have the pilot and plane and I give you a sixth part of everything.'

'It's nice work to get. The pilot will be ready soon,' I promised.

Antonio stood and brushed the pleats back into his trousers before he guided me away from the others. Arm around my shoulder, he looked me in the eye.

'My family needs this to work Cole.'

'So do I, Antonio, so do I,' I said as I winked at him.

'Then make it work,' Antonio replied as he squeezed my shoulder blade.

Antonio had just given me one share of the entire scam, which was worth many millions of dollars. A lucky break for law enforcement but his generosity came at a price. The pressure was on to find our pilot. The Italians were to look after the rest: source the drugs, bribe all the officials, pre-sell the drugs, finance the deal and more. They had a guy in the Papua New Guinean army who had a tribe of natives growing 'Buddha sticks' in the hills. Once harvested, the drugs were to be ferried in a fishing boat across the strait from Papua New Guinea to somewhere in the Torres Strait islands, onto a light aircraft, and home to Griffith. It all seemed too easy, too organised, but, after all, it was supposed to be Italian organised crime. It was.

The 'necessity is the mother of invention' rule applied to the Italians this time. The constant spying of satellite cameras on the crops made it increasingly difficult to grow marijuana plantations in Aust-ralia, so they came up with a cost-effective, clever way to maintain their drug supply. All they needed was a shonky pilot and safe plane, and me.

Our Papua New Guinea meetings were like any other business meeting, insofar as we nutted out the whys and wherefores, the obstacles and hurdles that we saw as the plan unfolded. Antonio told us that we needed a 'dry run', a rehearsal. He wanted a few of us to fly the route we were to take and work out our timing, loads and landings.

Cody lost himself at headquarters wading through the personnel files of anyone who listed themselves as a pilot. Labouring over his list, browsing the files, tossing them aside, 'too young', 'too old', 'too police in appearance': there were more pilots on our database than we had realised. On the rejects went, one after another, till we got down to the last three and went door-knocking these possibles. We were scared backwards by the short-back-and-sides haircuts and Hitler moustaches of the first two. We finally lucked onto our man, working in uniform at the Coroner's Court; he was a hobby pilot. After the usual 'hello' at the entry, he sat us down in the modest suburban lounge room of his three-bedroom brick-veneer home, where he lived with a wife and 2.5 kids, a dog and a family station wagon. Once the cups of instant coffee and lamingtons were served, we went straight for the jugular.

'How would you like to work undercover with the Mafia and fly a plane-load of drugs into the country?'

All of a sudden his lamington didn't taste so good, nor did his coffee. He wiped the dribbled coffee from his chin, as he asked to see our identification again. He had the oddest appearance for a cop, looking a bit like Zig, the clown from the Zig and Zag kids' television program that started in the 1950s. I nicknamed him Ziggy and he fell into the gig as our pilot. He was that sort of guy; I figured he must have been waiting half a lifetime for two crazy men to come knocking on his door with this wild and absurd proposition. We laughed about it for years later. I was so pleased, as I considered him one of the nicest cops I had ever met. Ziggy only took a couple of days to loosen up. He made copious notes on what the Italians had been asking and went about his aeronautical calculations, working out the type of plane we'd need, based on the loads, number of people in the aircraft and distance between fuel stops.

Within the week I was ready to face another meeting with our Italians, going through my paperwork, planning another trip to Griffith. I was startled by a ring on the doorbell at my apartment, a sound that always scared the living daylights out of me. After all, none of my friends ever knew the address, and the task force detectives were banned from visiting. The buzzer meant it could only be Antonio or his team, or someone with ill will who had worked out who I really was.

I was caught with the bedroom's secret panel open and all the tapes and books out, strewn over the bed. Startled, I went into fast motion, scrambling all my covert writings and tapes back into the hole. The buzzer kept ringing. I got to the front door trying desperately to look poised, feeling sheer relief as I opened it to the postman, asking for a signature. Rosario had been having trouble with his driver's licence in Victoria and had asked if he could use my address for his new licence. Of course, I said he could.

The postman handed it across and Cole Goodwin did his best moniker. As I looked at the sealed envelope addressed to Rosario, I thought it was a bit of a hoot. I closed the front door and sat on my lounge studying the envelope, turning it over a few times, putting it up to the light and giving it the once over. It looked fine. I wasn't really expecting to find anything odd about a cover letter and driver's licence. What had aroused my interest was the emblematic significance of sharing an address with one of the country's most active Italian organised crime figures; two opposites, with two contradictory view-points on the position of right and wrong.

That one simple envelope would forever represent the absolute achievement of our infiltration, more so than any drug deal we might share in our criminal future. Over and above any corrupt plane trip we may join forces on, to Papua New Guinea or any other far-away location. Well above the hundreds of tapes Vito, Jude and I eventually translated and transcribed, producing the many thousands of pages that would help a jury to understand how completely we infiltrated these crooks. The driver's licence would always prove the absolute success of our endeavours to penetrate the N'Drangheta in Australia. I wanted so badly to souvenir that licence, to hide it in a biscuit tin and bury it under earth somewhere safe, so that, when all the cops-and-robbers bullshit was well and truly over, when all the Italians had long gone to jail, when I had freed myself from the clutches of the police depart-ment, I might one day dig up my biscuit tin and look at that licence.

I held the envelope in my hands for perhaps an hour, letting my memory drift back to the first time I walked into Rodney's office, and the manner in which I was ordered to conduct this investigation. My mind wandered further: back to the Walsh Street days, bumping into other major investigations on its journey, past Karmein. Then again to the morning the two young constables were murdered. I saw myself standing on the road, shocked, angry and frustrated, with the sun coming up.

There still wasn't a day that went by when I didn't think of those two strapping young cops, at least for a second or two, and their mothers. Then I drifted back to the many times I had stood in the house of death with Dennis and watched the confidence glow from his bewhiskered face. Eventually, I locked onto the most shocking of all my memories, the slumped corpse of the cubicle girl, drained of life and blood. My mind held on that atrocious image for a time. Rosario's personal mail was now looking slightly the worse for wear.

I wondered whether that envelope and its plastic authority to drive a motor car represented my greatest achievement to date. Or whether it was in fact my greatest-ever failing. I questioned my own sanity, asking why I allowed myself to take on this investigation. By the time I had placed the envelope on the kitchen counter, propped up against the spice rack, I realised that the letter would, in a day or two, find its way into Rosario's wallet. I also realised that no matter what memories I might have that haunted me, or how far Rodney's ambition went, there was nothing I could do to change what the future held for me or anyone else.

I decided that I didn't want to open my secret panel any more for the day or make any more notes. I rang Connie and asked if she felt like a long lunch at a sidewalk restaurant; I could be around to collect her shortly. She seemed happy for the surprise, so I checked out of my police life for the night and stared into the eyes of a lady who had the capability of making me forget everything, at least for a while.

17

MY DISHRAG BODY

It was high time that my young brother got the budget tour of Griffith, so I threw him in the car and headed off to deliver the licence to Rosario. On the way up on the highway I went into great detail about the need to be in undercover mode twenty-four hours a day with these guys, even when they weren't in our company. No amount of relaxed mode was permissible. Brother Ben was flippant, believing the Italians would never catch him with his guard down.

Rosario had arranged our same hotel and we settled in. I was armed with aeronautical charts of the far north Queensland region and information on all the airstrips, at least enough to help make the vital decision about where the plane would land to meet the fishing boat full of marijuana. I was actually starting to feel like a shifty drug importer! Rosario was reluctant; something was bothering him. He brushed aside the charts and any discussion, suggesting instead we rest in our room and catch up over dinner. Then he left us alone; I knew instantly something was not right. Ben and I sat back and took the time for unwanted rest. Every now and again Ben paced the room; he was full of nerves and way too much energy.

'What's happening with these wogs?'

'Shhh, Ben.'

'What's happening, what are these dumb-arse wogs up to Cole?'

'Shhh, someone will hear you.'

'Who, they're only greasy wogs, take it easy.'

Ben's put-downs of our targets continued as he strode. I suffered a few hours of his inability to sit still and his constant ridicule of our targets. Each time I managed to silence him. As I finally lay back, about to drift off to sleep, Vito rang my phone, whispering down the line. As briefly as he could he explained that he had translated various mobile phone calls between Antonio and others and apparently there was a listening device inside our room, the Italians were listening to Ben's and my conversation. He warned that things could get dangerous; they were talking about us as if we were snitches.

I hung up and walked over to Ben, grabbing him by the collar and pulling him into me, whispering close to one ear: 'Shut the fuck up, they're listening to us.' I pointed to my phone and mouthed, 'Vito'. Ben went as white as a sheet, his head flicking around the room as he tried to comprehend the seriousness of our situation. He finally found the respect he needed. After a few winks to each other, we spoke fondly of our Italian friends, mentioning how 'smart' they were and how our pilot, Ziggy, would do a fine job with the plane, and anything else that might go well to prying ears.

That night, we sat down to another magnificent dinner at Antonio's restaurant, although the atmosphere was still somewhat cool. Vito called during the main meal with a worrying update; someone was in our room, searching through our bags. I knew we were safe there. I winked at Ben and he understood the game was still on. We offered nothing on the importation, just enjoyed their hospitality and laughed and ate. Our Italian hosts offered even less, as if they were going through the motions.

The real test would come two hours later back at our hotel. When we arrived back, Rosario suggested we visit another room he had booked for the night. It was odd, a local booking a room for himself, but hey, we just had to go with the flow. We moved into Rosario's room and were met by a couple of cheap smiles from two girls who were maybe twenty-one years old. Neither of them could be described as a beauty, yet they were pretty enough—just country hicks, really, you could tell by the cheap way they dressed. Rosario explained they were working girls. It evolved during conversation that both were locals, bored out of their brains, and the Italians had suggested they open up a brothel in town, to service the needs of the equally bored. They were really only junior burgers in a bigger and nastier game; they just didn't know it yet.

There was a knock on the door; it was the entire gang. Everyone I had met, dined with and had fun with over the past year, and not one of them smiled. One by one they filed into the room, crowding our space, none of them taking any notice of the female flesh on offer. Ben and I found ourselves surrounded by wall-to-wall N'Drangheta. This was a game of intimidation in play. Quite deliberately, no-one had much to say, they just stared in an obviously rehearsed move. I started to think of ways to escape; something was seriously wrong here. I tried to deflect the mood, to appear oblivious to the designed tension and create a few laughs. The feeling was so odd, so remote from any-thing friendly. Each of the men held their stare as Ben and I sat trapped on the two beds, nowhere to run. Ben was looking decidedly uneasy, as was I, willing to run, but knowing we had to stay and withstand the test.

Antonio's brother finally told the two prostitutes to leave, which they did, scuttling off to parts unknown, slamming the door hard on their way out. Antonio then went out onto the balcony and spoke seriously to Rosario. They glanced back at me mid-way though their chat, as if looking at an enemy, and shook their heads. Something was bothering them, and as much as they tried to look calm, in control, they looked like two men working a scam, and we were the scam. I ran the palms of both hands over my trousers, cleaning the sweat away, as fear gripped me. Ben went white again.

The nine men spoke in their Calabrian dialect as they looked us up and down, delivering more intimidation before, one by one, each man left the room, leaving Rosario, who didn't even look at me as he accepted a wink from Antonio on his way out also. The only word I could make out in all the theatre was *puttana*, Italian for prostitute. I realised what was happening; they were going to call the girls in, to soften us up. There's a rule in undercover work that, should you find yourself in a sexual situation with a criminal, undercover officers are not to have sex. The operative is required to deflect any sexual advance so as to not compromise the integrity of the investigation or the organisation he works for. Rosario bought the *puttani* into the room again and suggested Ben and I have sex with the girls. He then left, to a massive silence between two men and two apprentice prostitutes.

Obviously the 'not having sex at work rule' was written by a dill. One who had never been in a room full of N'Drangheta, or had a listening device transmitting their every word. Or had their room, bags and car searched by the Mafia. Or had ever felt a frightful sense of vulnerability and veiled danger such as existed that night in our hotel, surrounded by nine dark-haired unshaven men who had lost their sense of humour.

Ben and I had sex with the two prostitutes: quick, dull and unfulfilling sex. It would be the only sex I have ever had to preserve my personal safety. I played the Italian game, as did Ben, who toddled off to our room to prove his manhood. As I was lying on the bed immediately after, my girl, Regina, fussed with her hair. Peeping in the mirror, she spoke for the first time.

'You're nice, Cole. How come you and your brother know Ross and Tony?'

'They buy art from me, I'm an art dealer.'

'Cool, I like art; I want to be a painter one day.'

'Bet you do.'

There was a pause as she wrestled with her bob.

'You know, you're nice. Ross must be interested in you and your art then.'

'What makes you think that?'

'He wants me to tell him everything you did and everything you said.'

It was starting to make good sense.

'He must want to buy more of my art. He's a great guy, and Antonio, "clever".'

'Yeah, that's right, clever … I guess, yeah clever. You're nice though, Cole.'

I hate that word 'nice'. Both girls walked out of our lives as quickly as they had walked in. I wandered back to my room and met Ben, who looked equally unimpressed. Still, we knew the game and played a series of compliments into the hidden microphones, waffling on about how 'clever' the Italians were, and how much we 'enjoyed their company'. Once I'd put enough compliments into the night, I took the longest hot shower, listening to the snores of my young brother. During the night I took a call from a worried Sandra, hoping we were all right. She mentioned the boss was ropeable, believing that we may have had sex with the prostitutes; I was going to be dealt with when I returned. I only wished those criticising could have been in our shoes that night.

As I lay on top of my bed, staring at one or two silhouettes that highlighted an otherwise dark room, I wondered about this game of cops and robbers that had occupied my life for more than fourteen years. I tried desperately to understand why I disliked the company I worked for, yet loved the work I did. I wondered what it was that caused me to be addicted to scenarios that were both dangerous and exhilarating. Was it still a simple case of wanting to do better than my own father, to excel in my chosen career? Or was there some underlying subconscious drive to be 'good', as my Ma used to say? I felt sure the cubicle girl no longer claimed ownership of my professional exuberance. Maybe it was all of these ingredients. Or, as I came to be more satisfied with, maybe it had much to do with my earlier life with Titch; playing artful dodgers in the bad streets of Melbourne, keeping one step ahead of the rotten elements in town. There was fun in that game, when I thought back to it, being able to outsmart the street-smart ones. And there was an odd tinge of fun in the current infiltration game I played, again, being one step ahead of the rotten. All very well, as long as my game didn't swallow me up, didn't end before my final siren was due.

As daylight snuck into the room and my edginess faded, I was left thinking about management's focus on the sex-with-prostitutes issue, over and above the safety of two men alone in a town where people disappeared so easily. My thoughts frustrated me, keeping me awake to hear the roosters calling dawn. That morning Ben and I had just finished a country hotel breakfast and walked to our room when we noticed our door ajar. We peeped into the room and found Rosario's brother, mid-way through the act of standing up, placing something into his pocket. He was at the bar fridge and had obviously been squatting down; he was well and truly startled.

'Good morning *compadre*, how'd you get in here?' I said in a friendly way.

'The door was open, I was waiting for you, just wanted a drink of milk.'

I never did ask him what he had placed in his pocket, nor did I show any interest, knowing that Vito would pick up on the shenanigans later in the phone calls. Instead, I played the vague art dealer, back from breakfast.

'What's happening this morning?' I asked.

'Antonio wants to talk about the plane now.'

And so we did. Our tables had turned overnight. The room swelled with Calabrians, this time carrying smiles and backslapping, and there was a renewed vigour in discussing the importation of marijuana from Papua New Guinea. I threw the aeronautical maps onto the bed and the meeting went into a planning frenzy. We were back in business.

Whatever tests our Italians had conjured, we had passed. Whatever concerns our Italians had, we had laid them to rest. If their concern was Ben, they were now relaxed, willing to move to home base. After the meeting, my brother and I hit the road to Melbourne, knowing that for three days we had suffered the strongest scrutiny we could have endured. Rosario's brother had been removing a listening device from behind the bar fridge. Despite their efforts, we had come out on top. I hoped our relationship was now galvanised. Sadly for Ben, he was anything other than galvanised; he was mostly shattered by the Italians' cunning. He lost all confidence and drifted nervously through the rest of his limited role in the job.

Our conspiracy was fattening, with our Calabrian mates steering us towards Horn Island, an Aboriginal settlement in the Torres Strait, above the tip of Queensland: a 5-hour flight over the jungles of the Cape York Peninsula that boasted infestations of crocodiles and giant mosquitoes.

It was the closest Australian soil to Papua New Guinea. Antonio paid for hiring the plane and pushed for a dry run. In typical Mafia style, he wasn't fussed about meeting the pilot, believing Rosario could check him out. They decided on the Cohuna airstrip to land the contraband near Griffith, and Rosario would have four or five of his men there to unload the marijuana. We settled on a Navajo Chieftain twin-prop aircraft, a fourteen-seater. We needed a plane that size to fit the tonne of marijuana inside, once the seats were removed. In effect, what we were seeking was a very sophisticated plane able to land on a short airstrip in the dead of night, then, once loaded, fly out of the jungle at full weight and leapfrog home via two fuel stops. Our Italians were asking a lot, but then again, drug importers tend to take massive risks. As Antonio handed over $15000 in hiring fees, our game was running at full speed. The rest was up to us: to hire our plane and meet in Cairns in a week, so we could all go to see Horn Island.

It was a joy to see Ziggy sprinting through his work, finding an aeronautically worthy Navajo Chieftain aircraft, then negotiating the hire time and insurances. Once he had the plane, he needed the required tutorial to be legally capable, under the civil aviation laws, to fly the damn thing. Ziggy and I were having enormous fun, in a strange and legal sort of way. Our week of peak-hour work madness was halfway along when we were delivered a very rude awakening.

Geoffrey Bowen was the leader of the Adelaide arm of the NCA investigation into Italian organised crime. He too was reporting back to the parliamentary committee on the existence of the Mafia in his state. He had been working at a frantic pace, having charged a gang of hard-nosed Italians, mostly N'Drangheta. One in particular, whom Geoffrey had fingered as the main man, was facing trial for cultivating a massive marijuana crop. He was a man known for extreme violence, and he had developed an unhealthy dislike for Geoffrey.

On 2 March 1994, the day Ziggy received his ticket to fly the Navajo Chieftain, Geoffrey was accepting a parcel at his office. He opened it in company with his legal officer, a lawyer assisting him in his court cases. The parcel exploded. The entire floor of the NCA building was gutted, blown into the street eleven floors below. Staff and furnishings were tossed from one side of the building to the other; most workers sustained injuries. Geoffrey was killed, after suffering horrific burns. The bomb was made of red phosphorus, the stuff of match heads. It ignites instantly and burns with obscenely ferocious results. The lawyer suffered third-degree burns to his body and would lose body parts to plastic surgery.

Geoffrey had been my contemporary. With his death the landscape was very different, and we had to win, to crush the Mafia. Geoffrey and I had been each other's yardsticks, sharing the same endeavour to achieve the most basic and somewhat naive of all law enforcement philosophies: to see good triumph over evil. Twins in this aspect, I had good reason to wonder if perhaps we would end up twins in other respects. He was now alongside his only true contemporary, the brave Donald Mackay.

Absolute terror was delivered to the NCA investigation that day, causing us all to wake in fright, to consider who we were and what the fuck we were all involved with. The entire national NCA investigative effort stopped on that day, reducing us all to walking, disbelieving numbness. I sat alone in my apartment flicking through the television channels.

Two days in law enforcement can sometimes feel like an eternity. That's what I thought as I pondered the NCA bombing and chewed my fingernails down to their quicks. I was in Cairns, about to head even further north. I sucked in my gut as I searched for a little courage before this next venture. I felt naked as I wandered the passenger terminal at Cairns International Airport without a weapon. The humidity caused my hair to fall flat and my shirt to glue itself to my back. I had made my way up the east coast in the Navajo Chieftain to meet Rosario and two unknown thugs. Stress was ripping its pain across my shoulder blades. The end was near, I knew. I could almost smell it—and my armpits. I ached for that final day when I could walk away from my Italian targets and reopen the doors to my life.

As I paced the airport lounge I glimpsed an Italian-looking guy walking around, sneaking an occasional peek at me. I pretended not to notice him as he surveyed my every move, a big, powerful-looking man who obviously had a gym membership. He was standing with a sinfully fit-looking black guy, as black as midnight in a Melbourne winter. I reckoned these two belonged to Rosario and had decided to watch me through the crowd. It took me back to my own surveillance days at the secret squirrels, so I walked the entire length of the lounge area, just playing with them. I turned back on them occasionally and enjoyed their amateur attempts to look nonchalant. It was fun without a smile.

When Rosario disembarked from his Qantas flight into the jungle heat of the high tropics, we both said our hellos. He was full of business and airline food. He spat out an instruction that we'd no longer use mobile phones, just in case the cops were tracking them. I smiled inside myself again; he frowned. We slowly walked and talked, heads down, as his black and white sidekicks followed behind, like a couple of mugs in a B-grade movie.

Rosario went over his plan constantly until he was satisfied all was well, then broke his stride and called his two mates over to introduce them and we shook hands. The white one was Jim, a Calabrian tough, the number-two player in the Sydney N'Drangheta. Harley was the

Papua New Guinean army man, a sergeant in civilian clothing, whose contacts at home were growing the Buddha sticks. My first impressions held for the rest of my long day: two hard, streetwise blokes, not at all prone to small talk. I was in bad company.

A short taxi ride and we were at the private jet terminal, with the Navajo Chieftain parked, fuelled and ready to fly. I introduced the Mafia and Papua New Guinean contingent to Ziggy and Ben. We all bailed into our very fast twin-prop jet. So far, so good, nothing suspected.

We got on with vouching for each other, telling gangster stories (as you do, when you first meet), and before long Ziggy pulled our door shut and kicked some life into the engine. He seemed to be enjoying his role as an unshaven mosquito-coast drug runner. He threw me the quickest wink and hit the runway with full throttle. We were off!

Rosario and his men relaxed, mentally counting their millions, as we headed towards Horn Island. Our journey took two and a half hours, allowing me far too much time to go over the deal. Every so often I spied Jim staring at me, as if he was trying to look inside me. 'Crook's paranoia,' I guessed. Rosario caught him out once and calmed him down, telling him I was 'a trusted man'. He chilled out somewhat and went back to spotting crocodiles from high above.

The only comfort I had was a loaded .32 pistol hidden somewhere in the stuffing of a seat, just in case the shit hit the fan. The trouble was no-one had bothered to tell me which seat. I prayed that Jim or the army sergeant wouldn't find it. I also wondered what the army sergeant was carrying in his kitbag; it looked awfully heavy for a lunch box. Otherwise, it was high-altitude flying, with no cabin service and with Rosario and Jim's chatter to replace any inflight entertainment. I had to stop myself from contemplating a worst-case scenario, should things go wrong at 15 000 feet. I was never one for skydiving.

During our flight Rosario became lost in the moment. He seemed to enjoy sitting up, gazing across Australia. As he looked down at the rich greens and olive colours of the bush below, he opened up and talked freely, probably for the first time since I had known him. Usually, he was a serious dude who handed out orders and worried over the 'family', crops being pinched by the cops and new frontiers that had to be opened, yet today, for once, he started to drop his guard.

We discussed every twist and turn of the plan so that the hidden microphones could transmit it all back to Melbourne. I was able to ignore my usual money-laundering talk and realised I had them cold, in the bag. As of that instant, we had enough evidence to lock our targets away for many years for a massive conspiracy. The rest would be icing on my cake. The peculiar mix of stress and anxiety I had been surviving on over the last year or so lifted, temporarily.

Rosario told me his 'family' was importing 100 kilograms of cocaine. They had arranged most of it, with the shipment coming via Canada and America. He had a Calabrian cousin flying in to discuss the finer details. With as much pride as a passing student on graduation day, Rosario mentioned he had met the head godfather in Calabria some years earlier. It had been a proud moment for him; he was smitten. I seized the moment, knowing that I had Rosario's ear. I was feeling supremely confident and needed to know a secret only he or Antonio could reveal. I leant into his body odour.

'What's all this business … about bombing the police?' I asked, meaning the NCA bombing.

'The guy that got it, he hit one of our guys hard. It's only revenge,' he uttered without a twitch.

'Who did he hit?'

'One of our guys in Adelaide.'

'Aren't there a few people dead?'

'No, only one, the guy who hit our guy,' he said, in a very knowing voice.

Rosario then silenced me on the subject. Too late, I thought; he had said enough. I would ask him more some other time, maybe, when his head was in the clouds again. That's how it went in this sort of work, getting snippets of information at a time.

All of a sudden Horn Island was in sight, and the Papua New Guinea mainland was just beyond. The scenery was out of this world, beautiful, so astonishingly remote. I heard the screech of our tyres and the plane surged forward as Ziggy brought our jet into a perfect landing. We had arrived at the smallest airport in the hottest location imaginable. Ziggy freed our door to allow our stench to escape, along with the five of us. Ben headed off to smoke a pack of cigarettes and the rest of us milled around, looking conspicuous at trying to be inconspicuous.

Ziggy busied himself refuelling the plane as we discussed the logistics of handling a tonne of contraband. The army sergeant kept his heavy bag close at hand as Jim pointed here and there and slowly worked out the plan. Everyone was nodding: 'Yes sir, no sir, one plane full sir.' It didn't take long for us to decide that three-quarters of a tonne was the maximum possible load if we were to achieve a faster turnaround time. Our chosen airport was a customs port with a lone 24-hour guard in place. Rosario vowed to kill him if he interfered. Things were mighty thick by now.

Harley took particular notice of the distance from the airstrip to the edge of the island, where his men would arrive at 5 a.m. with a boatful of Buddha sticks. He was talking of using a fishing boat with a quiet motor and a dozen hands on board that could load our plane in double-quick time. Once we had answered all our own questions, Ziggy fired up his jet engines again. It was time to go home and undertake the final preparations. It was time for Harley to fly to Papua New Guinea. A few hours later, we landed back at Cairns airport, where we split up and went our separate ways; a move Rosario thought would shake off any cops who might be watching.

Our flight home in the Navajo Chieftain was without our conspirator mates and Ben, who had gone missing with a headache, flying comfortably home with Qantas; he was in Melbourne in a few hours. The young bloke was struggling; I only hoped it was not too obvious to the Italians.

Ziggy and I would spend two days trekking home, refuelling the plane every five hours. We enjoyed a boys' night in the cowboy town of Charleville, accepting the fine country hospitality of a local hotelier, free of obligations, microphones, prying ears and too many demands. The only real pressure we had was on which pretty cowgirl, in tight jeans and Cuban heels, would get our attention. We sat back to a slow-cooked meal and a bottle of Heathcote shiraz as I got to know my pilot a little better; I liked him for his part-time dash at my work, and his bravery. I also learned he was a man with a sense of humour, reminding me I hadn't laughed in well over a year.

Back in Melbourne, it was time to transcribe more tapes and fill another notebook, but the moment I opened the front security door to the apartment, I knew something was very wrong. My front door was ajar, just slightly. I dropped my bag and backed away across the road to sit in the park and call Cody, who arrived in no time. Now I had Dirty Harry with me, I felt a lot safer going back. We searched meticulously through every room. Cody called a forensic locksmith who snuck into my apartment via the back gate to offer his opinion on the break-in.

He said my lock had been professionally picked; there were minute scratches on each of the pins. The four screws holding the face plate over the fireplace cavity in the lounge room had been removed; the paint was missing from the screw heads. None of the covert cameras had been tampered with, nor any of the secret listening devices. And luckily, none of the documents, still hidden under the floorboards, had been found; my precious notebooks that would send the N'Drangheta to jail. It appeared an intruder had gained entry, snooped around enough to earn his fee, then left, unable to relock the door.

Another test, another level of scrutiny, another day in my life, a life that had become saturated with pressure. Ben, too, was feeling the pressure, possibly on a far greater scale. The young undercover bloke was in real strife. Little did I know at the time, but apparently he had gotten so worried for his own safety that one night he had placed his handgun to his head and thought long and hard about shooting himself. He anguished for weeks; his fears of Mafia retribution had overtaken him and he had withdrawn into himself, telling no-one but his psychologist. My reactions took a different turn. I thought back to the Walsh Street days: the bomb threat, the death threat, Annitia's decision to leave, even Chelsea's decision to leave home … this type of work leaves its mark. The very real threat of payback violence haunts all undercover operatives—in some ways, I understood Ben completely. But I had experienced other things that Ben hadn't; the lack of results for Walsh Street and Karmein also haunted me. I desperately wanted—needed—a win.

The hierarchy had decided to allow the undercover purchase of drugs, at least in quantities that would ensure our targets received substantial jail sentences. Somehow Cody had convinced the dills from the top floor to cough up the money. Thank God there was a controller on the job.

Over the next few weeks, to break the monotony of transcribing tapes, I took Ben under my wing, to try to settle him down. First, we took a drive to Griffith to catch up with my Italian mates, and purchased six kilos of 'skunk weed' for $50 000. It was the highest-grade marijuana, buried in massive blue plastic tubs between the orange groves on Rosario's farm. Once we were given the drugs, we smuggled them back over the border, dodging the highway patrol cars along our way in true drug-runner fashion.

The next week I drove alone to a house in Fawkner, in Melbourne's northern suburbs, with $185 000 of marked police money, to buy pure cocaine worth a million dollars in street value. It was part of a 10-kilogram shipment that had just arrived. I met the N'Drangheta in a rear garage of the house they had 'borrowed' for the night and felt completely safe. I enjoyed such a high level of trust by this stage that I had lost fear. The exchange was done after some fine Calabrese hospitality in the front of the house with a small group—some of whom I had not met before—sharing olives and a glass of wine.

Another time the N'Drangheta arrived in Melbourne unannounced, offering me 100 kilograms of marijuana. To tease me into buying, they gave me three huge garbage bags of the drug before offering the entire crop, worth well over $10 million. They suggested I take it on consignment and pay them back in the weeks to come. The offer was so tempting, if only more money were available. Cody and I convened an urgent meeting in the basement of our Collingwood warehouse. We pleaded for the money and for the necessary authority to purchase some or all of the entire crop on offer. Despite the predictable refusal, the evidence was taped and was hidden away for another day, for our day in court. A few weeks later, I received another visit from the N'Drangheta, this time offering 1.6 tonnes of marijuana. It was so much choof that I couldn't even be bothered to work out how many millions of dollars the load was worth. It was the end of the harvest and drying season and it was all getting ridiculous, with offer after offer coming at me!

We realised that we had purchased, spoken about, sampled and taken possession of enough drugs to end the run of almost the entire cell of the Griffith N'Drangheta. What remained was the importation of the three-quarters of a tonne of Buddha sticks, and the possibility of 100 kilograms of pure cocaine being imported via America. Tactically, the cocaine importation had to go by the wayside. We didn't have any arrival dates and the Italians were pressuring us to be ready, at a moment's notice, to fly to Horn Island and collect the shipment. As winter arrived, we waited.

I was sitting at home with headphones glued to my head, frantically trying to keep pace with my transcriptions, when my house phone rang. It was Big Bird from Sydney.

'You've managed to break free of the Sydney crims to call lucky me, got more bad news?' I said, knowing he only ever had rotten news.

'You've got a shipment of Buddha sticks coming in soon.'

'Trust in you ... how'd you know?'

'Who doesn't? Too many bosses down your way bragging about it.'

I knew Big Bird had more to say; he was just waiting for the moment.

'There's been another shooting,' he said.

'Fuck. Tell me.'

'Another Italian, in Griffith. They thought he was a snitch, held him down and put a shotgun to the back of his knee. Blew his leg completely off.'

'Was he a crook?'

'Oh yeah, one of their own, he'll survive, missing a leg though.'

'Was he the snitch?'

'You know that answer. Stay safe, you fool. I'm waiting for that drink you keep promising.'

Having dropped the phone, I poured a red wine and sat alone on Jude's comfy couch, pondering Big Bird's call. By now one man was dead, riddled with shotgun pellets; his only sin appeared to be that he had been mistaken for a snitch. Now another Italian had felt the bloody violence of a shotgun, his bocce-playing days well over. It was getting way too serious. Yet, despite the violence that clouded my landscape, I was still driven by the need to be successful. Quitting, or failure, could never be an option. Not after the years of emptiness that had followed Walsh Street. My thoughts then turned to concern, for Jude. I saw an image of her, sitting cosily on this same couch, legs tucked up under herself, as she did on the days we planned the moves in our sting: a mix of dedication, perseverance and easy-on-the-eye looks. Even though she was now removed from the equation, I couldn't help but worry whether the violence might descend on her as well. Would it follow both of us, once the proverbial shit hit the fan and the Italians were all locked away? It had been so easy for us to ignore the potential dangers as we savoured the flavours of Antonio's good company and fine food. I was now aching for the end of the job to come round.

In Calabrian terms, waiting also meant staying in touch and talking. Italians love to talk, to work out every iota of a plan, and so we would all get together, in secret, with my mobile phone listening device capturing every word.

In Griffith I was asked by a respected member of the Calabrian community, their local doctor, to value some art works. My lifetime hobby was being tested. The good doctor showed me a watercolour painting by the Belgian artist Jules Marie Armand Goethals, painted in 1868. The picture was in excellent condition, a pretty depiction of a small village; sadly the doctor thought it was worth a small fortune. I didn't know the artist but I knew enough to know watercolours fetch meagre prices compared to oils, especially when the picture is of a European village. I assessed the value at about $200. I followed up my valuation with an appraisal from Sotheby's; the picture was valued at 'up to $300'. I was glad to get it right and Rosario seemed mildly pleased, as if the valuation was really meant to be of myself.

During this waiting period, I was informed by Antonio that a cousin of theirs was coming to Australia from Calabria, the purpose of his visit being to root out the snitch. The cousin had considerable experience, Antonio continued, in eliminating these sorts of problems in the home country. His abilities, prior to his arrival, were spoken of with an almost princely reverence. My heart sank; I felt the need to be anywhere but involved in a covert investigation against the Mafia. The only positive was that at least I was aware of the cousin, and his plan. Our team at the task force all provided fabulous support, tracking the tough guy's movements into and subsequently around Australia, before he finally settled in Griffith. He was a hard man in his early thirties who had a history in Calabria involving serious drug trafficking and links to several murders.

I figured, with all my visits to Griffith, that the new hard man and I were bound to meet up at some stage and, sure enough, one night, he walked into Antonio's restaurant and sat down opposite me. His steely face looked me over critically as we greeted. It was the oddest of feelings to come face to face with a man who unknowingly had just shaken hands with his quarry. I conjured a nickname the Italians were never aware of: Hades, the god of the underworld. His knowledge of the English language was limited and our conversation was sporadic, but we did share a meal with Antonio and the others. From what I could understand he had been working all day in the orange groves, which did not seem to be to his taste. Despite the tone of complaint in his voice and general demeanour, he was very respectful to Antonio, who thankfully vouched for me, using the easily recognisable Italian words *amici*, *va bene*, *forte* and others. I kept the role-play going as best I could, despite the anxiety pulsing through me, working the table in a relaxed good humour, hoping to make the same impression on him as I had on the others. Especially as I was unarmed.

I ended up having dinner with my very own personal hit-man on one other occasion as well as seeing him twice over the coming months at Antonio's home. We were always pleasant to each other and thankfully nothing more evolved. Hades would never come to know of the massive impact he had on my life for many years.

Sometime later I met Antonio's accountant under the guise of laundering money through my art consultancy. Through the accountant I became privy to many secrets to do with the land and houses his clients owned. He unwittingly spoke of overstating the value of art works to hide the real black money for his clients. We saved him up for a rainy day, so he could get a stern visit from taxation investigators once our job was over.

Even though I sometimes struggled with my lot as a result of my infiltration of the Mafia, I'd often think back to Donald Mackay's ordeal. He had been the lone voice in a desert town at a time when politicians were too busy to listen or act. I often pondered his disappearance and subsequent murder. It kept me focused and was a thought that I shared with no-one. It was about this time I was introduced to Barbara Mackay, his widow. Bizarrely, like so many others, she had become aware of my infiltration work and we had a private conversation. I can still hear her soft, inquiring voice. She asked if I could try to find out anything about her husband's last day, for reasons of closure. I did try to talk his death into conversations with my targets, only to be told I was a 'sticky-nose'. I never learned anything of value. I failed on that score. I only wish I could have returned something to someone who had suffered so much.

It had been more than six months since our Italian friends had seen Jude, although they often talked about her. It was convenient that I had found myself totally absorbed in criminal activity, thereby offering the best excuse possible for not having Jude with me on my visits to Griffith. Still, she was always mentioned and it was important to reinforce the charade that she still existed. To this end we staged an engagement party to keep my cover story alive. We actually booked the Old Melbourne's reception area for our grand night for Sunday, 31 July, 'an informal cocktail party'. I hand-delivered an invitation to each of our Italian friends, written in Jude's handwriting, and they all promised to be there, with equally grand gifts!

Cody and I had figured our work might be complete by the end of July, so we'd never have to actually get engaged, which was a shame. I liked Jude and missed her very much. Still, her boyfriend may have had trouble with her accepting my promise of marriage.

A few days before our scheduled engagement party, at half-past five on a cold, rainy, mid-winter morning, I received a phone call from Rosario's mobile. He was standing at my front door, waiting to be let in. I'd made an error in judgement by spending the night with Connie, who coincidentally lived only two blocks away and still had no idea what I was up to. I sprinted out the door and was around at my own apartment in five minutes, telling him Jude was in Sydney with her dying mother and I had spent the night with an old girlfriend nearby. Rosario laughed, assuring me that he wouldn't say a word to Jude. He was carrying guns and Rocco was with him.

The importation couldn't come quickly enough; every week the Italians asked me to take more cocaine. The constant pressure to continually buy was starting to take effect. Undercover work is truly a game of 'put up or shut up'; once you put your head in the ring and you gain acceptance, it's time to play. I had reached the required level of acceptance, now I needed the cash to bankroll the drug purchases. The Italians would never understand that the police department didn't have any money left. With my wishing-well of bullshit almost dried up, my credibility was saved by the Papua New Guinean importation.

Rosario and Rocco sat down in my apartment, mentioning they had promised a couple of handguns and a machine gun to Harley and they wanted the guns hidden on our plane: a .38 revolver and an M1 Carbine military-assault weapon. They handed them over. Rosario spoke about Lindsay, who was to travel with me on the drug run. It transpired that Lindsay had been Rosario's trump card, tucked away until the final day. He was Harley's brother-in-law and the go-between to the Sydney Italians. He was waiting at the Old Melbourne Hotel to meet us at nine in the morning, and our tickets to Cairns were booked.

Lindsay and I were to fly by commercial aircraft to Cairns and meet up with Ziggy. The guns would travel on the Navajo Chieftain, which would be stripped of its seats. From Cairns, Lindsay and I would fly with Qantas to Weipa, a remote town and Aboriginal settlement south of Horn Island, where we'd meet Ziggy and then all make our way to Horn Island, arriving at dawn when Harley should be putt-putting along with a boatload of drugs. Easy, I thought. Fabulous, Rosario thought.

I had a couple of hours to see anyone special in my life, pack a bag and get ready. I raced through the city traffic, back to Connie's apartment, only to find she had already gone to work. I rang Chelsea at home and her phone rang out. I could only guess she had knocked off late the night before with her chef's job and was getting some serious sleep. I wandered back to my apartment to shower, and hit a wall of sheer loneliness, riddled with 'what ifs'. What if something went wrong and I never got to see Chelsea again? What if … I silenced my negativity, before catching the final briefing by Cody at our secret basement headquarters. There was a cast of dozens in attendance.

Rodney had the chair; he was in full flight. I was in a rush and interrupted, asking one favour; a very simple, yet important, favour: 'Complete radio silence at Horn Island; the white noise will scare them away.'

I doubt whether anyone took any notice as the briefing rambled on about a mess of stuff my head didn't need to hear just then. Cody dragged me away, making sure he and I had some quality time. I would say goodbye to him in minutes and be on my own for the next three days. Again I pleaded for radio silence, reminding Cody how remote Horn Island was, and that any use of police radios would be picked up by the smugglers' boat radio. He promised to pass it back.

With time running short, I hiked it to the Old Melbourne. As a handy bonus, I negotiated for half a kilo of 'pure' cocaine to be collected by Ben in two days' time while I was away; just the right amount of drugs to tickle the jury on our day in court. Now, there was nothing to do but to meet Lindsay and to end this job.

Lindsay was sitting inside the hotel room, a knockabout sort of a bloke, the type who would be in a shit sandwich if given a chance. We took to each other instantly; we both had years of vouching on our sides. He'd be the one to work with Harley loading the marijuana into our plane. Rocco slipped me two grand to cover expenses and, after a pep talk, we hit the airport and caught our flight to Cairns. On the way Lindsay broke the ice, sharing a few drinks, enough to loosen up. As I let a Scotch whisky ease my eyes shut, I sat back and thought how clever Rosario, Antonio and Rocco had really been. Perhaps they were far cleverer than I had originally thought. On the eve of the actual importation, the three main Italians had removed themselves from all risk, handing it to a couple of skippys in Lindsay and myself; very damn clever.

In Cairns, we took a pair of rooms on opposite sides of the same floor—as Lindsay said, 'far enough away from nosey coppers making inquiries'. As we were to spend a couple days together we nattered along freely; mostly it was gangster talk, confirming that he was best friends with Jim and that he was the one who had been liaising with

Harley daily throughout the growing process. Now it was only a matter of being at the Horn Island airstrip to collect the drugs at 5 a.m.
the day after tomorrow.

The next day, after spending much of Rocco's petty cash eating
crayfish at a local restaurant, we boarded a Qantas flight to Weipa, a
dust town on the west coast of Cape York Peninsula. While in the
departure lounge I snuck a final call to Cody, who went shy with
worry over the phone, though not before letting me know there was
a cast of thousands setting up on Horn Island, to lay in wait until it
was time to arrest everyone. I was worried what consequences that
might stir up in such a remote region.

We stayed the night in a dumpy, far-too-expensive motel in
Weipa, fighting off bats, giant mosquitoes and drunken locals till three
when our alarm sent us back to the airstrip. There was a magnificent
carpet of stars pinholing the pitch-black sky. The silence was perturb-
ing: not a sound other than the croaking of an occasional toad in the
distant mudflats and the gentle thud of our own feet as we walked
along the tarmac. We heard a tinkering in the immediate distance;
Ziggy had opened the door to his plane and was wrapping up his pre-
flight check. He had waited patiently in the quiet, ready to fly; his
empty plane was fuelled and our guns hidden. We climbed aboard.

Our jet was devoid of seats, forcing Lindsay and me to sit on the
floor, with just enough height to see out of our windows. Ziggy
looked back at me as he rubbed his hand over his whiskery chin and
winked, then gave me a nod that could only have meant 'good luck'.
I nodded back. We were off again!

It was only fifty minutes into the flight when Ziggy leaned back
to us, pointing downwards. As we peeped out our windows I could
see the water, like a sheet of black glass, dead calm and perfectly flat.
The canopy of stars cast a silver coating on the water's surface, high-
lighting the dark blob that was Horn Island. A few light dots indicated
fishing boats on the water. There wasn't a single cloud in the sky.

Ziggy brought our cargo plane to an abrupt halt at the chosen
end of the runway and killed the lights. He popped the door, allowing

us to step free into the pre-dawn stillness. I didn't care too much for the complete darkness and silence, despite knowing the Queensland SWAT team were dug into foxholes in the mangroves, covering my arse just in case things turned to shit and foul play took over; my feeling of uneasiness was only exacerbated by the serene cool that drifted across the runway, indicating daylight was near.

Lindsay and I confirmed the time and, without a word passing between us, we both started to walk to the edge of the tarmac to wait for the sound of a boat. Time ticked over and so did our brains as we stood, listening patiently for a sound. Only once was the silence broken when a crane scurried from the mangroves and leapt from a branch into the sky. It scared me, momentarily, till I fathomed what it was.

Lindsay began to get anxious, knowing that the game was on his shoulders. As he paced around in a small circle, he reassured me that Harley had confirmed the boat's crossing only hours earlier by telephone in Weipa. A sound pierced our silence. We looked at each other, jolting our heads, turning our good ears to the water. A boat motor putted in the distance. We stood frozen, frustrated by the effort involved in such a simple task of listening. The sound of a motor boat was definitely coming towards us. We looked back at each other. Lindsay nodded; our day had arrived.

Lindsay ran back to the plane, fetching one of the torches we had to help with the loading. As he listened to his boat getting closer he started shining his torch onto the grassy verge, as if he were looking for a pathway to the water. I called him back, throwing the fear of snakes into him, advice that fell on deaf ears. He walked a few more steps, then stopped and started to urinate on the grass.

At that moment something stirred near to him. The grass moved. It was more than just a rustle, and it wasn't made by any animal. It startled Lindsay, causing him to yell out in fright.

'What's that?'

'Come back Lindsay, back, back,' I pleaded with him, realising the problem.

He stood with his torch focused on the rustling.

'Who's that?' he demanded, losing all interest in the boat noise.

The grass began to lift upwards. With disbelief I watched the foliage rising from the ground, to get pushed aside as a SWAT man leapt to his feet, and then another. The grass was alive with the SWAT boys, brandishing machine guns, charging at us.

'Freeze, police! Freeze, police!' they screamed, coming from all directions in a chain reaction. Lindsay stepped back in shock. I stood yelling, 'No, no, no, no!'

Instantly, we were forced to the ground, handcuffed and left laying face down. Ziggy, too, was arrested and left lying on the tarmac, as SWAT men took charge of us. Radio noise was buzzing around the tarmac as each of the cops spoke into his handset, one to another, to headquarters, to anywhere, to everywhere. I lay slumped down, with giant mosquitoes landing on my face and neck, hearing the sound of the motor in the distance. Faint, but still alive. Then, the noise faded slowly away, until it had gone, leaving only the sound of radios and constant chatter.

It would be twenty minutes before I was lifted from the grass and placed in front of an officer, away from Lindsay. I got my only opportunity to whisper, 'I'm the police officer.'

'I know, well done mate, big effort.'

'No, the boat, it's going, you have to go after it, the motor. It's out there.'

'I'm sorry mate, I don't have those orders. I'll pass it on though. Well done.'

'It's not well done ... we're not done yet!'

I snatched the satellite phone from their hands and demanded to be told how to use it. They keyed in my office number and once connected I urgently prattled out my story, telling of the cluster fuck by the SWAT team, the escape of the motor boat, demanding a searching of the water. My pleas fell on deaf ears. I was told to report back to Melbourne: 'It's all over', just 'come back'. Apparently, there was no contingency plan to hunt down a motor boat, should it flee.

By the time the sun was starting to bite, Lindsay was locked up in Cairns and Ziggy and I were in the sky, with an empty plane and empty feelings. We had two days of travel ahead of us. My kindly pilot had suggested I fly home with Qantas. Of course, I couldn't do that, leave my mate to himself. I chose to lie on my back on the floor of the plane, scratching my face and neck, and rolling over the past two years and all that had gone before me.

Somewhere over central Queensland, a few hours from our fuel stop, I broke down and cried and cried. Ziggy politely and instinctively let me be.

18

THE SPYING GAME

As Ziggy and I cruised home, we would have, with the ideal flight plan, flown over Griffith. What a slice of irony, to be above the town that was in such turmoil. At that very moment, detectives were swarming all over houses and properties owned by the N'Drangheta. Sheds, yards, orchards, orange groves and cars were either dug up or searched to secure the largest collection of documents ever taken from the so-called Mafiosi. The NCA would gain years of insight into their seasoned adversary and eleven men would be taken from their grass castles, their heads bowed in silence, their wrists shackled.

It was a quiet Sunday morning when the posse galloped into town. Antonio was in his usual place of worship, celebrating his daughter's christening. The choir boys had just reached their high note when the doors were rudely flung open by Leigh and his deputy sheriffs. They marched up to a doting Antonio Romeo, halting his ceremony, and escorted him to the police cells, leaving a family in shocked disbelief. Rosario Trimbole was caught dashing from his home to his soldiers, wondering what on earth had gone wrong. He, too, found a bed in a concrete suite, the same one as the godfather's.

Honest locals took prime seats on the main street, with their deckchairs, to watch the passing parade of captured. The circus had come to town! And so it went, for many days, across the country, as more than two hundred police beat the drum against Italian organised crime. The media splashed front-page headlines, while leaks—some planned, others not—spruiked the largest undercover infiltration in Australia's history. It felt safe to be way up in the sky, secure amongst the clouds, away from the angst and fallen shoulders of the Calabrese who jostled for a seat in the Remand Court. The only presence absent from all the raids was the Calabrian tough, Hades. For good reason, I guess; he wasn't, to my knowledge, trafficking drugs and he certainly hadn't reared his head on the final day when the plane was due in. Still, he found his place, tucked in the corner of my mind.

By the time our tired jet arrived back in Melbourne, the only soul to greet two weary, smelly men was Rodney. He offered a handshake and then made a quick exit; he was on his way to headquarters. Of course he was, he was an ambitious man. I was an ambitious man no longer. I snuck home to an urgent appointment with a hot shower and a tub of face cream. Later that night, I got to see my girl again; Chelsea had been oblivious to all the nonsense her chameleon father had been up to. As was Connie, whom I fell into, emotionally and every other way. Funny how strong 'coming home' can be.

I gave myself ten days, a ruthless schedule, really, to transcribe sixteen cassette tapes and draft dozens of affidavits, not to mention cataloguing the hundred or so exhibits. Sandra worked alongside me; we took this time to ponder our journey together thus far. I had always put her right up there as one of the finest investigators I had ever worked with; there was a little bit of mother in dear old Sandra as she fussed over me, taking care of business. She did a lot of that over this hectic period, dotting my *is* and crossing my *ts* as we raced through the workload, making sure my date with an international flight would go unhindered.

I didn't tell her where I was going or when I'd be back; I knew she was worried. Endings are strange, really; they can feel like nervous beginnings. Once I had arrived home from Horn Island, not one boss gave a thought to my future safety or well-being. They were all missing, running their cheap suits around the chief commissioner's office, vying for a brownie point or two. There was no suggestion of how to dodge the long-reaching tentacles of the Mafia; it was a department without a contingency plan. I was yesterday's news.

There was a wonderful lady who worked in our task force, a woman I could rely on: Anna, my typist. She pounded away efficiently at her keyboard daily, typing my court documents. Privy to all the evidence and worried constantly about my safety, she reckoned the Italians would spend forever looking for me, hunting me down. Anna took it upon herself to arrange a hide-out in a farmhouse owned by her family in Montenegro, in the old Yugoslavia, believing the Mafia would never find me there. Her cousins would protect me. I was deeply touched by the concern this woman showed to me, serving to accentuate the lack of assistance offered by my own bosses.

Anna was right; the Mafia wouldn't find me at her cousins' farm. But I headed the other way, to New York, to enjoy the no-fuss hospitality of a couple of Australians who were living the tightrope-life of working in the stock exchange, earning huge salaries. I wondered how I could achieve such a pay packet; certainly risk was something I had reasonable experience with. I succumbed to five days of blissful, massive sleep-ins and relaxed fine dining along Lexington Avenue. My two Aussie mates and I enjoyed each other's company; they were unaware of my past. Their brother, another operative, had sent over a simple request: 'Look after this one, he needs rest.'

A week later I was lying alone on a Greek island, still asleep. I continued to sleep my way around Europe for six weeks, averaging twelve hours a day, the pressure and weariness leaching out of me. It wasn't until I arrived back in New York that my sleep pattern became something close to normal. My hospitable Australian friends failed to recognise me when they opened their door to me again; I had lost six kilos, tanned up and wore a smile. We laughed aloud, then went and dined some more.

The next year I was back up to my neck in work, back running at my usual pace, this time at a covert investigation unit. It takes a special type of person to become a skilled covert operative, one possessing a mix of qualities not normally sought after by police: attributes like cunning, strategic thinking, a quick mind and an inner discipline, and the ability to foresee the next four moves in the most dangerous of games, spying. For covert work is nothing more than spying—a very deliberate, long-term attempt to befriend a person and unravel their secrets. At the CIU we were trained like spies; this was a fairly new concept, much like the heralded undercover units in America that I had visited in the 1980s. It was a past director of the CIA who once said that only 3 per cent of their effort went into covert activity but it solved 97 per cent of their problems.

Covert investigation is a game requiring more than any textbook can ever explain. I have always believed my own upbringing was the finest initiation I could ever have had for covert work, and all police work, for that matter. I was able to comprehend the bad side. I could appreciate a peasant's need to be a king, if just for a day, or sympathise with a loser's desire for the niceties of life, even if it meant breaking the law. I understood the rationale, yet never condoned the outcome; I preferred the thrill of the chase.

I was offered the role of permanent controller at this elite unit. For reasons of national security, I shan't name the facility or its secret location. The unit was a hidden-away-from-the-world group of well-travelled spies, led by two odd men. The unit achieved fine and at times outstanding results, targeting the country's most hideous rabble.

As a group, they were real candidates for a Coen brothers' screenplay, a dozen hand-picked cops looking like tough dregs. An extraordinary effort went into their appearance and a few of the boys were truly villainous, the perfect lures. We created background histories that could fool the best, or worst. Our training was done in secret, at a specially built facility where we took our groups of hopefuls and ran them through their paces for weeks at a time. With access to every type of state-of-the-art equipment, we tested their reactions to a multitude

of scenarios, with enough twists and turns to intrigue a Russian nov-
elist. They were worked day and night, until their thinking sharpened
and their reactions came naturally. Their training roles would change
dramatically each time: one minute a 'coke' buyer, the next a negotia-
tor for submachine guns, then a thief of corporate secrets, then a pervert looking for child porn, and on we worked. Everyone got to
participate in the learning that came from debriefing. They were
tough courses; it wasn't uncommon to have a 30 per cent fail rate, and
failures along the way were given one hour to pack their belongings
before being driven home. It was the only way to develop a covert.
The ultimate risk in real life for a spy is death; there are no second
chances. In time, the graduates also went home, unable to tell anyone
who or what they were.

I would eventually become course director, with my main interest
in teaching the 'art' of infiltration, the slow, prolonged process of getting close to someone. The greatest mark of success is to one day find
yourself considered as one of your target's closest friends, without the
target quite knowing how it all happened. Clever work, if you can do
it. Very few operatives have the patience, yet it has been proven, worldwide, that the most important arrests come through infiltration.

One of the constant issues in training and managing covert operatives is dealing with their egos. Ego is a necessary attribute for the work,
but there are times when it can get in the way, and it can become a
dangerous liability. I came to be working closely with a new guy, Hani,
who had the potential to be one of the finest operatives of all. He was
brilliant, versatile and adaptive, which worried a few of the other
threatened egos in our stable, and they reacted the same way as stallions,
planning to kill off the threat. Hani had a small amount of choof planted in his locker, just the sort of thing a boss could stumble over, and I
had the god-awful task of packing his bags and driving him home, along
a lonely treacherous road. What a waste. Oh yes, ego is a dirty word.

Since the arrest of Antonio and his gang, I had spent my life hiding
out, sleeping here, there and everywhere, staying low until the Italians

faced the courts. Connie was unforgettably supportive during this time, glad to see a little more of me. But every now and again I disappeared to another flophouse, just to make sure prying eyes weren't upon me. My civilian friends were starting to sense something significant had happened in my working life.

My greatest infiltration, Antonio and Rosario, would finally come to face me again; the trial was at last listed for hearing. I had spent six days standing in the witness box at the earlier committal hearing, sweating through cross-examination from nine barristers, each one trying to discredit me. Now, I was ready for closure. One thing was for sure: we, as a task force, were never going to allow the likes of another Walsh Street verdict. Sandra and the team had put together a sensational brief, considered the largest document the courts had seen. My own statement was many hundreds of pages.

It was crucial that I was in court on the day of the pleas. I needed to look each man in the eye, especially Antonio and Rosario, for one last time. It was an extraordinarily emotional time for me, yet I believed my being there would give a sense of honesty to a process that took over three years. I waited nervously for that day.

I was, by now, well known for having little or no respect for the rank structure. Middle managers fell into the practice of either avoiding me or acquiescing to my ways. I had stopped caring about the 'big picture' and my reputation had suffered a blow; those who oversaw my work considered me 'difficult to manage'. My only focus was to gather evidence and to lock up the crooks we targeted. I had become a strategic investigative machine, devoid of any career aspiration past team leader or detective sergeant. And, much to the frustration of the hierarchy, I wasn't climbing the promotional ladder or currying favour with the heavyweights on the top floor. All I ever wanted to be was a detective and I'd fulfilled that desire. My tolerance for fools was spent.

As I walked into the courtroom I was met by a tidal wave of faces. Not just journalists, but the families and friends of the accused as well as each of the detectives who had played a key part in the task force.

Many of the Italians in the public seating gallery I knew well; I had eaten with them, sat in their homes and cuddled their kids. Perspiration trickled down my back. Every seat in the largest courtroom in the building was taken, except one, which Sandra had reserved for me. It was a confronting experience, shuffling in front of a near-dozen pairs of knees to get to my pew, being watched by a dozen pairs of eyes from the dock. The hatred was palpable.

In sitting down I noticed one of my bosses from the drug squad lean into Sandra and ask, 'What's that cunt doing here?' He ignored my uneasy smile and looked straight ahead. That comment alone represented the reason I lost all loyalty to my employer. It galvanised a basic flaw within policing structure, a department awash with its 'us and them' mentality. The department had a mere three ranks working the streets, all constantly at odds with the seven upper-level ranks who spent far too much time behind their desks ensconced in idle self-promotion and criticism of the lower levels. What a strange organisation, so often at odds with its community as well as with itself, one that calls its achievers 'cunts'!

Sandra, in her quiet wisdom, ignored the boss' question. Instead, she made sure I was comfortably seated. As I shuffled past the boss and his silence I received two 'hellos' from the Italian contingent. I was relieved when the judge's gavel came thundering down, shifting the feast of eyes away from me and onto business.

Eventually, our eleven Italians stood in the dock, the upper echelon of the Mafia in Australia, and not a smile amongst them. I could almost hear a drum-roll as I waited for their pleas. It was then that I felt a tear gather on my bottom eyelid as I heard: 'guilty, your Honour', 'guilty, your Honour', eleven times, to hushed voices in the gallery. I slowly breathed a sigh.

Strategically, the guilty pleas would allow each man up to a one-third discount in jail-time. I understood the strategy; a third of a whale is still a big feed.

Antonio Romeo stood forward in his fine fashions to hear his sentence: thirteen years. Likewise Rosario Trimbole, who by now had found a tailor: thirteen years. And on the morning went, sentence after sentence, as the numbers stacked up.

I sat and watched Antonio being dragged from the court, surrounded by a mess of high security. As he disappeared from life as he had always known it, he flicked two desperate glances back into the gallery. One at his wife and the other at myself, frozen on my seat, till the anger faded, till the theatre emptied. I left through a fire-escape door to a narrow laneway, choosing to walk alone back to my office, to my detectives, who rejoiced in the result. Once the media release was written and I shuffled a few pens on my desk, we decided to turn the clock back a few years and went in search of sushi and sake again. It had been a long ride together ... and I would always remember their loyalty.

A few months later, far too early one morning, I received a call from a detective mate in the major crime unit. Apparently the Australian billionaire Kerry Packer had had his safe broken into overnight. He was now very light on in the gold bullion department. An unknown crook, supposedly from Melbourne, had delivered his message through Kerry's personal assistant, demanding a ransom of $210 000 to surrender it. The idea was for the PA to bring the cash to Melbourne by a Qantas domestic flight at 4 p.m. that day, then hire an Avis rental car and travel to the Bruce County Motel in outer-suburban Mount Waverley, and wait. The caller knew the PA's name and would contact her once she had checked into her room.

The scramble was on to come up with a way to catch the crook. I raced through all the lockers in the covert office to find a suit—there weren't many of them in our midst! Luckily, I scored enough bits and pieces to look like an executive. I slicked back my hair, borrowed a briefcase and in two hours I was on a flight to Sydney along with a new covert operative. She didn't know it but she was about to become the PA to Australia's most wealthy man.

She had done some small stuff with the unit, was older than most other undercover staff, and was showing signs of greatness. She fitted the age group we needed for the job and so she met me on the plane, wearing shockingly dowdy clothes; I think she borrowed her mother's Sunday best, which was exactly what I had asked of her. As we walked into Kerry Packer's office we noticed his real PA, Simone, to one side, getting on with business. There was a reasonable likeness between Simone and my operative; the two of them now had an hour to sit and become one.

I got to meet the great man himself and sit in his office chair, to familiarise myself with his world, of course. I didn't care for the oil painting of a lion above his desk, nor did I think much of the safe that he had; it must have been as old as he was and would, I thought, have been easily opened with a screwdriver. I met his financial director and I was glad that he was my age, and even gladder that he was a few kilos heavier than me. I was about to become him. The real PA and financial director were sent home and told not to answer any telephone calls, and 'my' Simone and I left Mr Packer's office with a case containing $210 000 and two tickets to Melbourne: first class of course!

I figured Kerry would never allow his PA to travel to Melbourne alone with that sort of dosh; he would have his financial director accompany her. By 6 p.m. we were laying back on our vibrating bed at the suburban hotel, snapping the screw-tops from a couple of mini-bar drinks, waiting. The loot was burning a hole in the bottom of my briefcase and the telephone looked lonely. Then, just like clockwork, it rang. Simone sprang into action. I could hear her one-sided call.

'He's my boss … I had to … Mr Packer insisted … no, please … hello?'

She looked at the handpiece as if it had farted, then placed it down. She was beaten, despondent.

'Don't sweat it, he'll ring back. You're doing well; play the scared secretary.'

'He hit the roof about me not being alone,' she said, nervously.

'Of course he did, but he'll get back to you. He enjoys your fear.'

Our crook had obviously been watching the hotel. Common sense should tell him that a woman would never have gone alone.

All he needed to do now was relax about the presence of the financial director: greed would help that decision. After an hour, the phone rang again.

'Yes, he's my boss … my boss, really … yes, I'm writing it down: 015 309 333.'

His jitters had obviously waned. Simone had been given an address and she had passed on our mobile number. There were instructions for us to sit and wait in our car—'and bring the fuckin' money!' The crook made it clear he was watching us; we figured from another room.

The hotel clerk approached us as we sat in our rental car to say that a call was waiting for Simone at reception. 'This guy's smart,' I thought, 'very damn smart, to try to separate us.' Simone took the call and returned to the car, saying that there was now a call waiting for me, in our hotel room. Surely he was checking the way we reacted; we went back to our room.

Ten minutes later and we were back in the car, with the loot, driving in circles. For two hours we were told where to drive, where to turn and where to stop by an abusive crook in a game of cat and mouse as he tried to weave us around his little finger, looking for who might be following us. He was good! We played happily, knowing the secret squirrels were out there, in the dark, watching our backs. Eventually he had us stop in a busy shopping-centre car park and wait. Each minute or so a new stream of cars was permitted in by the adjacent traffic light. Using the stream, he was able to buzz past us, making it difficult for us to work out which car was his. So far, he had succeeded in confusing us and remaining far enough away from being spotted. He had put some serious thought into his plan and either he had watched too many cops-and-robbers movies or he was the real deal.

The crunch came when he instructed us to place the briefcase of cash on the asphalt and leave; the location of the bullion would be disclosed the following day. Simone and I found ourselves in a stalemate. We were role-playing two scared executives, not street-smart cops with a bag of cunning alternatives. We had to stick to our parts, otherwise he would smell a rat. It was time to bite the bullet.

We sat in a full, pitch-black car park, watching cars come and go; headlights on and off, lone drivers, as well as families. Our crook rang again, demanding for the last time that we drop the money or it was all over; I could tell by his voice that he wasn't kidding. Brilliantly, and to plan, Simone started crying, sobbing profusely. I tried talking to the target, only to be howled down by a woman in obvious distress. Her tears got louder and louder, until our crook couldn't hear at all; he loved it. Eventually, he agreed to one concession, to drive past us and flash his lights, and then I'd drop the money.

I have no doubt it was the tears that got the concession. And he did it; he followed a stream of traffic into the car park, flashed his lights and kept moving. We passed his car details onto the squirrels. I placed the money onto the asphalt and went back to our car. Another stream of cars drove into the car park, past the briefcase, and instantly it was gone. The chase was now well on and less then five minutes later the squirrels had run him to ground. No use fleeing a crime scene with $210 000 and driving down a dead-end street!

I stood over him in my now-wrinkled suit and said only two words as he lay prone in a pool of his own urine: 'Got you!' Then I left to buy a clever woman a drink.

A few days later I was sitting at the covert office when the phone rang; it was the NCA in Adelaide, wondering if I would fly over and talk. They asked if I would take over the investigation into the death of Geoffrey Bowen. They had run into too many brick walls and wanted a 'Griffith Mafia treatment' on their suspect. I laughed at how naive that sounded. Apparently the way had been cleared for me by my own chief commissioner and the director of the NCA. I wasn't going to get in the way of a damn smart idea. I booked an airfare.

Days later I was sitting at the NCA office in Adelaide in front of a dozen disheartened detectives. I made it clear that under no circumstances would I be an active covert operative during the investigation. My days of being undercover with Italians were well and truly over. These good men didn't know it but I remained forever conscious of the shadow of the Calabrian tough: Hades. I had hung up my covert identities for good. But I agreed to run the job, pick the operatives and strategically manage the investigation to the end. First, I needed to read everything they had on the bombing.

Apart from that initial briefing, I was given an office and left alone to digest the written material on the case. The investigators were obliging, handing file after file to me, allowing me total access to the most secret information, the 'scuttlebutt', as we say. I settled in at the computer database and lost myself for days. When I needed air, I'd ask to be driven around all the addresses in the files, so I could, where possible, spy on the players from a distance.

The investigators had fingered an N'Drangheta member for the crime; he had a heated history with police. The bomb that shook the law enforcement's foundations was made of red phosphorus (red P), a unique ingredient, not readily available in the general community. It's a chemical that's used by pyrotechnic companies and is also required in small amounts in the recipe for making speed, therefore it's highly restricted. Either way, it's harder to get than leprosy; I liked that. I saw a way through already.

Often the best starts in a covert job can be achieved by latching onto the unusual, making a feast out of something that might otherwise be dismissed as too hard. The fact that red P was so highly restricted was a bonus: it allowed me to come up with a potential way into the suspect Alfonso. I burrowed down into my research to find out where red P came from, who made it, who supplied it and what volumes were available. After three days I had square eyes and a backache, but I was happy to brief Kym and his mate Quarters, the detectives in charge of the case who had done great work, so far.

There were two problems that would make a normal investigation near impossible: firstly, Alfonso was a paranoid individual with an extraordinary cunning for police procedure. In other words, he was a suspect who was difficult to target; he was too smart. Secondly, there was a private investigator floating around, Gianni, a guy who was, by the very nature of his work, also acutely aware of police procedure. Any wonder the original investigation had been stymied. I checked out Gianni's private eye business and found that it was wide and varied. He was a dog's body, covering everything from security and witness statements to marital disputes. My final assessment was simple.

'We'll be talking to Alfonso in six months,' I said.

'No way!' replied Quarters.

'We need six months. Alfonso will talk about red P.'

'Six months, it's very expensive.' I could feel Quarters adding up the dollars. They needed results but they just weren't aware of how valuable time was to this work. They scratched their heads and looked at the ceiling, hoping for quicker solutions.

'How do you know Alfonso will meet undercover police. How?' from Quarters.

'Because I know. Give me the time and we'll give you Alfonso.'

Kym and Quarters looked a little bewildered. They adjourned our meeting and headed for the tea-room for an urgent confab of their own. Half an hour later they stepped back into my office with four wide eyes and ears that listened. They needed something that could be sold upstairs, to get funding. I put down a script, to outline how we could infiltrate Alfonso and have him meet and talk freely with undercover police. The detectives leaned into the table as I reeled off my script. It went something like this:

Cast
The Husband, a 32-year-old knockabout with past drug arrests
The Estranged Wife, a tough blonde, with looks and attitude
Jack the Maori, a 40-year-old crook and cook of amphetamines
Jimmy, a 40-year-old best mate to Jack and all-round crook

Targets
Alfonso and his private eye, Gianni, and anyone else who wants to play!

Act One

We create an Italian couple of Calabrian background, covert operatives, of course. The husband is rough and tough, an ugly son-of-a-bitch; we'll give him a bad background. He'll run earthmoving equipment for a living.

The wife will have an air of queen harpy about her; she'll tease interest from those wanting to play, to get to know her. We'll make sure we create the right bank histories, birth and marriage certificates and all the usual backstopping.

Our couple lives in a smart apartment in St Kilda in Melbourne, down a seedy side street. Problem is they are going through the motions of a messy separation. The wife runs off to Adelaide. The husband finds out via the wife's best friend, who gets a postcard. Our jealous Calabrese husband attempts to retrieve his estranged wife and searches out private eyes in the Adelaide phone book, spotting Gianni. There's a nice Calabrese connection with the names.

Act Two

Our husband employs Gianni to locate his wife, whom we hide in an apartment by the beach. He comes across to Adelaide to meet Gianni and offers information that might help find his wife: wedding photo albums, etc.

Gianni befriends our husband, who, little by little, offers up information about his own background, his dodgy past: being charged by police for drugs, being involved in a marijuana plantation and that he can get specialist chemicals for making speed. The game is on. After a couple of months of calls and visits, a friendship is brewing. To help matters along we have the wife 'located' in Adelaide by Gianni, who, apart from feeling smart about himself, offers to negotiate her return home.

Lovely work, we think, allowing the infiltration to be prolonged. It's now three months since the husband first telephoned Gianni.

Many social occasions have happened and the infiltration is running well.

At the same time, we run another infiltration in parallel. Kym and Quarters already have an informer—a genuine informer, not a covert operative—who is prepared to introduce undercover police to Alfonso's network. We introduce our man Jack, a Maori. His ethnicity provides the perfect deflection from suspicion. Jack and his mate Jimmy play crooks involved in making speed. They enjoy the company of the informer, giving them the opportunity to meet Alfonso's friend. In time, Jack tells the friend that he cooks speed for a living. Everyone gets on swimmingly. The friend talks of Alfonso wanting to make a large amount of speed. Everything is taped.

Months roll by, as do the many meetings between the friend and our two boys. Alfonso himself finally wants to meet our Maori and talk about a massive cook of speed. Coincidentally, on the other side of Adelaide the husband has told Gianni that he can get red P, to help make speed. The bait is now set; all that is needed is to wait. By now, it's seven months since the start.

Act Three

Alfonso and his friend set up a large laboratory on the outskirts of Adelaide, along with three other Italians and our two boys, the Maori and Jimmy. A cook of speed is on. Our two boys help in the laboratory for three days, working around the clock, then ... the issue of red P comes up.

And that's pretty much how it rolled out in actuality. Sure, it was a bit more complex but, to the amazement of Kym and Quarters and the rest of the select few in our gaggle, that's how it panned out. It took eight months to get to the end of Act Three, but we still weren't finished. It was red P we were after and my operatives had work ahead.

It was a few days after New Year's Day and Jack and Jimmy were inside a laboratory with at least three edgy Italians, making a massive amount of amphetamines. It was a nervous time, yet the operatives showed no signs of withering: they were totally committed. I was controlling the investigation from the safety of my Adelaide hotel room, where I had lived all this time. Sneaking out late at night to brief them on the next phase of our cunning game, I sometimes met them in a motel room, at other times in a coffee shop or down a country lane. Often we sweated over the right words to use, how much to say, how little to offer. Each meeting was crucial to advance onto the next day, the next step forward. The core team of Jack, Jimmy, the wife and the husband were highly disciplined, a joy to control, to lead.

Once I had briefed them and discussed the endless possibilities and contingencies that ran with the job, I sent them back into the night to mix it with their targets. They had each other as cover and support but the level of danger at this point of the job was extreme, particularly for Jack and Jimmy.

I remembered being alone many times in Griffith, without a weapon or any way of calling for help. Month after month, it's steely work. Jack and Jimmy were faced with that same eerie feeling. I was on their wavelength as I listened to their conversations from inside my room, as Vito had done two years earlier for me, second-guessing the next move in our game of human chess, sending off instructions that might keep them safe or advance the infiltration. It's the ultimate sport of camaraderie: covert operative and controller. They need each other like solder needs flux. It's that simple.

A speed cook normally takes about three days. Our crooks and undercover boys had gotten the mixture to the stage where red P was needed to finish the process. Trouble was, Alfonso made it clear that he wouldn't be touching the stuff; he was adamant red P was a no-talk zone and that Jack was to be responsible for accessing the powder. I didn't like that. We needed to pull off a sting, a plan to get Alfonso to talk about red P. The cooking process was almost over.

This was the moment we had been waiting for. I designed a scam that went like this:

Jack mentions that he has a small quantity of red P left over from a past cook in Sydney, just enough. He'd freight it overnight to Adelaide. Alfonso is pleased. In the meantime, I'd get a tin of the red P and place it in a carton, crushing the side to make sure the phosphorus tin was dented, spewing the red powder everywhere. We'd then dampen the powder, nullifying the phosphorus and rendering it useless. The carton is freighted to Adelaide.

When the carton arrives, Jack and Jimmy feign shock and horror at the loss of the red P. Alfonso is present at the bleak discovery. Jack puts the problem fair and square back onto his shoulders. Alfonso chats away explaining that he wouldn't access the powder; nothing would budge him on that, but his friend knew another (Italian) who had some. The subject of red P was now freely spoken about between the undercover boys and our target.

Alfonso accepted the loss of the powder. The sting seemed to free him up, to encourage him to talk more about his taboo subject. He mouthed to Jack and Jimmy the word 'BOMB' while pointing to himself. Our work was all but over. The pressure on the shoulders of Jack and Jimmy started to ease.

For the pièce de résistance, Alfonso set into motion a request for some red P, contacting Gianni, who in turn contacted the husband, our undercover man. Within twenty-four hours our husband had delivered the powder to Gianni, and the massive mix of amphetamines was almost complete. Thirty detectives pounced on the laboratory, locking up Alfonso, Gianni and four other Italians. Oh, yes, and Jack and Jimmy, who were in the middle of drying the amphetamines, worth many millions of dollars, getting them ready to sell.

With all the crooks locked up, Jack, Jimmy and the posse went for a very long celebration drink before I packed up nine months' worth of dirty laundry and headed back to my Melbourne office. I had on my rose-coloured glasses, looking for new horizons.

I spent a long time with the covert unit and was involved in dozens of jobs. I had a mix of good times and the average, but was starting to tire of the egos and the insecurities that follow this type of work. Operatives can be a handful. I have always believed covert cops are the bravest of all police but I found myself dulled by it all, in need of a change. It's like being part of a movie sometimes, an overly long dirty western, with far too many bad guys and not enough Clint Eastwoods. I decided I wanted to feature in a romantic comedy for a while.

19

'NO GLORY FOR YOU'

My last year as a cop would prove to be the most tumultuous of my career, with more frustration, more spite and more disdain experienced than at any other time. And yet I never saw or spoke to a crook.

David and I hadn't worked together since the Mr Cruel days. He was now the boss of the detective training academy, writing new courses, improving the standards. Since our failures at Walsh Street, David had vowed to improve the skill base of investigators, and he was a man of his word. His directing staff at the academy were a fine bunch of lecturers and the school was enjoying a renaissance, now competency accredited to the University of Melbourne.

I accepted David's invitation to join his team and to write a new course for junior-burger cops, getting them skilled at an early age. This meant sitting in the law library for many months, drafting lecture notes. I thought that sounded perfect, especially as I could enjoy a cold beer at the end of a nine-to-five day and get weekends off. So I went to see my tailor, who measured me for a few suits and lectured me on my waistline.

I was now living quietly on my own and I wasn't prepared to surrender to anyone. Connie and I had said our goodbyes some time earlier. As gorgeous as she was and as much as I liked her, she wanted marriage and children; I still wasn't ready. She drifted off to face the singles scene. She had long been a great friend, as well as a lover.

My little, now 91-year-old lady had died in hospital (not of red phosphorous poisoning) and that had caused me to catch the renovation bug again. I started knocking down walls, turning my fantastic best-in-the-world apartment into something unique. But first, I had to clear it out—and it was filled with rubble. Magazines and newspapers dating back to the 1950s were stacked to the ceiling. Packets of food that had passed their use-by dates ten years earlier lined the cupboards. It was a mess. My old buddy Charles rolled up his sleeves and we spent a week taking everything to the tip. Sadly, the old dear hadn't had a cash tin stashed away, at least not one that I found. Unless Charles … ?

One wet weekend I lost myself to pottering with paint samples. The renovation was almost complete. For reasons unknown, I started to get a tad melancholy. My mind drifted off to all the relationships I had had and lost, as guys tend to do at times. I was quietly dwelling on the beautiful and smart women I had shared time with and lost. I found myself lost to cosy wistfulness, reliving qualities, delicious moments and special times. I missed Connie badly. I missed Annitia just as much.

I drifted on into a history of the work I'd been involved in. It seemed an easier subject to reflect on. I scanned my life as a cop, loving some of it, hating the rest. That's life, I figured. My mind slipstreamed past the many fine people I had had the pleasure to work with and befriend. I enjoyed exploring this mental territory, until I started ticking off a list of the dills who had graced my life: the men who took and never gave back, the ladder-climbers who grabbed fistfuls of my achievements so that they could keep hoisting themselves up on their way to the top. I tried to understand their ambition but didn't have enough inside me to do the subject justice.

My mood swung sharply, becoming melancholy, dark and horribly lonely. I went looking for Connie again but she was gone, as was Annitia. A wave crashed over me and before long I had fallen into the darkest depression. My final recollection is of sitting curled up in a ball on my sofa, thinking of ways to escape my life. The room was black.

I woke up three days later in the Melbourne Clinic—the nuthouse for overworked business executives, celebrities in hiding and burnt-out cops. Apparently Cody had found me, still on my sofa. I must have been there for hours. I did some of my best detective work over the next few months, trying to find those missing three days, but I lost that case badly. I have never been able to recall anything much, only four snippets. I have an image of waking up and seeing Ma and Ray at the end of my single bed, then an even shorter image of Connie, sitting alongside my gown-clad body in the visitors' lounge, then another of Chelsea, holding my hand, with a face full of tears, and a final vision of being handed a tiny white paper cup by a nurse, filled with about twelve different coloured pills and capsules. No wonder I was in noddy-land.

I lay in my bed with the all-too-familiar smell of linoleum and the sight of pyjama-clad stress-heads staring at the ceiling. A guy in the next bed was manically arranging and rearranging the contents of his little timber cupboard, over and over: folding his shirts, fussing over his ties, sorting himself mad. The bloke opposite had a stare that could kill a brown dog. I felt uneasy. For the first time, I was not a team player. I didn't like this task force much.

I went into analysis.

'Too long at the grindstone,' one said.

'Too obsessed with trying to better your father,' the psychologist intoned.

It wasn't for me to argue the truth; I was guilty as charged. If I was going to be completely honest with the psychologist I might have added to his list, 'with behavioural traits like perfectionist, fear of failure and the constant worry of what might become of my daughter, the one person I cherish'.

But I kept those beads to myself, electing to get my health back, as fast as possible. I teamed up with a big bloke, bespectacled and overfed. He stooped. He told his story, of being a CEO of something important and how he had crashed and burned: 'mental exhaustion', they called it. Plus too many long lunches, I reckoned. The CEO and I marched around and around like dogged tin soldiers, till the wobbles wandered off and our backs straightened. Then I bid him farewell and walked out the front door, never to return.

My own doctor, Marshy, and his wife, Clair, were far better medicine then a cup full of pretty tablets, so I knocked on their door a little more often than usual. Of course, my entrance fee was always a 'darn good red'. Over many meals and many bottles of Heathcote shiraz, the three of us decided the only future for me was divorce—from the police department. They reminded me that Chelsea had grown to a fine adult; there was nothing to worry about anymore. I reminded myself that I had let go of the image of the cubicle girl. All that was left was timing, and I knew a lot about that. So promises were made and I waited for the right day. My day.

I struggled back into my lecturer's job with the total support of my fellow instructors and David—all good people, some having crashed and burned themselves, such is life for a cop. I finished writing that new course and we opened in the nick of time, to a room full of new wannabes. As course coordinator, I took enormous pride in teaching my trade, sometimes passing on my tricks, my ways, and always giving a left-eye wink when I mentioned the enemy—my bosses—which raised smiles. Most of the young guys had heard the gossip over the years, knew the hurdles I'd faced. I liked their fresh endeavour, their willingness to learn, but wondered what lay ahead for them. The department had developed management cancer.

After we put the course to bed and graduated the lucky ones, I got stuck into setting up the next course. There was a rush of gossip running around about an old friend of mine, Gerry, a very reputable private investigator, one of the most likeable characters I have ever met. The internal cops had a bug in Gerry's office. They had been fishing for a shark and the trail had gone cold, but my name came up, so they settled on a minnow instead. A couple of years earlier, while off duty, I had helped Gerry with another cop, following someone. A favour for a mate, I thought, yet my assistance to Gerry was considered 'unauthorised part-time work', a misdemeanour. Cops can't have part-time jobs.

I had some explaining to do. My only blush in eighteen years of police service was presented as a gift to some with long memories. I could hear their hands rubbing before the knock came on my door. I awaited their arrival.

Meanwhile, I was due to be presented to the chief commissioner and handed a commendation for 'dedication to duty, and outstanding courage', a belated award for my work on the Mafia job. Awards often take years to come around in the police. I was deeply touched, especially because of the lack of praise I had received to that date. There was a separate report from the South Australian commissioner, recommending that I receive a 'commendation of the highest order' for dedication, professionalism and tactical ability on the bombing investigation. And I was also cited to be named the 'national investigator of the year' by the NCA for my infiltration work. A good day was looming. I rang Chelsea to see if she'd like to partner me.

The night before I was to be paraded before the media, and graced with gilded handshakes, the internal cops tapped on my door. I knew the head-hunter who was seeking my scalp; he had been trying for promotion for years and was unable to cut the street work, a dill on the rise. It was all very simple, really. He knew of my indiscretion, years earlier. All he wanted me to do was snitch on the other cop involved. I laughed, it was that ridiculous. He saw it as serious, the sort of stuff that promotions are made of, and pushed on, asking me eleven times in total to name the other cop. And ten times I shook my head, explaining it was a favour to a mate. My mind failed to comprehend the earnestness with which this was being handled.

Then it dawned on me; my number had come up. The collective energies of so many of those dills I had upset was now bearing down on me. I was being moved on, which both angered and saddened me. On his eleventh request I told him to 'get fucked'. He was taken aback by my bravado, momentarily recovered, took a deep breath and suspended me with pay. Like a pimply kid out of favour in the schoolyard, he dropped his trump card: 'And … don't come tomorrow, there'll be no glory for you!'

He left me shaking my head in disbelief, completely gobsmacked. I walked home in the rain, minus a badge but with my integrity, in complete disbelief that I could be treated in this way. Sure, I had become 'difficult to manage', but I failed to see the outcome as being justified after years of faithful, honest service.

That night my dark cloud paid me another visit, asking if it could stay a while. I feared the worst. I imagined the door to the Melbourne Clinic in my mind's eye, and I shook like hell. I stayed in this horrid state until midday the following day, the time of the media announcement. Journalists were throwing questions about my absence and the chief commissioner nervously batted them off. Apparently the award ceremony, which thankfully included Sandra as a recipient, failed to impress the sceptics, who asked where I was. My awards were never forthcoming. Nor was there proper recognition given to Jude, the real catalyst in the first six months of the infiltration; she, too, was ignored, yet the senior management of the task force nominated themselves for 'highly commended' awards.

'It's odd how we treat our own,' I pondered, sitting at home, fidgeting. I guessed it was my turn to fall on my sword, like many others in the past. What should have been a celebration of talent and performance was comprehensively overshadowed by a blemish that could have been easily dealt with across a table in the time it took to make two cups of coffee. The ancient Jewish prophet Meir ticked a simple truth when he observed that 'the tree itself supplies the handle of the axe that cuts it down'.

By mid-afternoon I had come to terms with my fate. I was no more than one cog in a very large machine, a machine that drove a big dirty game known as 'cops and robbers'. There were certainly no rules there, that I knew.

I regrouped and sent my demons packing. Finding an inner strength and lashings of dedication, that stuff I was supposed to be commended for, I vowed to myself to hold tight, to ignore the nonsense. My day had finally arrived; the one Marshy had alluded to. But first I wanted to send the internal cop nuts and go out with a smile. I wanted him to know that you don't take ambition to a shit-fight; it's smarts that you need.

I had sold my apartment only a week earlier and purchased an old warehouse shell that I intended to renovate as a trendy city-loft apartment. On went the overalls, out came my tools and I went to work. After all, I was on paid suspension leave, so I decided to take advantage of the 'paid' element. For six months I buried myself in my renovation, transforming my warehouse into a treasure. For six months the internal police tried every trick in their grimy book to find me, without success. I had avoided thugs, gangsters and death threats of more worrisome significance in my career. To avoid the internal police was a cinch by comparison. Pimples knocked on doors, followed a couple of my friends and exhausted himself hunting for me, all to no avail, so out came the dirty tricks.

He sent a letter to Ma, saying I was 'corrupt'. Of course I wasn't, but it was his best strategy to try to flush me out. Ma just laughed. A mother knows her son! I kept renovating. A letter arrived, ordering me to see the police doctor. Pimples hoped I would be assessed as fit to return to work, that way he could get another dip at me. I saw the doctor and told him the whole sordid story. We sat for two hours, enthralled, swapping bad management yarns. I learned that the doctor, too, had become jaded with the ways of the top floor. He wrote a warning to the chief's office that they were 'not to contact Colin under any circumstances'. Marshy also sent a letter of medical warning to the chief. I kept renovating.

A couple of the internal sods heard I was somewhere in Fitzroy, playing handyman, so they went looking, staking out the coffee shops in the area. I sprung a few of them sitting in a cafe, eating falafels; I lost them down the laneways as they scuttled about. After six months I had finished my renovation and stepped down from my ladder, spotted with paint. I walked into David's office, in my overalls, and resigned. It was that easy. The Keystone Cops were still running around Fitzroy, except now they were looking for a civilian. Marshy, Clair and I went to dinner that night and pulled a couple of corks. There were no laughs, nor were there any tears. But there was plenty of smiling; I was well and truly over it by then. The quail was delicious.

I had had a good run in what would become known as the most volatile time in policing, a time when police shot first and asked questions later, a period when the hierarchy was out to lunch. Between 1986 and 1996, thirty people were shot and killed by Victoria Police. Any other police department in the civilised world would blush with figures that bad. To have my own career peak over that same period was a fascination. I was close to it all, involved in much of the controversy and wanted for nothing, professionally. I had no reason to hit the phones and find out what was going on, to seek inside gossip on the dramas that rolled out. I was in the middle of them, batting the balls, surviving the game. And I'm glad I was on the right team, always. It was a good time to be a walloper, even though it was a strange time for a police department.

The former highly-thought-of chief commissioner Mick Miller, who had shaken my hand at my graduation, must have sat back in his easy chair in his retirement, wondering what on earth was happening. Perhaps his world had gone mad. I know mine had, almost. But, hey … that big wide world was still out there.

In leaving the police department, I only left behind one loose end: Hades, who was still in the country, playing the system. Senior federal law enforcement officials were trying everything in their power to block his application for residency, which had found its way into political circles. I only hoped as I entered civilian life that he would either be returned to Calabria or shrivel up and blow away.

20

THE HEAT IN THE KITCHEN

By late 2002 I was up to my neck in concrete. No, the N'Drangheta hadn't found me, nor had any of the other lowlifes I had played with for nearly two decades. I was building an Italian villa, with concrete footings, limewashed walls, granite and Carrara marble.

Italy would always be in my system, one way or another; it had been from the days when I was ogling Mrs Bongiorno's beautiful daughters or just hanging out with Vinnie and his brothers and scoffing homemade wine and his mother's delicious Sunday lunches. I had been to Italy at least a dozen times and it was only natural to desire my own slice of it: my own villa and my own trattoria, the one Chelsea and I talked about for all those years. The trouble was that my 'Italian' villa was in the stunningly beautiful Buckland Valley, near the town of Bright at the foot of Mount Buffalo, in north-western Victoria. While I adored the Italian culture, I wasn't prepared to say goodbye to my daughter just yet. So, I was building a villa in Australia. Why not?

I first hit on the idea during an earlier visit to northern Italy. My partner and I (another soon-to-be-doomed relationship) had arrived the night before, ushered in under inside-out umbrellas during the worst storm in years. We were staying in a villa on Lake Como. After we had run through grand glass doors, past a reception desk where officialdom had dwelled for a century, and dropped our passports onto the old leather-bound register, we headed straight to the best room. My partner thought it okay; I thought it was among the best rooms I had ever stayed in, laced with charm from another era.

As the owner bid us '*Buona notte, signore e la signora*', I ordered '*due digestivo*' and a plate of *formaggio* before settling in for a routine evening.

We had arrived from Milan airport an hour earlier. What was meant to be a brief meandering along the beautiful autostrada towards Lake Como turned into a 2-hour crawl as hailstones pelted down and sheets of rain formed shallow, fast-moving rivers along our road. The Italian heavens were falling in. Cars were abandoned, some after colliding with the safety barriers, others just dumped, with bonnets left up. Drivers and passengers skedaddled to the emergency phones, drenched, wearing clinging, see-through clothes. Ambulances buzzed in all directions to locate injured or distressed motorists in a night of calamity. It wouldn't let up until dawn, when the sheer beauty of the region would return, glossed with fallen water.

The choice of Italy and Lake Como wasn't a difficult one. I'd nearly lost count of the number of times I'd criss-crossed this magnificent land, revelling in the unique offerings in the north and south. I had patiently and blissfully explored each region. And, as far as sublime locations are concerned, there's no finer vista than Lake Como.

Dawn arrived. The sun peeped its rays through the gaps in the weathered shutters. The other side of the mattress was sound asleep, near comatose, as I edged out of our squeaking bed, aware of the aroma of last night's cheese on the bedside table. My feet felt cool on the old parquetry tiles. After my first steps, I could feel the age of the villa in the uneven timber floor. I felt welcomed, at home. I stood in front of an equally old four-drawer credenza under the window and leaned an elbow on its marbled surface, fidgeting for a release catch for the shutters. I flung both shutters wide open. The morning glare hit my face.

Both shutters clanged against the masonry wall before settling for the day. I straightened my jetlagged back and took my first real look at daytime Lake Como. At that exact delicious moment, both hands braced the cold marble top of the credenza. The scene was heaven, like no other view I had ever seen. It was as if I was seeing the finest view the world could offer. The villa garden below was a gift in design, pattern and form, with nurtured Tuscan pines reaching to the sky, one after the other, lined up like new centurions and framed by a continuous run of perfectly grown box hedge. Inside the hedgerow were large sections of the greenest turf, peppered with frangipanis. Orange trees, cumquats, mandarins and limes sprung up without order. And for good measure there was the occasional carved statue of a Milanese *duca* standing proud, overlooking the glass-like water.

Where the lake met the villa, a scattering of brightly coloured, timber-hulled rowboats, moored to weathered upright posts and covered in gull droppings, jutted from the water. Then, the pièce de résistance: a kilometre across the lake, the stunningly beautiful village of Bellagio, often called the prettiest town in Europe. I stood at my window in awe. My eyes moved from the foreground across the lake to the village, over the mountains and back again, many times over. I was completely and utterly in love … with my view.

I knew then that I would build my own Italian villa, one day, with equally awe-inspiring views. One day soon, I hoped.

I had left the police vowing to never lease a backwater pub or become a gumshoe chasing unfaithful husbands through bedrooms. I also knew there was nothing more ex than an ex-cop; once the door closes, it's all over, it's time to get on with life. Sadly, many don't, choosing to fall on the bottle or hang around barbecues talking old days crap. The savvy ones reinvent themselves. I had to.

I started my own workplace relations business. My background helped me to understand the complex legislation. The *Workplace Relations Act* was a massive document, far too much for any busy company executive or middle manager to digest. I had no difficulty unravelling it and, more importantly, working out the safest way to rid the workplace of dodgy workers. It was fun for a while and, as a business, lucrative. In parallel I undertook some property development, which was also enjoyable. I even tried my hand at private investigations, flushing out a nest of old Gestapo from World War II, handing the results to the media group that hired me. But the truth couldn't be ignored; I realised my heart wasn't in any of it.

I had found myself rethinking my own dream, to build an Italian villa. Whatever spare time I had, I mustered to the project, despite an abundance of advice not to build it. And the advice was correct. It makes sense: Italian villas are mostly over a hundred years old, seriously aged structures with weathered limewash walls, old marble and handmade tiled floors, manicured gardens of Tuscan pines and petunias spewing from cast-iron pots. Yet, each day I relived that same image of Lake Como. I knew there had to be a way forward. Before long I was sketching, putting ideas onto paper and playing with my new 'project'. I met my loyal bean-counter and dear friend Paula, asking her to work out my net wealth to see if I could fund a villa. She gave me the thumbs up and I set about planning my longed-for escape.

A friend introduced me to a master builder who came highly recommended. It wasn't long before the town planner gave the go-ahead for the construction of my villa, with its forty-seat restaurant, in-house cinema, nine suites with bathrooms and marbled terraces throughout, all of a luxury standard. The day my building permit arrived in the letterbox, I was so thrilled I could have kissed the postman.

The first thing the builder asked for was a deposit; he wanted 10 per cent to start the job, as well as progress payments along the way. Nothing too hard there, I thought, so I handed over a fat cheque, eager to get the project started. While I waited for the arrival on site of my new employee, I set about creating a landscaped garden, planting more than five hundred trees, shrubs and bushes over a hectare of ground.

Weeks rolled by, but still no builder, and no return phone calls. I did some covert background checks. I learned he had a history of ripping off clients: taking deposits, then shooting through. The more I delved into his background, the more carcasses I discovered strewn across the country. I'd been stooged. My deposit had been stolen. I made contact with the fraud squad and filed an official complaint. Tipped off that he was in the County Court, answering fraud charges from another of his 'stings', I grabbed a car and raced to Melbourne, just in time to confront him on the court-house steps. He almost collapsed when he saw me. After his initial fright, he ran back inside, into the sanctuary of the courtroom, still shaking.

I wasted weeks trying to get that sod to work, to no avail. I threw money at lawyers, who did little more than further frustrate me. After too much angst, I cut my losses and signed him out of the project, giving me complete control over my dream. As I was walking away from him I wished him cancer of the balls, and immediately the stress started to lift from my shoulders.

Returning to Bright as an owner-builder, I soon formed a close, richly rewarding relationship with a young local builder, Craig, who worked alongside me. He proved to be an outstanding fellow, with a small team of talented tradesmen, and before long the site was a hive of activity. The camaraderie was akin to any previous task force I had been part of, a team that oozed dedication and commitment. The rapidly growing building was looking a treat. As it grew, so did my garden. Ma and Ray had followed me to Bright, electing to live nearby. They delighted in helping with the garden, planting Tuscan pines, hedgerows, lemon trees, limes and a feast of Italian blooms. It was so rewarding to have them as part of my life, creating my dream.

Building the villa was among the hardest things I have ever undertaken, right up there with raising an infant in nappies. It became my second baby. After nine months of construction my body was ruined, riddled with aches and pains, torn and inflamed. I went overboard, especially lifting and carrying the stone at the local quarry—more than forty tonnes of it! A couple of weeks before opening day, I was in real strife. I had torn my spleen and was passing blood, I had three degenerated disks in my neck and my shoulder muscles were a mess. I needed more than a hundred remedial massage sessions, acupuncture, physiotherapy and stretching classes over the next two years to knock my twisted form back into shape. All because I stupidly tried to keep the building costs down, to compensate for the money lost from the deposit.

And then came the bushfires. The fires of 2003 were among the worst Victoria had suffered, raging across the state, destroying property after property. The villa was surrounded by fires for weeks; it had been a long time since I had been so scared. Yet, we survived, and the villa opening was a grand afternoon. As I hobbled about, offering a taste of Italian cooking and local wines, the sound of backslapping could be heard for miles. The mayor, travel journalists and VIPs from the hospitality industry marvelled at the only purpose-built Italian villa outside of Italy. It had been an exhausting and richly pleasurable journey.

Hospitality can be a cruel profession, with long hours and fierce competition. It is the vocation of fools, yet, it can be explicitly rewarding. There was something wonderfully pleasing, forever memorable, in opening my villa: welcoming guests and seeing their faces, looking in all directions at once; watching them walk, filled with curiosity, through the doors. I delighted in their enthralled, fascinated looks as they explored their weekend indulgence or romantic getaway, and in hearing their feedback at the end of their stay, in seeing a smile as they turned back and glanced at the front door again, just as their car left the driveway.

My dream villa was eventually given a name, chosen by Chelsea over a long afternoon of wine and food: 'Villa Gusto', meaning 'big house of tastes'. Chelsea had made the smart decision to go back to school and pick up a degree in speech pathology. She was the first in our clan to gain a degree. I will never forget her graduation. I nursed a lump in my throat as I sat in the university auditorium, waiting for her name to be called. Of course, the 'macks' are always in the middle. Later that same day, in driving back to the villa, alone, that night, I recalled the shaggy-haired, confused teenager I once was, with news of looming fatherhood, and how I wrestled with my decision to stick it out, to take the role of sole parent. That classic crossroads decision had shaped the rest of my life.

I would never have chosen to have a child in the circumstances in which Chelsea arrived, and the life I had lived was almost incompatible with bringing up children—that one child had been squeezed into it was something that amazed me. It wasn't something I'd inflict on another. Yet I never regretted Chelsea for one minute (well, maybe just once or twice, very briefly, in those early nappy-flinging days). My girl, my little girl, had filled my life with more happiness than that long-ago stunned teenager could ever have imagined. If I was to be true about anything in life I'd have to acknowledge that Chelsea, more often than not, kept check on me—more than I did on her, as I weaved my way through a life littered with pressure, challenges, intrigue and business ventures. She always seemed prone to leaving little notes, or cards, words of love, encouragement. If only she knew how much strength she gave me and how often I read her notes. There is always one such note tucked away snugly in my wallet, which I pull out and read in odd places around the globe.

As I was driving home one day, the car radio squawked the news. The lead item was about my old adversary, Antonio. He had been released from jail after only eight years (for good behaviour) and had just been found dead at the back of his orange grove. He had only been home a few days when he paid the ultimate price for his behaviour. His body was found ripped to shreds by shotgun pellets, a horrible death for a man for whom I held a strange respect. The Italians have a saying: the cause of death was a vendetta and the problem is now gone. I might say, the monkey that I had carried on my back for those eight years, and the fear of reprisals, was now gone. Still, I couldn't help but wonder about Hades, who was now a legal citizen of this country.

Of course, the township of Griffith played its own version of three monkeys that day. No-one saw anything, heard anything or said anything. It seemed that the new N'Drangheta were doing a bit of housekeeping, out with the old and in with the new. Sandra called me to say hello and to suggest that I keep my eyes open, just in case. It was an uneasy time at the villa for a few months as I tried to second-guess the Italians, especially in the wee hours of the night. For the past eight years I had often worried about a vendetta. Such musings would always have me think twice when opening my letterbox, or standing aside at the sound of a knock on my door. I was glad Antonio was gone; I only hoped it was to a better place. I always knew that with the click of his fingers, or the wink of an eye, he could easily have delivered the same fate that someone bestowed him upon me. Yes, I respected him.

I spent five years running my villa, delighting as the business grew. I learned about marketing, menu design, regional wine lists and training staff. I had a ball.

Shortly after we had started, my guests began looking for evening meals to accompany the gourmet breakfasts and lunches on offer, so I decided to try my hand at cooking. For four nights a week I offered a set menu. After six months of cooking, I came to the realisation that I was a very good gardener! So the kitchen stepped up its skill base and I hired a head chef. Those were exciting times. We hosted Opera Australia as they put on a range of stunning events matched to regional food and wine in our garden.

By the end of our first year, the villa was winning awards for accommodation, food and wine lists. A premier US guide labelled us 'one of the world's top establishments'. The *Good Food Guide* awarded us a chef's hat two years running.

Our many awards were due, in the main, to the extraordinary team we had gathered, to the different chefs who passed through the kitchen, the front-of-house staff, waiting staff, housekeepers and gardeners. The head housekeeper, Judith, was a wonderful support and a real friend. But the real trumps in the success of Villa Gusto were Ma and Ray. For five years they worked tirelessly behind the scenes; ironing our Ralph Lauren uniforms, making biscotti, fussing their way through my work life. I relish the memories, which will always be linked to my mother's twilight years. I can see her now, wandering 'her' garden with secateurs in hand, glancing at her wristwatch, knowing it was half past one and the guests would soon be arriving. She would quietly stroll over to one of her hundred rose bushes and cut an assortment, stopping to check for aphids or black leaf. Happily, she'd end up with a range of different colours, then into the villa, to Ray waiting with a dozen watered vases and love in his eyes. They'd clip away and chat away, sublimely happy, as they arranged their blooms.

'Someone arriving Colin?' she would say to the noise of a car on the driveway.

'First ones in, they've probably had a long journey,' I'd answer.

'Like you and me both. I'll make them a cup of tea.'

'Ma, Italian villas don't serve tea … only coffee.'

'Mrs Bongiorno, I got her onto a cuppa.'

'You sure did. I think you influenced a lot of people, Ma.'

By now the vases were full; it was time to wipe down the bench as the doorbell rang.

'Better answer the door son, there's bills to pay.'

'I'll take a cuppa if it's offered.'

'If you're good.'

As my business grew, I began taking guests around Italy on guided gourmet food and wine tours, fourteen nights of eating around southern Italy, to Calabria and Sicily. An odd quirk of fate really, considering my undercover career. I reckoned I could share some colourful snippets on those parts, more than most tour guides. On one trip I took a detour from my main group of guests and drove into the small town of Plati, the ancestral home of Rosario and Antonio. It truly was a hovel. I parked my car and went for a walk in the worst town of any I had seen in my Italian travels. I remembered the saying, 'There's nothing more inconspicuous then the conspicuous'.

As I walked, I was met by many sad faces on aged women wandering in and out of the only shop in town, gathering the most basic of food produce. Bullet holes aerated the street signage and burnt-out cars littered the roads into town. There was a tough guy on every corner, picking his teeth. I simply couldn't imagine Antonio walking these same streets. Yet I could see him strolling through the chic porticos of Bologna in the north, window-shopping for a cashmere suit, or eyeing a pastry over espresso. I didn't stay too long on those dusty streets, just long enough to close a very big chapter in my life, to see the birthplace of a once-held acquaintance. Then I went back to my guests and my new life.

The summer of 2006–07 would prove to be the hottest on record. It had been four years since the last bushfires, which authorities had claimed were 'one-in-a-hundred-year' fires. I wanted badly to wave my finger at the authorities to let them know the worst was now upon us! By early December flames had started to race through the region, to shocking effect. The villa lost all its bookings; each phone call was another cancellation. The loneliness of a bushfire gripped me as I sat in my empty villa, eyes burning from the smoke. Nights I spent on top of my vast roof, watching the embers fall: long spears of bark, alight, like falling javelins, blazing through the air, piercing the night.

I brought in water, by tanker, from 100 kilometres away; it was a precious commodity.

For ten days I followed the same routine: up all night spotting fires, all day mingling with local farmers to second-guess the direction and severity of the flames, and constantly dampening the edge of the villa and hedgerow. My staff had all fled to their own homes, to undertake their own fire safety procedures. All except my new head chef, Christos, who toughed it out with me, day and night, as we fought off ruin.

On the tenth day I drove to the airport to fly to Sicily to meet a tour group. The villa was hosting another gourmet tour of southern Italy and there was no way of postponing. I boarded that plane with stinging eyes and the heaviest feeling of doom, knowing that my chef would struggle alone with the fires. With only the help of Ma and Ray, who I was blessed to have, he kept a vigilant watch.

My food tour was filled with worry. Each day I contacted the villa, only to hear more dreaded news. I wasn't the perfect relaxed and amicable host to my lovely travelling guests. I faced them of a morning drained, knowing overnight the villa had survived, had been spared yet another threat. There was little I could say. My guests had every right to enjoy their gourmet holiday and I regretted that, by the end, they were far too aware of my Australian problems.

Upon my return from Italy I was forced to reach into my financial reserves to prop up the business. The fun was all gone from Villa Gusto; it had turned into a heavy millstone.

By February, I was totally demoralised. But then one day my doorbell rang. A young and talented couple stood on my front steps, wanting the business. They were both chefs who had won Michelin stars and their timing was perfect. I think I would have handed the villa over to a dog by then. The kitchen was far too hot for me. I packed my bags for the umpteenth time in my life and out my front door I walked, leaving behind a small group of wonderful, inspirational neighbours and friends. I didn't know where I'd end up, other than an airport. I farewelled Chelsea.

I took a flight to America. All I had were my clothes, a pocket full of Visa cards and a head that wouldn't sleep. A day and a half later I arrived in the jungles of Guatemala, in Central America, in the town of Antigua, a maze of laneways and horse-drawn carts at the base of a not-too-active volcano.

There was a female version of myself waiting to open her life to me. She too was one of the equally obsessed, willing to guide a weary traveller into her cool and charming colonial guest house. I knocked on her very big timber door. A tiny maid opened an equally tiny shutter and a light came shining through. She squinted at me, then at the taxi driver, and smiled. 'Señor Colin, Señor Colin,' she yelled, as the shutter was slammed closed and she scuttled away to find the hostess.

I dropped my heavy load to the floor and heard the release of a metal latch as Alexandra pulled open her door. Barefoot, with red-painted toenails and both hands on her hips, she looked delicious in her buttoned shirt and messed-up cotton skirt. She blew hair from her face, looking me up and down. It was nice to know she was still full of attitude. Then she threw me the most brilliant smile I had ever seen. I caught it.

'What kept you Aussie … give up your bags and get in here.' And I did, as she stepped aside. The door slammed shut and I was home, for a while.

EPILOGUE

I'm sitting on a bar stool at Sangre, a swanky bar-cum-restaurant on Fifth Avenida in Antigua. The owner, a Yank, fleeing from corporate madness, has settled here. He now madly wipes his bar top and experiments with cocktails to pass the time of day. And he's never been more content, as he mixes cucumber martinis and seeks my opinion. He reaches for another glass. It tastes fine, as does life again; I've been here a while.

There are three other stools and I've befriended the occupant of each. Murray the Texan cowboy is on the run from corporate shock and now sells trinkets to tourists. Bruce, in the middle, was once a partner in a fast-peddling team of financial advisers; he's bolted from his pressures to open the hotel just down the road. The stool closest to mine is Alexandra's; a runaway from the New York money markets, she landed in the jungle to open a guest house. As I travelled about, I was constantly drawn back to her embrace. We fitted nicely together, for a time.

I figured it out: the older you get, the more you run from. All my new friends are playing truant with reality. It's a life worth snatching, escaping home-grown problems and living in another world. Usually the entrance ticket is decades of pressure and years of tolerating dills.

Our bar-stool club of runaways swap tales and laugh a lot. We reckon there's safety in numbers and we share a real happiness.

I also discovered there were bar stools all over the Americas. I just joined the line, like so many others, and found my utopia, dropping anchor for a while to detangle my lot. Initially, yarns of failure or success were common talk. The more I dallied with my mix of like-minded chums, the faster my horrors faded, into American sunsets. I became blissfully calm and started to think of home again.

When I arrived back home, it was to a raging Australian winter. In no time at all, Vinnie and his girlfriend were knocking on my door, showing off broad smiles and a new-born baby girl. Had I been gone that long? Apart from the run of kisses and hugs, Vinnie told me he'd opened his own restaurant; he wanted to play the game. Oh, I had much advice to give them, on both new babies.

Vinnie sat me down and passed on all the news, or at least the headlines he thought I might listen to. A chief commissioner was apologising for taking free first-class airline tickets and accommodation overseas. An assistant commissioner was on multiple charges of perjury. Senior police were interfering in the carriage of prosecutions against street gangs, and the quality of life on the streets for many citizens had deteriorated dramatically. Do as I say, not do as I do, I thought. It never changes. I was more fascinated to hear the news that an importation of illicit drugs of massive proportions had been seized and that Hades had been found stuck fat in the middle of the scam.

Thankfully, normality called; Chelsea felt it was more than time for an extraordinarily long lunch. She proffered a trattoria near where she lived: 'It's got Heathcote shiraz on the wine list.' I told her to book a table for four and a half.

We jumped in my car and went looking for my girl; I'd missed her far too much. As we drove along the idyllic country road, I thought back over a life of half a century. I figured I had done well thus far, ticking a few boxes as I cleared most of my hurdles. And I relished the wonderful company I was about to enjoy.

An hour later, as our wine glasses were half-full and the Italian feast started to roll out, I looked over my dining table. Watching Chelsea fuss over the antipasto and Vinnie confiding a story about the latest dramas with his brothers, it wasn't long before all that had gone before me in recent years was forgotten. I realised how very simple life actually is: good friends, fine wine, great food and family. Those very ingredients were on my table.

I wondered why some people had to make their lives so damn complicated!